Illustrators
Cheryl Buhler, Sue Fullam,
Keith Vasconcelles, and
Theresa M. Wright

Editor
Karen J. Goldfluss

Editor-in-Chief
Sharon Coan, M.S. Ed.

Art Director
Darlene Spivak

Cover Artist
Keith Vasconcelles

Imaging
Rick Chacón

Product Manager
Phil Garcia

Research and Contributions
Patricia Miriani Sima and
Bobbie Johnson

Publishers
Rachelle Cracchiolo, M.S. Ed.
Mary Dupuy Smith, M.S. Ed.

Ou_
Fifty States

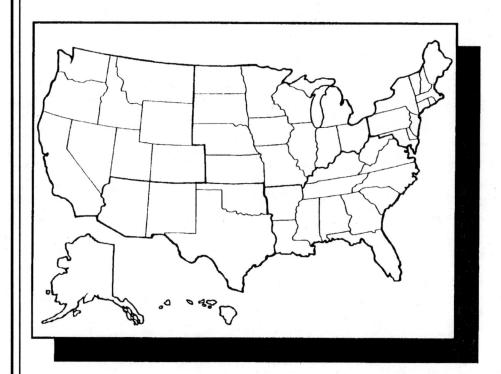

Author

Janet Hale and Richard Rayburn

Teacher Created Materials, Inc.
6421 Industry Way
Westminster, CA 92683
www.teachercreated.com

ISBN-1-55734-470-1

©1993 Teacher Created Materials, Inc.
Reprinted, 2002

Made in U.S.A.

Table of Contents

Table of Contents *(cont.)*

Before You Begin

Introduction

Our Fifty States is designed to help students acquire basic knowledge about each state. The 288 pages within this book include reproducible maps of the United States and its regions. In addition, informative state profiles and related activities are provided to help reinforce and enhance your students' knowledge of the fifty states.

Unit Organization and Management

The fifty United States presented in this book are divided into the following regions:

Each regional section includes:

- a regional map
- a fact sheet for each state, complete with a state flag
- a blank outline map of each state
- background information connecting important and interesting facts to related activities for every state in the region
- clip art, highlighting important people, places, and products from each state
- regional activities at the end of the section to help students assimilate the information gathered throughout the section

---

Clip art may be cut out and glued to a state map before, during, or after studying the state. You may wish to make clip art flashcards by cutting out the region's clip art and pasting each picture to a piece of construction paper. On the back of each card, write the name of the state to which the picture belongs. Have pairs of students use the flashcards to reinforce their knowledge of each state.

Before You Begin *(cont.)*

States Trivia Game

The trivia game found on pages 267-274 provides students with an enjoyable way of reviewing the information they learned while studying the fifty states. You may wish to use the States Trivia Game as a culminating activity for *Our Fifty States*.

Idea Bank, Bibliography, and Resources

The Idea Bank on pages 275-280 includes additional suggestions for using maps and activities that extend the unit into other areas of the curriculum.

A bibliography for each region and suggested resources are provided on pages 287-288.

Enlarging Maps

If you wish to enlarge the maps provided in this book, here are two easy ways of doing so.

Method I

- Use an opaque projector to project the state outline onto a large piece of heavy paper.
- Trace the projected lines with a thick black marker.
- Color, label, and display as desired.

Method 2

- Enlarge a state outline using a copy machine equipped with enlargement capability.
- Select the desired enlargement size.
- Choose the paper size appropriate for the enlargement.
- Print out the enlarged copy.
- Color, label, and display as desired.

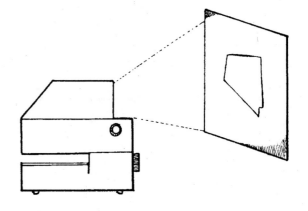

The Southeast

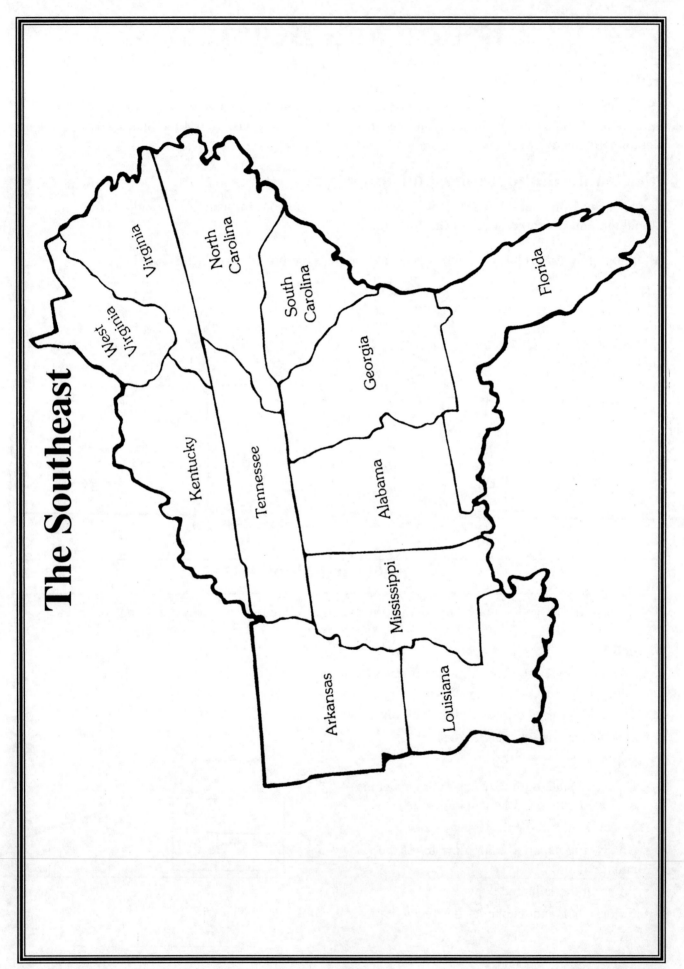

West Virginia

Virginia

North Carolina

South Carolina

Florida

Georgia

Kentucky

Tennessee

Alabama

Mississippi

Arkansas

Louisiana

6

Alabama
"The Heart of Dixie"

Basic Facts
Capital: *Montgomery*
Statehood: *December 14, 1819*
Admittance: *22nd state*
Motto: *We Dare Defend Our Rights*
Song: *"Alabama"*
Bird: *Yellowhammer*
Flower: *Camellia*
Tree: *Southern Pine*

Abbreviation: *AL*
Area: *51,705 square miles (133,915 sq. km)*
Elevation: *(above sea level)*
Highest: 2,407 ft. (734 m) – Cheaha Mountain
Lowest: Sea level along coastline
Average Temperatures:
July: 80°F. (27°C)
January: 46°F. (8°C)
Average Yearly Precipitation: *56 in. (142 cm)*

Population
How Many: *4,062,608 (1990 Census)*
Where They Live: *62% urban, 38% rural*
Largest Cities: *Birmingham, Mobile, Montgomery*

Alabama State Flag

State Government
Governor: *4-year term*
Senators *(35): 4-year term*
Representatives *(105): 4-year term*
Counties: *67*

Federal Government
Senators *(2): 6-year term*
Representatives *(7): 2-year term*
Electoral Votes: *9*

Economy
Agriculture: *chickens, beef cattle, eggs, soybeans, peanuts, cotton, hogs*
Fishing: *shrimp, oysters*
Manufacturing: *paper products, chemicals, rubber and plastic products, textiles, metals, transportation equipment*
Mining: *coal, petroleum, natural gas, stone*

Interesting Facts
- The first electric streetcars in the United States began operating in Montgomery in 1866.
- Little River, located on Lookout Mountain in Northeastern Alabama, is the only river that runs its entire course on top of a mountain

Interesting Alabamian
- George Washington Carver gained a reputation as one of the world's greatest agricultural scientists from the research he completed at Alabama's Tuskegee University.

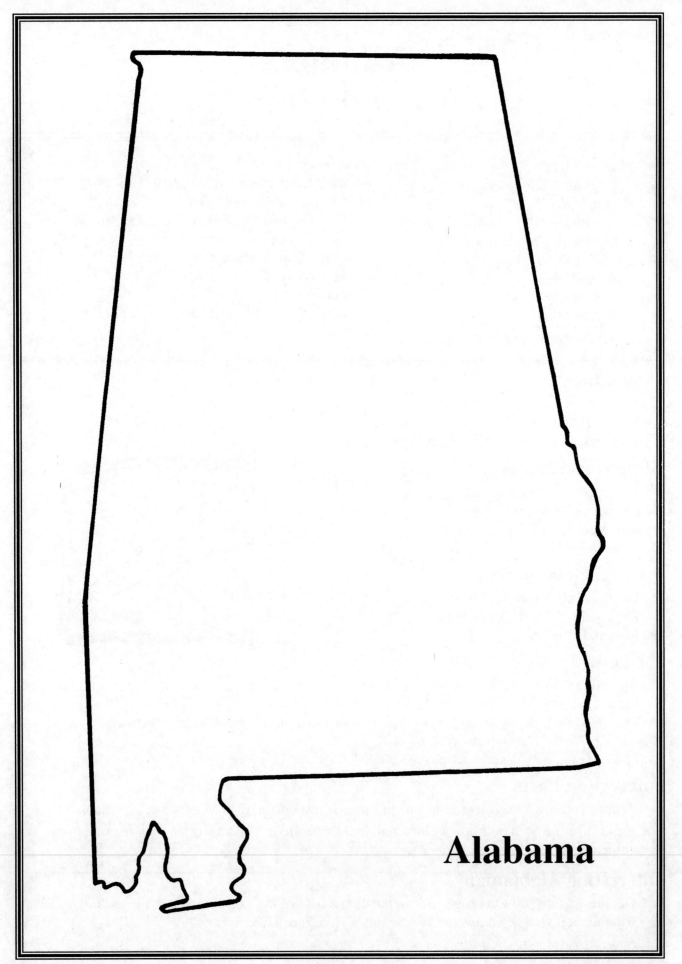

Alabama

8

Heroic Heritage

A hero or heroine is a person who shows great strength, courage, pride, or noble purpose; someone who can act bravely in dangerous or difficult situations. Heroes and heroines are people whom we can look up to, individuals whose brave actions display the best part of the human spirit. They are an important part of our nation's tradition.

Two famous heroic figures from Alabama are Rosa Parks and Dr. Martin Luther King, Jr. Read the following background information about these two Alabamians. Then complete the activity at the bottom of the page.

Like many states in the 1950's and 1960's, Alabama had many racial problems. In 1955 and 1956, Rosa Parks and Martin Luther King, Jr. led the Montgomery bus boycott. On December 1, 1955, Rosa got on a bus to go home from work. She refused to give up her seat to a white man. Rosa had paid her fare just like the white man and was not going to stand on the bus just because of the color of her skin. Rosa Parks was arrested, causing public reaction which led to the famous boycott.

During the boycott, many blacks refused to ride the public buses of Montgomery. They walked, carpooled, took mules and horses, and found various other methods of getting around the city. This resulting boycott lasted 381 days. Finally, in 1956, the courts desegregated the buses.

In March of 1965, Martin Luther King Jr. led a five day march from Selma to Montgomery to protest discrimination in voter registration. This turned out to be a dangerous march because the law did not protect the marchers, making the marchers easy targets on the lonely road. Despite the danger, many individuals took part in the march. Congress passed the Voting Rights Act in August of 1965, which made blacks eligible to vote.

Like many heroes and heroines, these two individuals stood up for their personal rights as well as for the rights of many others. They did so with pride, determination, and without violence.

Activity 1: My Hero

Find and cut out articles in a newspaper or magazine that fit your description of a modern-day hero. Personalize the article by stating reasons why this person is your hero, and what makes him/her the hero/heroine you respect.

Heroic Heritage *(cont.)*

Activity 2: Songs of Freedom

Picture yourself striving for something important to you and your classmates. Learn the lyrics to songs such as "We Shall Overcome" and "Ain't Gonna Let Nobody Turn Me Around" (*Martin Luther King. The Peaceful Warrior* by Ed Clayton, Simon & Schuster 1986). You may personalize the song by substituting certain words with lyrics that pertain to you. As an alternative, create your own song to a familiar melody. Follow the directions below to perform a dance as you sing or recite your songs.

Have everyone take hands to create a large circle. If you have a large group, create a smaller, separate circle inside the larger one. After one line of your song or chant, slide 8 steps to your right, then slide 8 steps to your left. After your second line, slide 4 steps to your right and then 4 steps to your left. Now speed things up. As you are singing, slide 2 steps to your right and then 2 to your left. Next, slide 1 step to your right and 1 step to your left (this can almost be a leap). At the end of the song, take 3 steps toward the center of the circle, jump up in the air and then clap. Depending on the length of your song, you may need to lengthen or shorten the number of steps.

Arkansas
"The Land of Opportunity"

Basic Facts

Capital: *Little Rock*
Statehood: *June 15, 1836*
Admittance: *25th state*
Motto: *The People Rule*
Song: *"Arkansas"*
Bird: *Mockingbird*
Flower: *Apple Blossom*
Tree: *Pine tree*

Abbreviation: *AR*
Area: *53,187 square miles (137,754 sq. km)*
Elevation: *(above sea level)*
  Highest: 2, 753 ft. (839 m) – Magazine Mt.
  Lowest: 55ft. (17m) – Ashley County
Average Temperatures:
  July: 81°F. (27°C)
  January: 40°F. (4°C)
Average Yearly Precipitation: *49 in. (124 cm)*

Population

How Many: *2,362,239 (1990 Census)*
Where They Live: *52% urban, 48% rural*
Largest Cities: *Little Rock, Fort Smith, North Little Rock*

State Government

Governor: *4-year term*
Senators *(35): 4year term*
Representatives *(100): 2-year term*
Counties: *75*

Federal Government

Senators *(2): 6-year term*
Representatives *(4): 2-year term*
Electoral Votes: *6*

Arkansas State Flag

Economy

Agriculture: *broiler chickens, rice, beef cattle, eggs, wheat, cotton, turkeys*
Manufacturing: *food products, electric machinery and equipment, lumber and wood products, chemicals, metal products*
Mining: *petroleum, natural gas, bromide, stone, sand, gravel*

Interesting Facts

- The Crater of Diamonds, near Murfreesboro, is the only diamond mine in the United States.
- Norfolk National Fish Hatchery is the largest trout hatchery in the United States. Over two million trout eggs are hatched there each year.

Interesting Arkansan

- Bill Clinton. from Arkansas, became president of the United States in 1993.

Arkansas

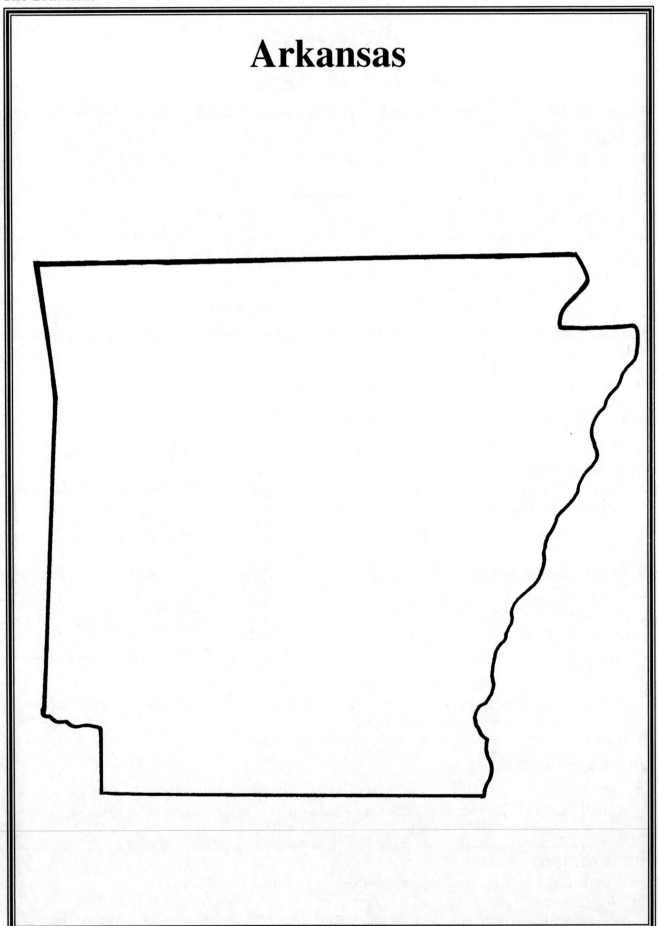

Sparkling Springs and Diamonds

Arkansas is well known for its spring water. Many of Arkansas' Mammoth Springs contain minerals. Five million people visit each year, hoping to cure a variety of ailments. Mammoth Springs yields about 235 million gallons (890 million liters) of water per day. The definition of a hot spring is a spring that discharges water heated by natural processes within the earth. Hot springs are a source of geothermal energy, which is the energy produced by underground steam or hot water. Sometimes geothermal energy is used to generate electricity. A spring can come in three different forms; one is a steadily flowing spring, another can be a calm pool of water, and the third is a bubbling pool of mud.

Crater of Diamonds State Park, located near Murfreesboro, boasts a diamond mine in which the visiting public can hunt for diamonds. It's "finders keepers" for those who might happen upon a diamond in the mines of the Crater of Diamonds. Over the years, thousands of diamonds have been found.

Activity: Treasure Boxes

Essentials

- old greeting cards, magazines, or catalogs
- cigar boxes or shoe boxes
- paint (gold or silver or any other color you desire)
- assorted trimmings (sequins, buttons, colored uncooked pasta, scraps of old material, shells, etc.)
- artificial "gemstones" from old costume jewelry
- scissors
- glue
- crayons, markers, pencils

Directions

- Paint a cigar box or shoe box any color you prefer. Make a colorful and interesting collage by gluing pieces of greeting cards or magazine pages onto the top of the box. Glue the trimmings around the box. Be creative!

- Have someone hide pieces of costume jewelry around the room. Pretend you are in an old diamond mine searching for diamonds or other jewels. Try to find as many treasures as you can within a given time limit.

- Use your treasure boxes to collect and store the items you have collected.

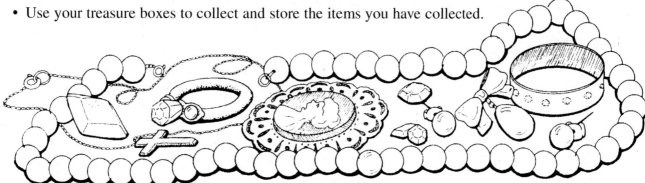

Florida

"The Sunshine State"

Basic Facts

Capital: *Tallahassee*
Statehood: *March 3, 1845*
Admittance: *27th state*
Motto: *In God We Trust*
Song: *"Old Folks at Home"*
Bird: *Mockingbird*
Flower: *Orange blossom*
Tree: *Sabalpalm*
Abbreviation: *FL*

Area: *58,664 square miles (151,939 sq. km)*
Elevation: *(above sea level)*
  Highest: 345 ft. (105 m) – Walton County
  Lowest: Sea level along coastline-
Average Temperatures:
  July: 81°F. (27°C)
  January: 59°F. (15°C)
Average Yearly Precipitation: *54 in. (137 cm)*

Population

How Many: *13,003,362 (1990 Census)*
Where They Live: *84% urban, 16% rural*
Largest Cities: *Jacksonville, Miami, Tampa*

State Government

Governor: *4-year term*
Senators *(40): 4-year term*
Representatives *(120): 2-year term*
Counties: *67*

Federal Government

Senators *(2): 6-year term*
Representatives *(23): 2-year term*
Electoral Votes: *25*

Florida State Flag

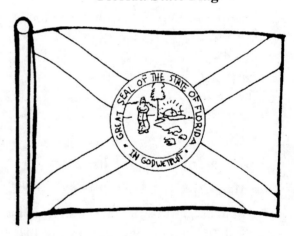

Economy

Agriculture: *oranges, greenhouse and nursery products, tomatoes, beef cattle, sugar cane, milk*
Fishing: *shrimp, lobsters*
Manufacturing: *food products, chemicals, printed materials, nonelectric machinery, transportation
          equipment*
Mining: *phosphate, rock, petroleum, stone*

Interesting Facts

- Florida has more lakes than any other state.
- All Navy pilots begin their flight training at the Pensacola Naval Air Station.

Interesting Floridian

- James Weldon Johnson was a famous American diplomat and author. He wrote the lyrics to the song "Lift Every Voice High," which has become the African-American National Anthem.

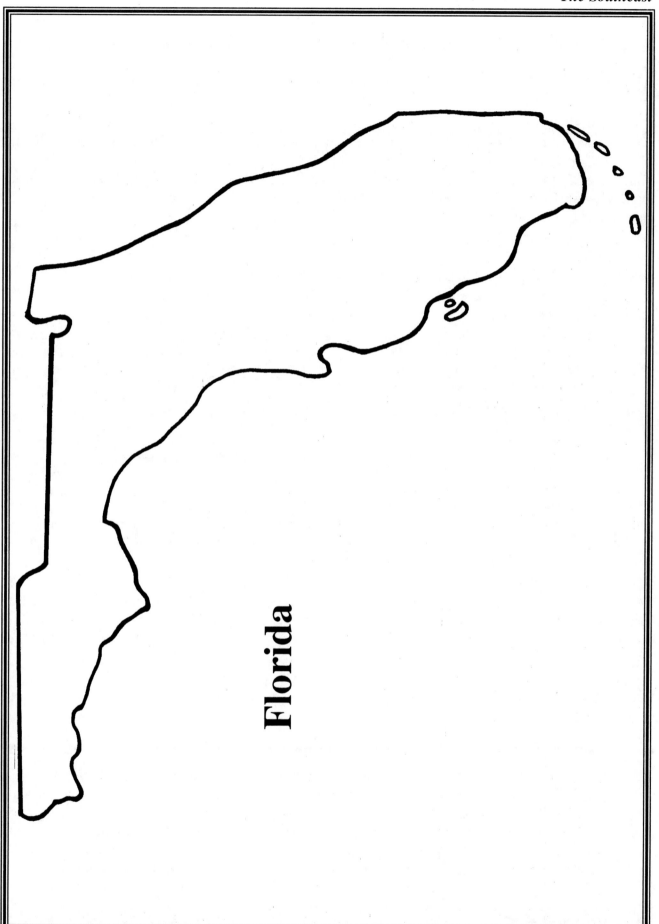

Florida

A Unique Ecosystem

The everglades are low, flat plains that begin at Lake Okeechobee, a large lake in the center of Florida, and end in the Gulf of Mexico and Florida Bay. They were formed by the natural flooding of Lake Okeechobee.

The Florida everglades are part of a very unique ecosystem. An ecosystem is a term used to classify the Earth's natural communities according to how living and nonliving things and their environment function as a unit. It demonstrates a cycle of life in which everything is delicately balanced. Periods of high water alternating with periods of low water have created a wet-dry habitat for a variety of plants and animals.

The everglades contain examples of aquatic (water) and terrestrial (land) food chains. There are three types of organisms in each of these food chains: producers, consumers, and decomposers. Plants are the producers. They store the sun's energy and convert it to food. Animals feed on plants and other animals, so they are the consumers. Bacteria and other small organisms that break down dead plants and animals are the decomposers.

The Florida everglades merge into saltwater marshes and mangrove swamps. Here you will find a completely different category of plants that can survive the salty waters. There are also alligators, turtles, snakes, otters, and many kinds of fish. On land, you may see bears, panthers, snakes, and deer. in addition to these animals, some 300 varieties of birds make their home in this area of the everglades.

Within each large ecosystem, smaller ecosystems can be found. A decaying tree within a forest and the decomposition of plant life in the everglades by bacteria are examples of these smaller ecosystems.

Study an ecosystem up close by observing the decomposition of wood. As wood decays, it returns to the soil and recycles minerals in a series of processes. Fungus and lichen, or other decomposers, permeate and then soften the bark. Insects, such as termites and beetles, attack the heartwood. In turn, animals feed on the insects. Waste materials from the animals are deposited on the ground, providing a rich fertilizer for the soil.

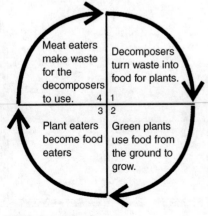

Activity: Create a Local Ecosystem

Locate information and pictures from books and magazines that suggest how some of the plants and animals in the everglades become part of a food chain. Two good sources are *Life on Earth,* by Linda Gamlin (Gloucester, 1988) and *Chains, Webs, and Pyramids: The Flow of Energy in Nature,* by Laurence Pringle (Harper, 1975). Use the materials you collected and the diagram on this page to design a food chain poster representing some plant and animal life in the everglades. Share your poster with the class.

Georgia

"The Empire State of the South"

Basic Facts

Capital: *Atlanta*
Statehood: *January 2, 1788*
Admittance: *4th state*
Motto: *Wisdom, Justice, and Moderation*
Song: *"Georgia on My Mind"*
Bird: *Brown Thrasher*
Flower: *Cherokee Rose*
Tree: *Live Oak*
Abbreviation: *GA*

Area: *58,910 square miles (152,576 sq. km)*
Elevation: *(above sea level)*
  Highest: 4,784 ft. – Brasstown Bald Mountain
  Lowest: Sea level along coastline
Average Temperatures:
  July: 80°F. (27°C)
  January: 47°F. (8°C)
Average Yearly Precipitation: *50 in. (127 cm)*

Population

How Many: *6,508,419 (1990 Census)*
Where They Live: *62% urban, 38% rural*
Largest Cities: *Atlanta, Columbus, Savannah*

State Government

Governor: *4-year term*
Senators *(56): 2-year term*
Representatives *(180): 2-year term*
Counties: *159*

Federal Government

Senators *(2): 6-year term*
Representatives *(11): 2-year term*
Electoral Votes: *13*

Georgia State Flag

Economy

Agriculture: *chickens, peanuts, eggs, soybeans, corn, hogs, milt beef cattle, tobacco*
Fishing: *shrimp, crabs*
Manufacturing: *paper products, chemicals, lumber and wood products, textiles, metals, transportation equipment, clothing*
Mining: *clay, stone, sand and gravel*

Interesting Facts

• The first effective use of ether during surgery occurred in Georgia in 1842. Dr. Crawford Long put James Venable "to sleep" to remove a tumor from his neck.

• Coca-Cola0 was first served in a drugstore in Atlanta in 1887.

Interesting Georgian

• Juliette Gordon Low founded the Girl Scouts of America on March 12, 1912, in Savannah. The national headquarters is still located there.

Georgia

The Nuttiest State

Georgia is sometimes referred to as the "nuttiest state" in our nation. When it comes to growing peanuts, Georgia is the leader. Two-billion pounds of peanuts are grown in Georgia in one year. To get an idea of just how many peanuts this is, it is helpful to know that there are 200 peanut pods to a pound and there are two peanuts per pod.

Facts About Peanuts

- A peanut bears fruit in the form of pods that contain one or two seeds.
- Georgia produces nearly half of the annual U.S. peanut crop.
- Peanuts are more closely related to peas than to nuts.
- Peanuts are nutritious. There are more energy-giving calories in roasted peanuts than in an equal amount of steak.
- George Washington Carver made an extensive study of peanuts. Carver is credited with having found more than 300 uses for the plant and its fruit.
- Peanuts are native to South America. The South Americans were growing peanuts at least 1,000 years ago.
- South Americans called the peanut a"goober."
- Worldwide peanuts are grown chiefly for their oil.

Activity 1: Homemade Crunchy Peanut Butter

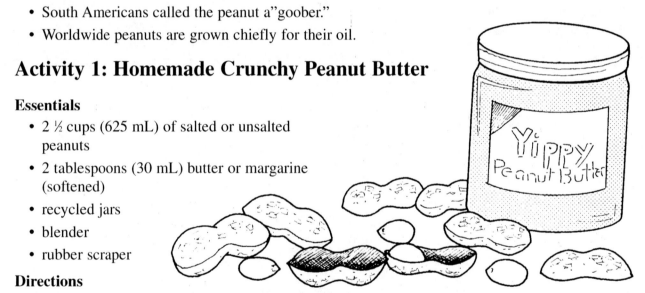

Essentials

- 2 ½ cups (625 mL) of salted or unsalted peanuts
- 2 tablespoons (30 mL) butter or margarine (softened)
- recycled jars
- blender
- rubber scraper

Directions

1. Measure out ½ cup (125 mL) of peanuts. Empty the other two cups of peanuts into the blender.
2. Blend on low speed for ten seconds or until peanuts are chopped.
3. Add two tablespoons of butter to the blender.
4. Blend for another ten seconds. Make sure the blender is off and scrap the peanut butter off the sides of the blender.
5. Blend for five seconds and repeat step 4.
6. Repeat step 5 until the peanut butter begins to get smooth.
7. Cover and blend for one minute on high speed.
8. Add the extra ½ cup of peanuts to the blender and blend on medium speed for three seconds.

Note: This recipe makes 1 cup (250 mL) of peanut butter. To make creamy peanut butter do not measure out the ½ cup of peanuts. Put all 2½ cups of peanuts in the blender and proceed with steps 2 through 7.

The Nuttiest State *(cont.)*

Activity 2: Plant Your Own Peanuts

Conduct an experiment to find out the best way to grow a peanut plant from a peanut.

Essentials

- raw peanuts
- 4 plastic foam cups
- tray filled with sand or gravel
- sand, pebbles, soil, water
- piece of paper

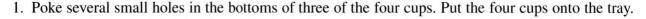

Directions

1. Poke several small holes in the bottoms of three of the four cups. Put the four cups onto the tray.

2. The cups with the holes should be filled two-thirds full. Place sand in one, pebbles in a second, and soil in the third. Fill the fourth cup without holes with water. Label each cup.

3. Put two raw peanuts in each cup at about one to two inches (2.5 – 5 cm) deep. (You can just drop the peanuts in the water cup.)

4. Set the tray with the cups close to a sunny window. Add water to the sand, pebbles, and soil until moist. Make sure these cups are in a warm place.

5. Predict which substance is best for growing the peanut plant.

6. Keep the substances from drying out by adding water when needed. Check for sprouts daily. Make a chart showing the best conditions for growing your peanut plant. Were your predictions correct? Discuss the results of your experiment with classmates.

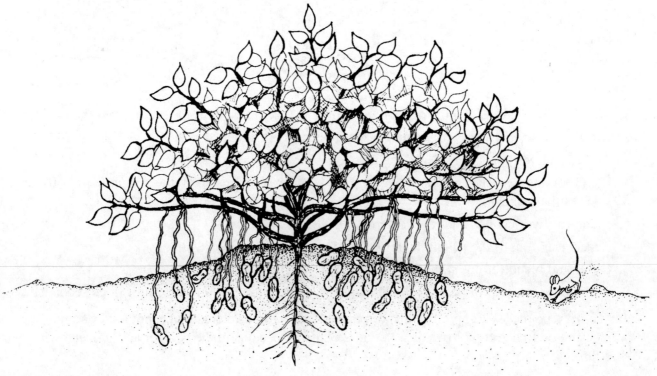

Kentucky

"The Bluegrass State"

Basic Facts

Capital: *Frankfort*
Statehood: *June 1, 1792*
Admittance: *15th state*
Motto: *United We Stand, Divided We Fall*
Song: *"My Old Kentucky Home"*
Bird: *Kentucky cardinal*
Flower: *Goldenrod*
Tree: *Kentucky coffee tree*
Abbreviation: *KY*

Area: *40,409 square miles (104,660 sq. km)*
Elevation: *(above sea level)*
   Highest: 4,145 ft. (1,263 m) – Black Mountain
   Lowest: 257 ft. (78 m) – Fulton County
Average Temperatures:
   July: 77°F. (25°C)
   January: 34°F. (1°C)
Average Yearly Precipitation: *47 in. (119 cm)*

Population

How Many: *3,698,969 (1990 Census)*
Where They Live: *51% urban, 49% rural*
Largest Cities: *Louisville, Lexington, Owensboro*

State Government

Governor: *4-year term*
Senators *(38): 4-year term*
Representatives *(100): 2-year term*
Counties: *120*

Federal Government

Senators *(2): 6-year term*
Representatives *(6): 2-year term*
Electoral Votes: *8*

Kentucky State Flag

Economy

Agriculture: *tobacco, beef cattle, soybeans, hogs, corn, milk*
Manufacturing: *tobacco products, chemicals, fabricated metal products, electric machinery,*
   transportation equipment
Mining: *coal, stone, petroleum*

Interesting Facts

- The Kentucky Derby, the oldest annually-run horse race in the United States, began in 1875 in Louisville at Churchill Downs.

- The gold depository for the United States is located at Fort Knox.

Interesting Kentuckian

- Daniel Boone was an American frontiersman. Though born in Pennsylvania, he helped settle Kentucky by hunting, guiding, and tracking for the new settlers. He led the colonists through the Cumberland Gap.

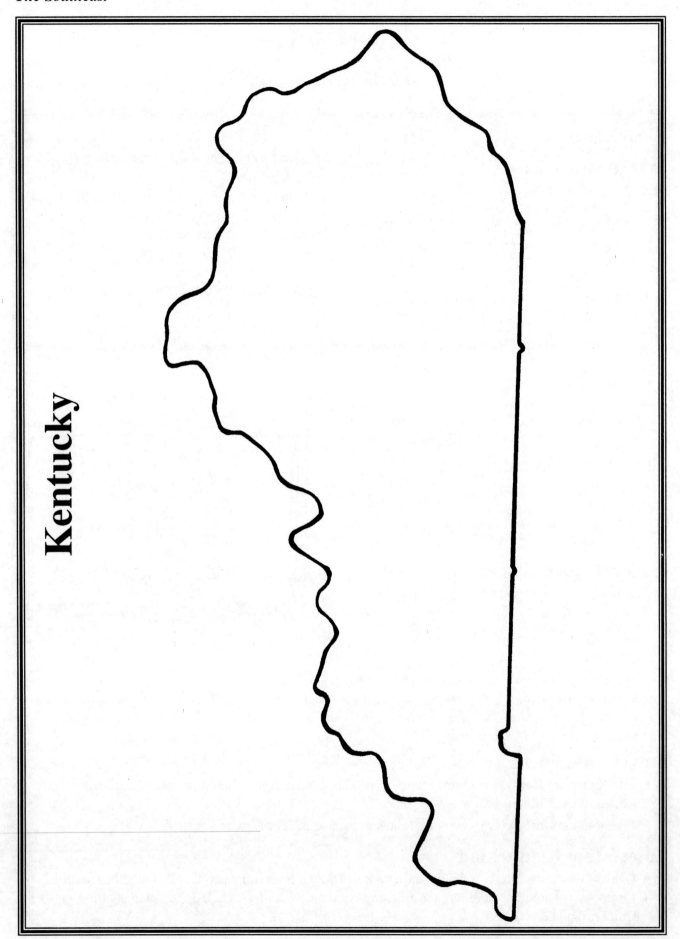

Kentucky

And They're Off!

Kentucky's name is derived from the Wyandot Indian word, Kah-ten-tah-teh, meaning "land of tomorrow." Perhaps a more appropriate name would have been "land of the derby," for it is because of the Kentucky Derby that Kentucky has gained world-wide recognition. First run on the 17th of May, 1875, this annual horse race has become the single most famous event in U.S. thoroughbred racing. Now held on the first Saturday in May at Churchill Downs in Louisville, the Derby is the first of the three races comprising the Triple Crown for 3-year olds.

Activity: Class Kentucky Derby

Find out more about the Kentucky Derby by reading books and other resources from your school or local library. Then use the materials and directions below to hold your own Kentucky Derby.

Essentials

- 36 copies of the horse pattern on page 24
- chalk or masking tape
- 3 dice

Directions

Using the pattern on page 24, have each student color and name his or her horse. It works best if there were 36 horses to start, so some students may wish to make more than one horse.

When the horses have been made, separate them into six groups. The groups will race against each other, with the winners of each race competing in the final derby. Follow the steps below for the race.

1. Using chalk or masking tape, make the race track. The track should be 6 lanes wide and contain ten spaces in each lane. (See diagram below.)

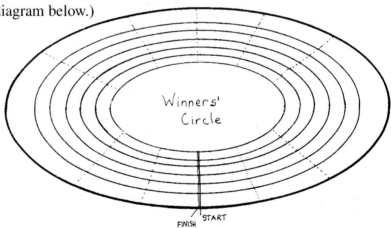

2. Assign each group of 6 horses a lane number. Number the horses 1-6, and place each horse in its starting gate. Roll the dice and move each horse one space every time its number shows. For example, if a three, a one, and a one are showing on the dice, the number three horse will move ahead one space and the number one horse will move ahead two spaces. Play continues in this way. When a horse reaches its start/finish line, move it into the winners' circle. In the case of a tie, roll one die until one of the numbers is rolled. For instance, if the number four horse and number five horse reach the finish line at the same time, roll one die until either a four or a five have been rolled to determine the winner.

3. The winner of each race will wait in the winners' circle until all six races are finished. The six winners will compete in one final derby. Award the winner with a garland of roses.

Horse Pattern

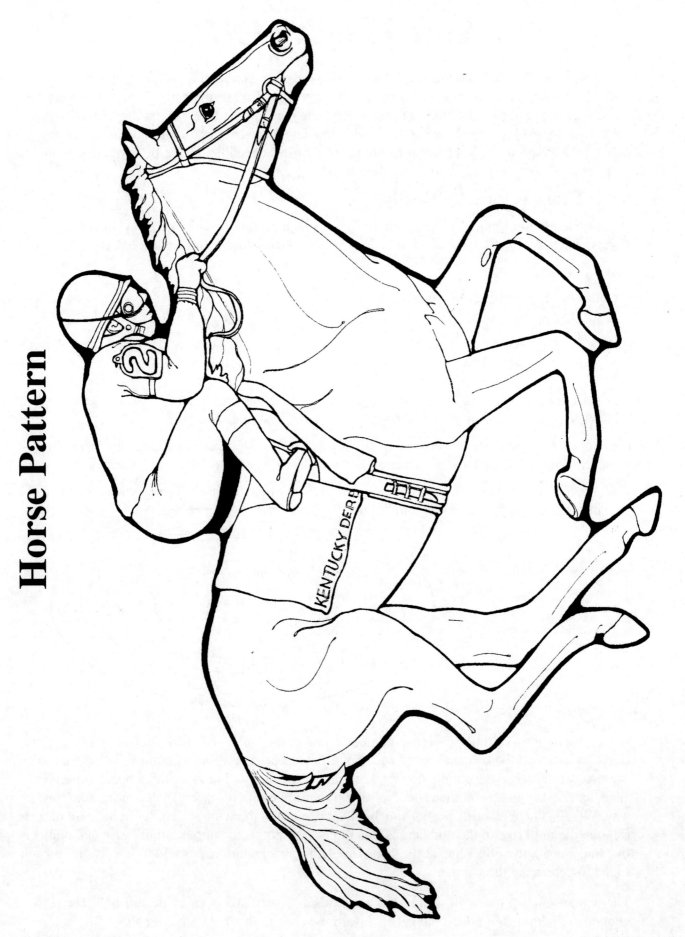

Louisiana

"The Pelican State"

Basic Facts

Capital: *Baton Rouge*
Statehood: *April 30, 1812*
Admittance: *15th state*
Motto: *Union, Justice, and Confidence*
Song: *"Give Me Louisiana"*
Bird: *Brown Pelican*
Flower: *Magnolia*
Tree: *Bald Cypress*
Abbreviation: *LA*

Area: *47,752 square miles (123,677 sq. km)*
Elevation: *(above sea level)*
  Highest: *535 ft. (163 m) – Driskill Mountain*
  Lowest: *5 ft. (1.5 m) – New Orleans*
Average Temperatures:
  July: *80°F. (28°C)*
  January: *50°F. (10°C)*
Average Yearly Precipitation: *57 in. (145 cm)*

Population

How Many: *4,238,216 (1990 Census)*
Where They Live: *69% urban, 31% rural*
Largest Cities: *New Orleans, Baton Rouge, Shreveport*

Louisiana State Flag

State Government

Governor: *4-year term*
Senators *(39): 4-year term*
Representatives *(105): 4-year term*
Counties: *64*

Federal Government

Senators *(2): 6-year term*
Representatives *(7): 2-year term*
Electoral Votes: *19*

Economy

Agriculture: *soybeans, rice, sugar cane, cotton, beef cattle, milk*
Fishing: *shrimp, menhaden*
Manufacturing: *paper products, chemicals, petroleum and coal products, metal products, transportation equipment*
Mining: *natural gas, sulfur, salt, petroleum*

Interesting Facts

- Tabasco sauce, a hot, red, spicy sauce made from tabasco peppers, originated on Avery Island.

- People come from all over to join the celebration of Mardi Gras in New Orleans. Wonderful parades, music, and costumes are part of this festival.

Interesting Louisianian

- Louis Armstrong was a famous American jazz trumpet player. He is known world-wide for his musical abilities and his special singing style. He was born in New Orleans.

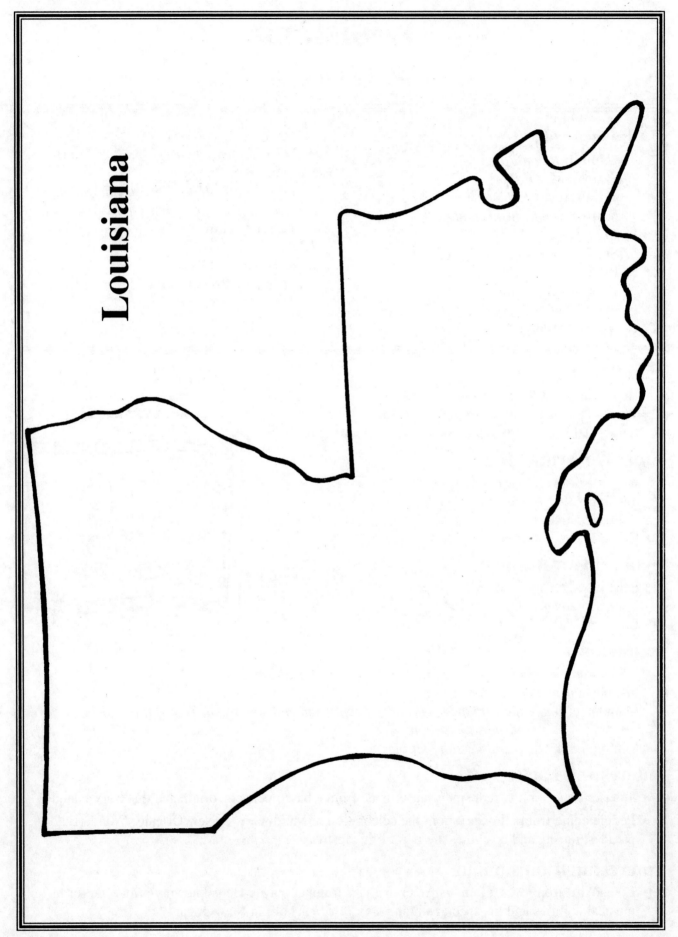

Louisiana

Festive Traditions

Louisiana was named in 1682 for France's King Louis XIV, but its connection with France does not end there. The culture of Louisiana is tied closely to the early settlers of the region. These descendants of France and Nova Scotia are known as the Creoles, Acadians, and Cajuns.

The Cajuns trace their origins from the mainly rural people exiled from Acadia (Nova Scotia) in the 1740's, while the Creoles tend to be city people from France.

Today New Orleans is one of the major tourist attractions in the U.S., drawing a million people a year.

Mardi Gras, a lavish festival introduced by the French colonists in the 1700's, has parades and costume balls nightly. The carnival ends on Fat Tuesday or Mardi Gras Day.

Dixieland jazz, born in New Orleans around 1900, is rooted to the culture of Louisiana. Originally played by brass bands at carnivals and funerals, it has, over the years, swept the globe. Dixieland jazz, along with Cajun music, which uses the fiddle and accordion, are Louisiana's best known musical contributions to the world.

Activity 1: Class Cook-off

Both Cajuns and Creoles are famous for their spicy foods. Find as many recipes from the two cultures as possible. Make one of each in class, or make the dishes at home and have a Cajun vs. Creole cook-off.

Activity 2: Mardi Gras Masks

Find out more about the New Orleans Mardi Gras. Then make Mardi Gras masks using the directions below. Create your own Mardi Gras magic with a class festival.

Essentials

- mask pattern on page 28 (Reproduce on index or construction paper.)
- scissors
- glue
- tag board
- paint, markers, crayons, or glitter for decorating the mask
- tongue depressor or craft stick

Directions

Cut out the pattern on page 28. Decorate the mask. Staple or glue a tongue depressor or craft stick to one side of the mask to use as a handle. Wear your mask as you dance to the music of Louis Armstrong (see activity 3). Display masks on a wall or bulletin board along with pictures and information about Louisiana.

Activity 3: Birthplace of Jazz

Listen to music by one of the most famous jazz musicians of all times, Louisiana-born Louis ("Satchmo") Armstrong.

Mardi Gras Mask Pattern

Mississippi
"The Magnolia State"

Basic Facts

Capital: *Jackson*
Statehood: *December 10, 1817*
Admittance: *20th state*
Motto: *By Valor and Arms*
Song: *"Go Mis-sis-sip-pi"*
Bird: *Mockingbird*
Flower: *Magnolia*
Tree: *Magnolia*
Abbreviation: *MS*

Area: *47,689 square miles (123,515 sq. km)*
Elevation: *(above sea level)*
   Highest: 806 ft. (246 m) – Woodall Mt.
   Lowest: Sea level along the coastline
Average Temperatures:
   July: 81°F. (27°C)
   January: 46°F. (8°C)
Average Yearly Precipitation: *56 in. (142 cm)*

Population

How Many: *2,586,443 (1990 Census)*
Where They Live: *53% urban, 37% rural*
Largest Cities: *Jackson, Biloxi, Meridian*

Mississippi State Flag

State Government

Governor: *4-year term*
Senators *(52): 4-year term*
Representatives *(122): 4-year term*
Counties: *82*

Federal Government

Senators *(2): 6-year term*
Representatives *(5): 2-year term*
Electoral Votes: *7*

Economy

Agriculture: *chickens, soybeans, cotton, beef cattle, milk*
Fishing: *menhaden, shrimp, red snapper*
Manufacturing: *food products, chemicals, lumber and wood products, electric machinery*
Mining: *petroleum, natural gas*

Interesting Facts

• As the Pasagoula River flows, it makes a noise that sounds like a swarm of bees.

• The world's first heart transplant on a human being took place in Jackson in 1964.

Interesting Mississippian

• Elvis Presley, a legend in the music industry, was born in Tupelo. His style of rock and roll music has influenced musicians around the world.

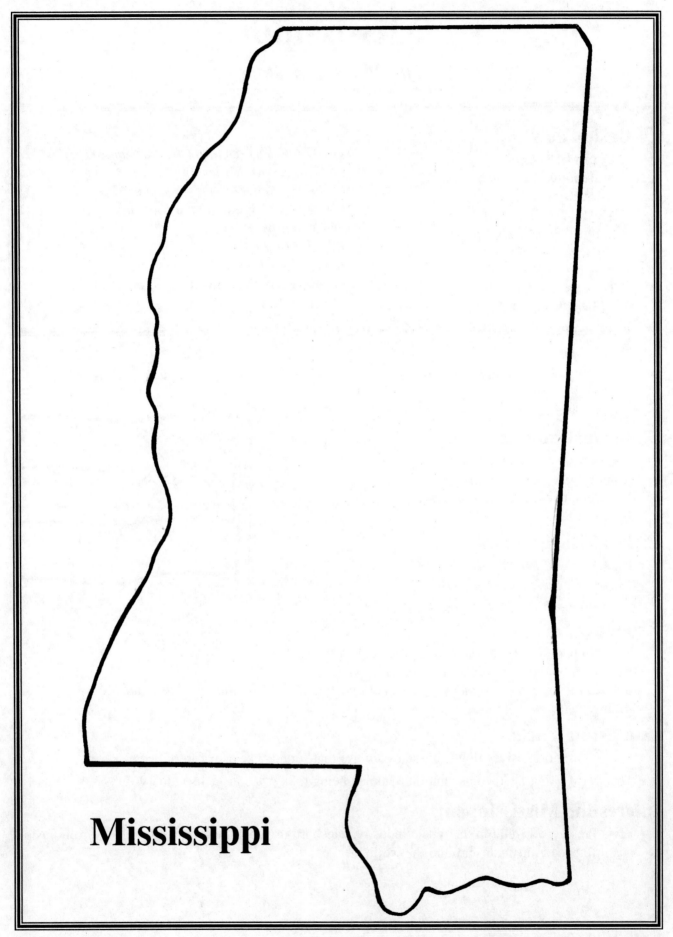

Mississippi

Mississippi Mud Pies

The 1993 flooding of the Mississippi River was not the first time the banks of this great river overflowed, creating havoc and devastation to surrounding areas.

In the spring, of 1927, the town of Greenville, Mississippi, was under water for over two months due to flooding. When the water finally receded, what remained was a tremendous amount of mud, "too thick to pour, too thin to plow."

Many of the Greenville residents lost everything and decided to move to other towns to start anew. Jenny Meyer was one such refugee. She took a job as a waitress in the town of Vicksberg. One warm day, while she was serving a piece of frozen pie invented by a chef named Percy Tolliver, Jenny remarked that the melting concoction reminded her of the Mississippi mud—and so, the Mississippi Mud Pie came to be named.

Activity: Make a Mouthwatering Mud Pie

Follow the recipe below to make your own mud pie.

Essentials

- ¼ cup (60 mL) softened butter or margarine
- ⅔ cup (8½-ounce/160 mL) package dark chocolate wafers
- ½ gallon (4.5 L) coffee ice cream
- whipped cream or nondairy topping
- Fudge Sauce (see recipe below)
- toasted sliced almonds

Directions

Crush the chocolate wafers in a food processor or place wafers on waxed paper and crush with a rolling pin. Mix the wafer crumbs with butter or margarine and press into a 9" (23 cm) pie pan to form a pie crust. Chill to firm up the crust. Fill the chilled crust with ice cream, packed to form a smooth surface. Freeze the pie until firm. Pour ¾ cup (about 180 mL) Fudge Sauce over the pie and freeze it until you are ready to serve. Just before serving, top your Mouthwatering Mud Pie with whipped cream or nondairy topping and sprinkle with almond slices. This recipe makes 6 to 8 servings.

Fudge Sauce

Essentials

- ½ cup (125 mL) butter or margarine
- 5 ounces (142 g) unsweetened Swiss chocolate
- ⅔ cups (156 mL) evaporated milk
- 1¼ teaspoons (6 mL) vanilla
- 3 cups (700 mL) powdered sugar

Directions

Melt the butter (or margarine) and chocolate together in a saucepan. Remove the mixture from the heat and add milk and powdered sugar, alternating each as you blend them into the mixture. Place the saucepan over medium heat and bring the ingredients to a boil, stirring constantly. Cook about 8 minutes, stirring constantly, until the liquid thickens and becomes creamy. Remove from heat and add vanilla. Place in refrigerator until ready to use.

North Carolina
"The Tar Heel State"

Basic Facts

Capital: *Raleigh*
Statehood: *November 21, 1789*
Admittance: *12th state*
Motto: *To Be, Rather Than to Seem*
Song: *"The Old North State"*
Bird: *Cardinal*
Flower: *Flowering Dogwood*
Tree: *Pine*
Abbreviation: *NC*

Area: *52,669 square miles (136,413 sq. km)*
Elevation: *(above sea level)*
  Highest: 6,684 ft. (2,037 m) – Mount Mitchell
  Lowest: Sea level along the coastline
Average Temperatures:
  July: 70°F. (21°C)
  January: 41°F. (5°C)
Average Yearly Precipitation: *50 in. (127 cm)*

Population

How Many: *6,657,630 (1990 Census)*
Where They Live: *52% urban, 48% rural*
Largest Cities: *Charlotte, Greensboro, Raleigh*

State Government

Governor: *4-year term*
Senators *(50): 2-year term*
Representatives *(120): 2-year term*
Counties: *100*

Federal Government

Senators *(2): 6-year term*
Representatives *(12): 2-year term*
Electoral Votes: *14*

North Carolina Sate Flag

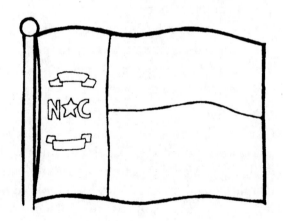

Economy

Agriculture: *tobacco, chickens, hogs, corn, turkeys, milk*
Fishing: *shrimp, menhaden, flounder*
Manufacturing: *textiles, tobacco products, electric machinery, food products, furniture, clothing, rubber and plastic products*
Mining: *stone, phosphate rock, sand, and gravel*

Interesting Facts

• The Wright brothers completed the world's first airplane flight near Kitty Hawk in 1903.

• The first interstate railroad was opened in 1833 between Northhampton County and Petersburg, Virginia.

Interesting North Carolinian

• Andrew Johnson, the 17th President of the United States, was born in Raleigh.

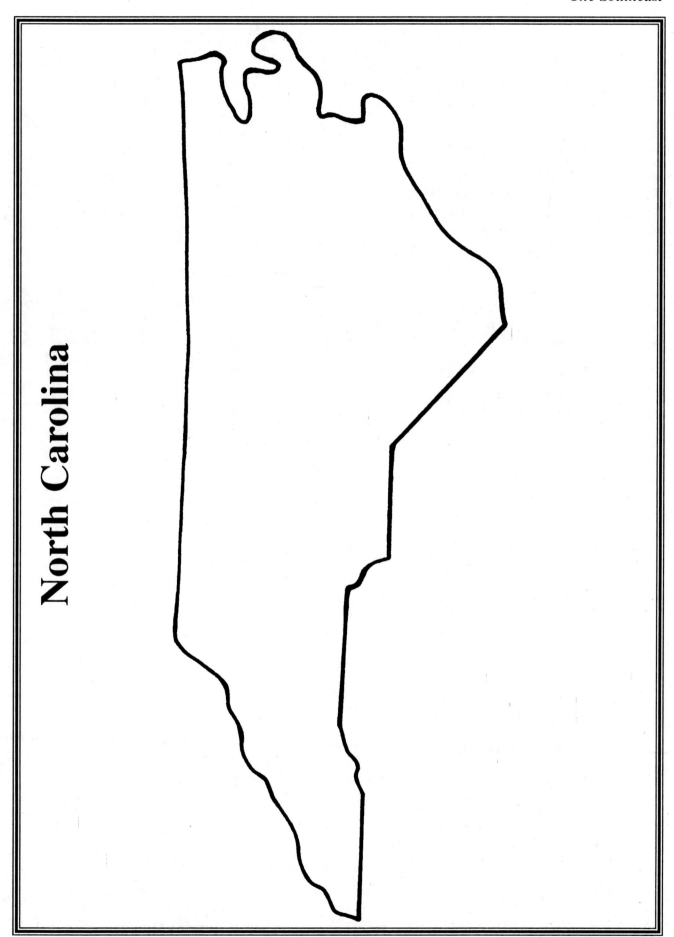

North Carolina

The Famous Flight

One of the most famous places in North Carolina is Kitty Hawk, where, from 1900 to 1903, the Wright brothers experimented with gliders and airplanes. The Wright Brothers National Memorial marks the site of the first successful flight.

Activity: Taking Notes

Create two columns on a piece of notebook paper by folding it in half lengthwise. Label the first column "About the Flight" and the second column "About the Kitty Hawk Flyer." Organize the following information about the Wright Brothers' Kitty Hawk Flyer into the two categories provided. First, write "clue words" for each sentence on the lines provided. Then, write your "clue words" in the correct categories on your notebook paper. The first one is done for you.

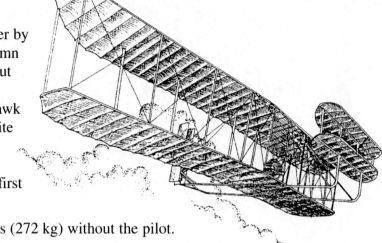

1. The Kitty Hawk Flyer weighed 605 pounds (272 kg) without the pilot.

   airplane weight
   _____

2. On the third flight, Orville flew 200 feet (60 m) and stayed aloft for fifteen seconds.

   _____

3. On Friday, December 17, 1903, at Kitty Hawk, North Carolina, the Wright brothers were successful in their goal.

   _____

4. There were two counter-rotating propellers made of laminated spruce wood.

   _____

5. The fourth and final flight was the longest and farthest.

   _____

6. The wood was covered with canvas and painted with aluminum paint.

   _____

7. The final flight covered 175 feet (53 m) and lasted 12 seconds.

   _____

8. The propellers turned 330 revolutions per minute and produced 90 pounds (40.5 kg) of thrust.

   _____

9. There were four flights that day.

   _____

10. The engine was made of four iron cylinders which produced 12 horsepower.

South Carolina

"The Palmetto State"

Basic Facts

Capital: *Columbia*
Statehood: *May 23, 1788*
Admittance: *8th state*
Motto: *While I Breathe, I Hope*
Song: *"Carolina"*
Bird: *Carolina wren*
Flower: *Carolina jessamine*
Tree: *Palmetto*
Abbreviation: *SC*

Area: *31,113 square miles (80,582 sq. km)*
Elevation: *(above sea level)*
   Highest: 3,560 ft. (1,085 m) – Sassafras Mt.
   Lowest: Sea level along coastline
Average Temperatures:
   July: 80°F. (27°C)
   January: 45°F. (7°C)
Average Yearly Precipitation: *48 in. (122 cm)*

Population

How Many: *3,505,707 (1990 Census)*
Where They Live: *54% urban, 46% rural*
Largest Cities: *Columbia, Charleston, North Charleston*

State Government

Governor: *4-year term*
Senators *(46): 4-year term*
Representatives *(124): 2-year term*
Counties: *46*

Federal Government

Senators *(2): 6-year term*
Representatives *(6): 2-year term*
Electoral Votes: *8*

South Carolina State Flag

Economy

Agriculture: *tobacco, beef cattle, milk, eggs, soybeans, hogs*
Fishing: *shrimp, crabs*
Manufacturing: *textiles, chemicals, machinery, electric equipment, rubber and plastic products*
Mining: *crushed stone, clay*

Interesting Facts

- More Revolutionary War battles were fought on South Carolina soil than in any other state.
- The first American Colony museum was opened in Charleston in 1773. The museum contained natural history items that had been found in South Carolina.

Interesting South Carolinian

- Dizzy Gillespie, a famous jazz composer and trumpet player, was born in Cheraw. He co-founded the "bebop" jazz movement in the 1940's.

South Carolina

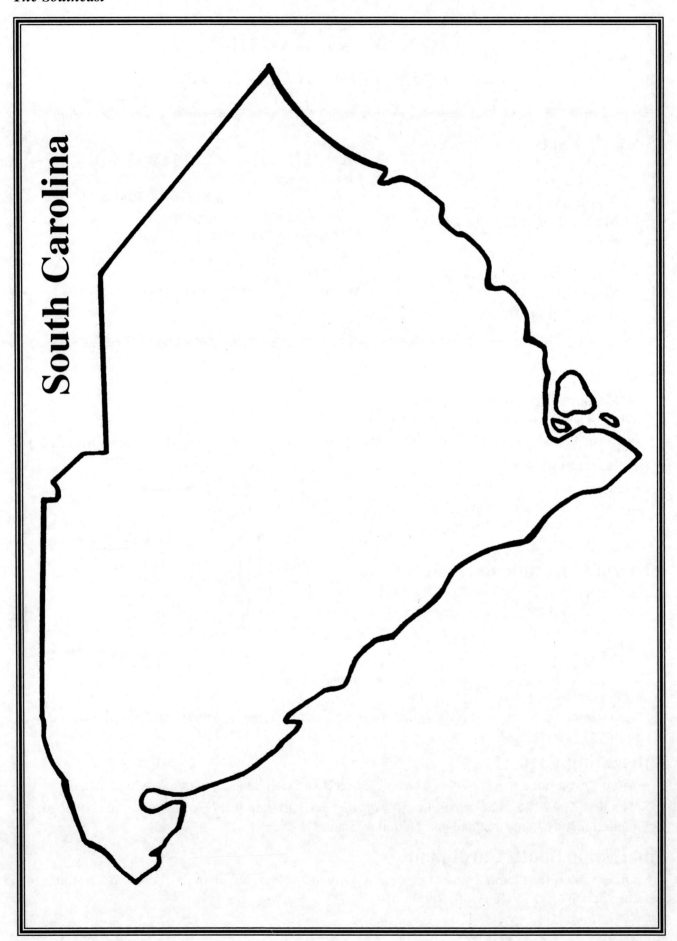

Two Kinds of Battles

South Carolina faces yearly battles with nature. Its location along the Atlantic coastline of the United States makes it an easy target for the powerful forces of hurricanes and tropical storms. A hurricane is an area of low pressure that forms over oceans in the tropical regions of the North Atlantic and North Pacific. Hurricanes are one of the most destructive forces on earth. They can stretch over hundreds of miles and sustain winds of up to two hundred miles per hour. The winds can uproot trees, cars, and homes.

Today, hurricanes can be tracked by weather satellites and radar. Information about the direction and force of a hurricane is essential to coastal communities such as those along the South Carolina shore.

During the Revolutionary War, more battles were fought on South Carolina soil than in any other state. While American soldiers and militiamen fought some of the battles, others were fought in swamp lands by American guerillas. Many of the Revolutionary War battlegrounds of South Carolina can still be seen today.

Activity: Make An Anemometer

The anemometer is an important weather instrument used to measure how hard the wind is blowing. Use the information below to make your own anemometer. When you are finished, use the anemometer to graph the wind speed for one week. Share your findings with the class.

Essentials

For each group of 3 or 4 students you will need:

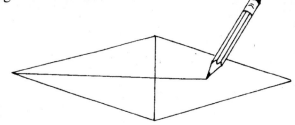

- 4 paper cups
- 12" (30 cm) square piece of cardboard
- 18" (46 cm) dowel
- long straight pin
- pencil
- bead
- ruler
- tape or glue

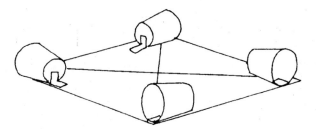

Directions

- Use a ruler to draw a diagonal line across the cardboard, corner to corner. Draw another diagonal line across joining the other two corners.
- Place cups on their sides and glue one to each corner of the cardboard. Be sure that the cup openings face the same direction (see diagram).
- Push the straight pin down through the center of the cardboard where the lines cross.
- Put the pin through the bead. Gently tap the pin into the tip of the dowel.
- Take your wind gauge outside and "find" some wind.

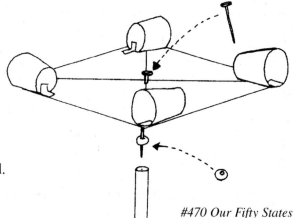

Two Kinds of Battles *(cont.)*

Activity 2: Revolutionary War Diary

"Bring to life" some of the battles that were fought in South Carolina during the Revolutionary War. You will need to research famous battles that were fought in South Carolina. Assume the role of at soldier fighting in South Carolina. Make a diary cover by coloring and cutting out the picture below. Attach several lined writing pages to the cover and write in your diary each day for one week.

Revolutionary War Diary

Tennessee

"The Volunteer State"

Basic Facts

Capital: *Nashville*
Statehood: *June 1, 1796*
Admittance: *16th state*
Motto: *Agriculture and Commerce*
Song: *"The Tennessee Waltz"*
Bird: *Mockingbird*
Flower: *Iris*
Tree: *Tulip poplar*
Abbreviation: *TN*

Area: *42,114 square miles (109,152 sq. km)*
Elevation: *(above sea level)*
   Highest: 6,643 ft. (2,025 m) – Clingmans Dome
   Lowest: 182 ft. (55 m) – Shelby County
Average Temperatures:
   July: 78°F. (26°C)
   January: 380°F. (3°C)
Average Yearly Precipitation: *52 in. (132 cm)*

Population

How Many: *4,896,641 (1990 Census)*
Where They Live: *60% urban, 40% rural*
Largest Cities: *Memphis, Nashville, Knoxville*

State Government

Governor: *4-year term*
Senators *(33): 4-year term*
Representatives *(99): 2-year term*
Counties: *95*

Federal Government

Senators *(2): 6-year term*
Representatives *(9): 2-year term*
Electoral Votes: *11*

Tennessee State Flag

Economy

Agriculture: *beef cattle, milk, soybeans, hogs, tobacco, hay*
Manufacturing: *chemicals, food products, machinery, transportation equipment, printed materials, electric equipment*
Mining: *coal, crushed stone, zinc*

Interesting Facts

- Kingston was the capital of Tennessee for one day in 1807.
- The city of Nashville is considered the home of country and western music.

Interesting Tennessean

- David "Davey" Crockett was a famous frontiersman in the early days of the West. He was a humorist, expert marksman, and also a member of Congress.

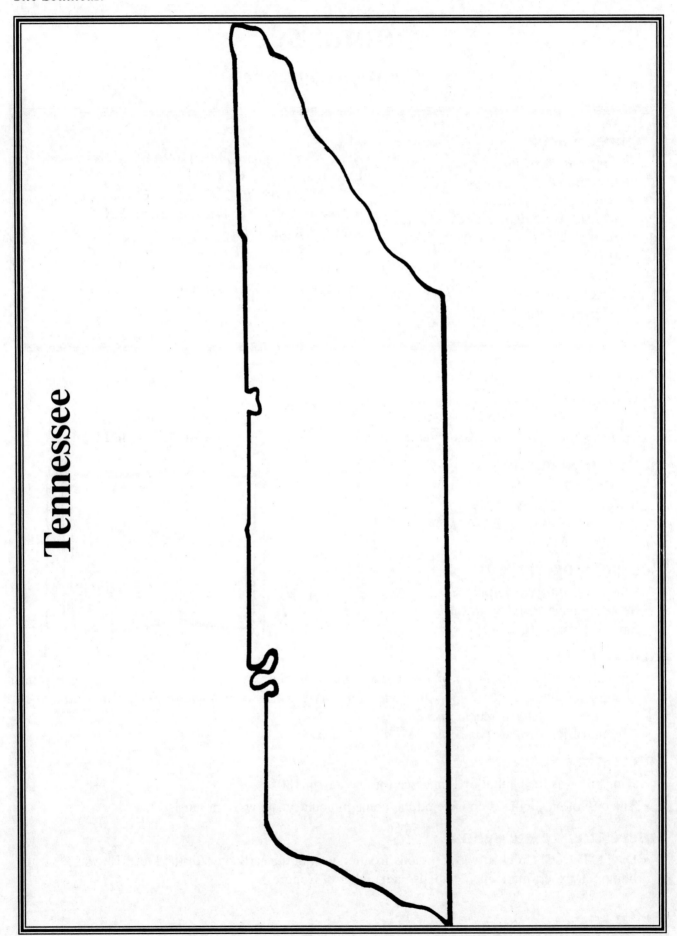

Tennessee

Frontier Folks

By the mid 1700's, many settlers had crossed the Appalachian barrier in search of pelts, and other desired resources. These hearty folks were accustomed to hardship and unwilling to stay in any one area for long. One of the most well known of these frontier folks was Davey Crockett. This real person has worked his way into the heart of American folklore and tall tales. Born on August 17, 1786, Crockett was not born too long after Tennessee received its statehood, and the two are said to have grown up together. His motto, "Be always sure you're right, then go ahead," reflected the national spirit of the times. He was a first-rate hunter and had a colorful career as a politician. Davey Crockett died in 1836 while fighting in the war for Texas independence.

The Making of a Legend

Davey Crockett loved to tell exaggerated stories, or "backwoods brags," often about himself. He told stories about hunting, claiming to have killed 105 bears in 7 months, and a raccoon who "just gave himself up" to Davey while he was hunting one day.

He was a cunning political opponent as well. He once memorized the standard speech given by his rival at a debate. Davey went first and recited the speech word for word. Stunned, his confused opponent was forced to make up a speech on the spot. Through the years, the life of this American hero has been celebrated in books, television shows, and movies.

Activity: Legendary People

A legend is a type of folk story. Most legends have as their subjects recognizable people, events, or places. Create and tell a legend of your own based on a real person from history.

In groups of four, make up a legend based on facts. Write and illustrate these legends. Share them with the class in the form of a reader's theater or dramatic play. Bind the stories into a class book of folk legends.

Virginia

"Old Dominion"

Basic Facts

Capital: *Richmond*
Statehood: *June 25, 1788*
Admittance: *10th state*
Motto: *Thus Always to Tyrants*
Song: *"Carry Me Back to Old Virginia"*
Bird: *Cardinal*
Flower: *Flowering dogwood blossom*
Tree: *Flowering dogwood*
Abbreviation: *VA*

Area: *40,767 square miles (105,586 sq. km)*
Elevation: *(above sea level)*
   Highest: 5,729 ft. (1,746 m) – Mount Rogers
   Lowest: Sea level along coastline
Average Temperatures:
   July: 75°F. (24°C)
   January: 36°F. (2°C)
Average Yearly Precipitation: *43 in. (109 cm)*

Population

How Many: *6,216,568 (1990 Census)*
Where They Live: *66% urban, 34% rural*
Largest Cities: *Norfolk, Virginia Beach, Richmond*

Virginia State Flag

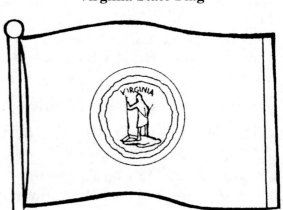

State Government

Governor: *4-year term*
Senators *(40): 4-year term*
Representatives *(100): 2-year term*
Counties: *95*

Federal Government

Senators *(2): 6-year term*
Representatives *(11): 2-year term*
Electoral Votes: *13*

Economy

Agriculture: *beef cattle, milk, chickens, tobacco*
Fishing: *menhaden, clams, crabs, oysters*
Manufacturing: *chemicals, tobacco products, food products, electric equipment, transportation
             equipment*
Mining: *coal, stone, lime*

Interesting Facts

- Eight United States Presidents were born in Virginia: George Washington, Thomas Jefferson, James Madison, James Monroe, William Henry Harrison, John Tyler, Zachary Taylor, and Woodrow Wilson.

Interesting Virginian

- Robert E. Lee was a highly honored general who commanded the Confederate Army during the Civil War. He was born in Stratford Hall.

42

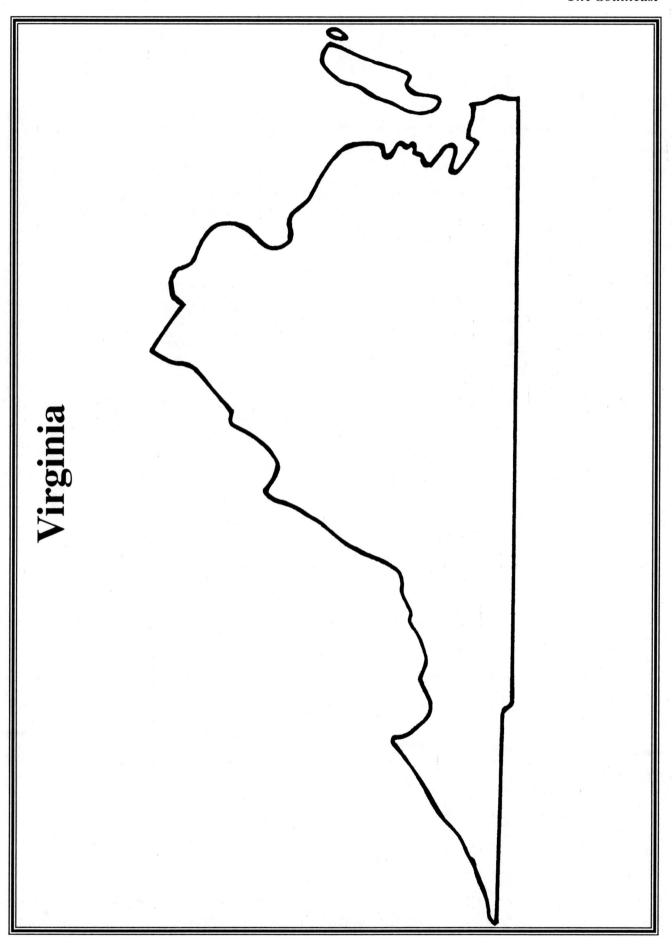

Virginia

Settling in America

The first permanent English settlement in America was Jamestown, Virginia. Captain John Smith and a group of English colonists established the settlement in May, 1607.

Settlers went there in hopes of finding gold and silver in the new world. Instead they found thick forests along the Virginia coastline and water that sparkled with fish. The settlers were disappointed. But in a few years, they would learn how valuable the forests and rich soil was in other ways.

One settler had an idea that would help the colony economically. John Rolfe had seen local Indians growing tobacco in their gardens. He filled his garden with different tobacco plants and worked to grow a plant that tasted good enough to send to England.

Activity: Investigating Plant Growth

Find out more about the effects of soil and other conditions on the growth of plants. Obtain four specimens of the same kind of plant. (Choose fast-growing plants that are already established, or start your own plants using dried bean seeds, such as lima bean seeds, soaked in tap water overnight before planting.) Place each plant in the same type of container and label the plants A, B, C, and D.

Provide the following growing conditions for your plants:

> Plant A—*water and good soil, but no light*
>
> Plant B—*light and good soil, but no water*
>
> Plant C—*light and water, but poor soil*
>
> Plant D—*light, water, and good soil*

Use the chart below to record each plant's growth over a period of time. What did you discover about the various conditions for growing plants? Discuss your ideas with other members of the class.

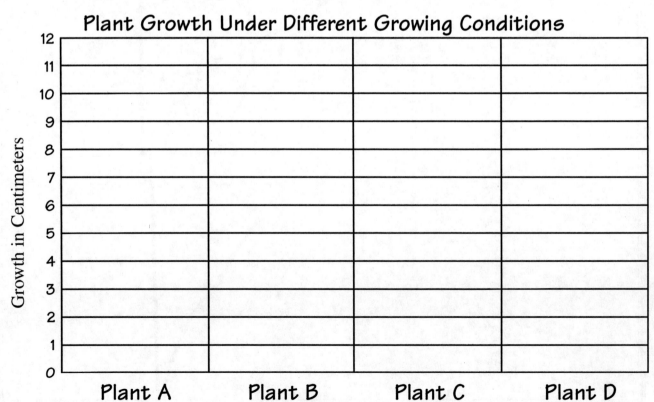

West Virginia
"The Mountain State"

Basic Facts

Capital: *Charleston*
Statehood: *June 20, 1863*
Admittance: *35th state*
Motto: *Mountaineers Are Always Free*
Song: *"The West Virginia Hills"*
Bird: *Cardinal*
Flower: *Rhododendron*
Tree: *Sugar maple*
Abbreviation: *WV*

Area: *24,231 square miles (62,759 sq. km)*
Elevation: *(above sea level)*
  Highest: 4,862 ft. (1,482 m) – Spruce Knob
  Lowest: 240 ft. (73 m) – Jefferson County
Average Temperatures:
  July: 72°F. (22°C)
  January: 32°F. (0°C)
Average Yearly Precipitation: *44 in. (112 cm)*

Population

How Many: *1,801,625 (1990 Census)*
Where They Live: *64% urban, 36% rural*
Largest Cities: *Charleston, Huntington, Wheeling*

West VIrginia State Flag

State Government

Governor: *4-year term*
Senators *(34): 4-year term*
Representatives *(100): 2-year term*
Counties: *55*

Federal Government

Senators *(2): 6-year term*
Representatives *(3): 2-year term*
Electoral Votes: *5*

Economy

Agriculture: *beef cattle, milk, hay, chickens*
Manufacturing: *chemicals, primary metals, clay and grass products*
Mining: *coal, natural gas, petroleum, stone*

Interesting Facts

- Most of the nation's glass marbles are manufactured in the city of Parksburg.

- The city of Weirton is the only city in the United States that has three different state borders: West Virginia, Ohio, and Pennsylvania.

Interesting West Virginian

- General "Stonewall" Jackson, a famous Confederate military leader, was born and raised on a farm near Weston called Jackson's Mill.

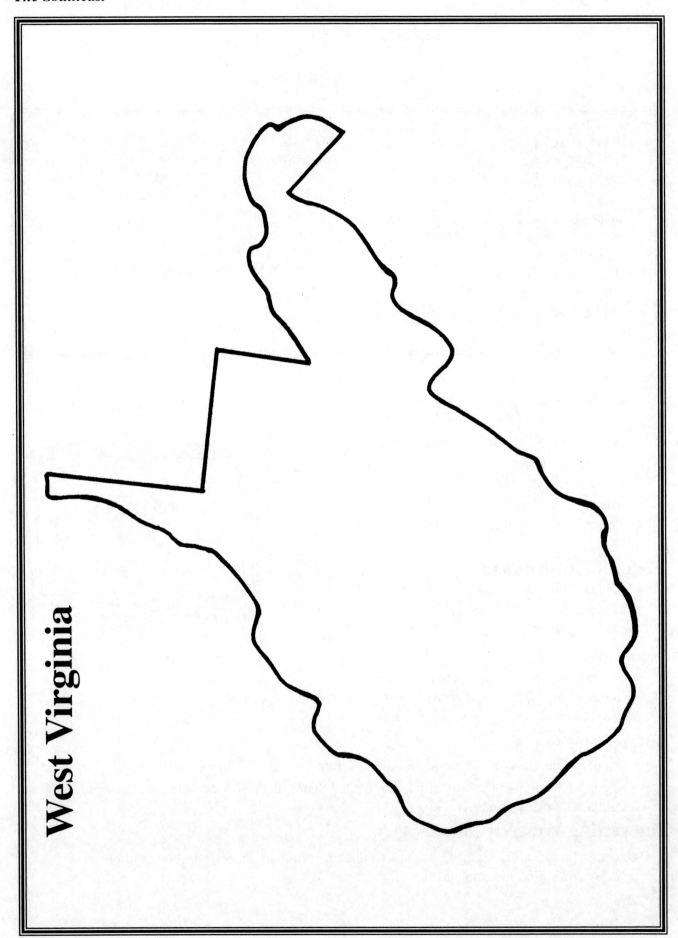

West Virginia

The Coal Producer

West Virginia is the third leading coal-producing state in the country. Coal appears as a black or brown rock. It is a raw material that can be ignited and burned. While the heat from coal is used to heat buildings and to process many products, coal is mainly used to produce electricity. About half the electricity used in the United States comes from coal-burning power plants.

Coal is classified as a sedimentary rock. Rocks are actually classified into three types: igneous; metamorphic; and sedimentary. Learn more about classifying rocks with the following activity.

Activity: Rock Sorting

Essentials

- bag filled with a variety of rocks
- newspaper to cover a work surface
- chart below
- 3 paper bags or shoe boxes

Directions

Spread the rocks out on the newspaper. Sort the rocks into three categories by matching the characteristics of each with the descriptions on the chart below. Did you collect samples of coal? How do you know? Discuss why you chose to classify each rock as you did.

Name	Characteristics	Cause/Effect	Usually Found
Igneous (granite, basalt, obsidian, pumice, quartz)	glossy, crystalline, coarse-grained	created when molten lava cools	where volcanoes have existed
Metamorphic (slate, schists, migmatite, marble, eclogite)	hard, crystals may appear, layers may develop	created when sedimentary or igneous rocks undergo a change due to pressure or heat within the earth	deep in the earth where pressure and heat can affect the rocks
Sedimentary (chalk, coal, sandstone, shale, limestone, dolomite)	contains fossils, soft layered	created when layers of sediment (mud, sand, gravel, and minerals) settle to the bottom of the ocean and over thousands of years are pressed together	where oceans or bodies of water once existed or still exist

Southeastern Clip Art

South Carolina

limestone

Middleton Place
Gardens

Fort
Sumter

cotton

Tennessee

Casey Jones Home
and Railroad Museum

Great Smoky Mountains

sheep

Grand Old Opry

48

Southeastern Clip Art *(cont.)*

Kentucky

Kentucky Derby

Birthplace of
Abraham Lincoln
(Hodgenville)

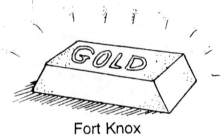

Fort Knox

Louisiana

oil

cotton

fishing

Evangeline Monument

New Orleans
Mardi Gras

forest products

Southeastern Clip Art *(cont.)*

Florida

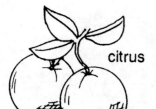

citrus

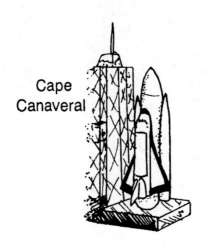

Cape
Canaveral

The Everglades

peaches

Georgia

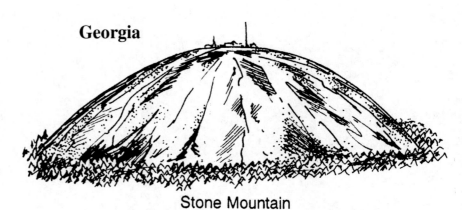

Stone Mountain

peanuts

Okefenokee Swamp

50

Southeastern Clip Art *(cont.)*

Alabama

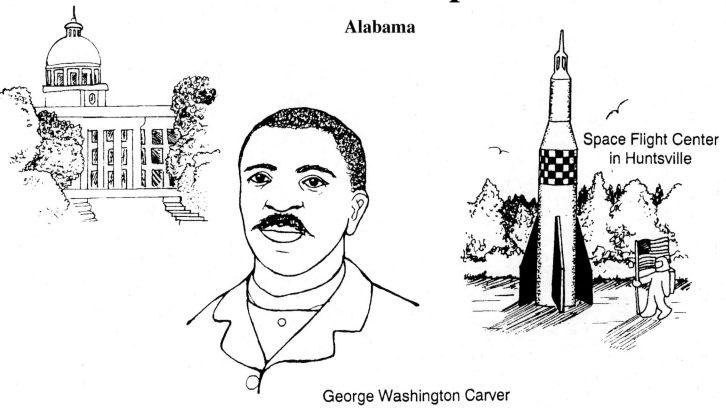

George Washington Carver

Space Flight Center
in Huntsville

Arkansas

Ozark Plateau

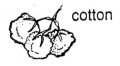

cotton

soybeans

Diamond State Park

rice

Southeastern Clip Art *(cont.)*

Mississippi

sweet potatoes

Vicksburg

cotton

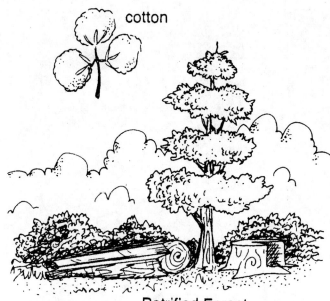

Petrified Forest

North Carolina

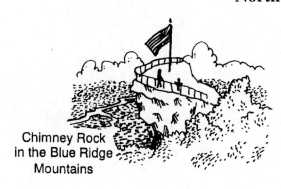

Chimney Rock
in the Blue Ridge
Mountains

Graveyard of the
Atlantic

North Carolina Zoo

Southeastern Clip Art *(cont.)*

Virginia

McLean House

Blue Ridge
Mountains

Tomb of the
Unknown Soldier

West Virginia

chemical industry

Seneca Rock

coal

Name _____   Date _____

Which State Am I?

Directions: Identify the state described. Write its name on the line.

1. I was one of the first thirty states in our country. I am sometimes referred to as "The Heart of Dixie." Both Rosa Parks and Dr. Martin Luther King, Jr. hail from my state. Cotton and peanuts grow well in my soil. Did you know that the first electric streetcars began operation in my state?

   Which state am I? _____

2. I was one of the first 30 states in our country. Although many people think my most valuable resource is petroleum, I think it is sunshine. Sunshine helps me produce oranges, tomatoes, and nursery products. In the waters off my shore, fishermen catch shrimp and lobsters. Did you know that I have more lakes than any other state?

   Which state am I? _____

3. I was one of the first 20 states in the United States. One of my most valuable natural resources is coal. Some of the important agricultural products that I produce are beef cattle, milk, soybeans, and hogs. A major river forms my western boundary. Abraham Lincoln was born here.

   Which state am I? _____

4. I was among the first 20 states of the United States. Among my agricultural products are rice, sugar cane, and cotton. I produce a lot of petroleum and natural gas. Jazz was first played here.

   Which state am I? _____

5. I was neither an early nor a late state. I produce agricultural products like rice, beef cattle, wheat, and turkeys. If you visit me, you might even find some diamonds. I am famous for my spring waters.

   Which state am I? _____

6. I was one of the first 5 states. I am well-known for my peaches. No other state produces more peanuts than I do. A drug store in one of my cities was the first place in the world to serve Coca-Cola®.

   Which state am I? _____

Name _____   Date _____

Which State Am I? *(cont.)*

7. I was one of the first thirteen states. I am well-known for textiles produced from southeastern cotton and synthetic materials. More Revolutionary War battles were fought on my soil than in any other state. Part of my name is shared with one of my neighbors.

   Which state am I? _____

8. I was one of the first 15 states to join the union. Most homes in the United States have some furniture that was made here. My coastline is one of the most treacherous in the world. The first successful airplane flight in the world was made here.

   Which state am I? _____

9. More than 30 states joined the Union before I did. I am well-known for my coal mines. If you collect glass marbles, many of them probably came from me. I am bordered by five states, but only two of them are part of the southeast region like me.

   Which state am I? _____

10. I was the 10th state to accept statehood. My valuable natural resources include coal, lime, sand, and gravel. Eight presidents were born here including George Washington. My Bill of Rights was the model for the U.S. Bill of Rights.

    Which state am I? _____

11. I was among the first 15 states of the United States. One of my most valuable resources is coal. I have outstanding military traditions, and for this I am sometimes called "The Volunteer State."

    Which state am I? _____

12. I was the 20th state to join the Union. I manufacture wood products, paper products and clothing. Flat boats used to carry goods down one of my largest rivers before there were railroads and trucks. I am the only state that has a singing river.

    Which state am I? _____

Name _____   Date _____

Identifying Southeastern States

Directions: Outlines of the states in the southeast region are mixed up with those of other regions. Identify the states of the southeastern region by coloring them green.

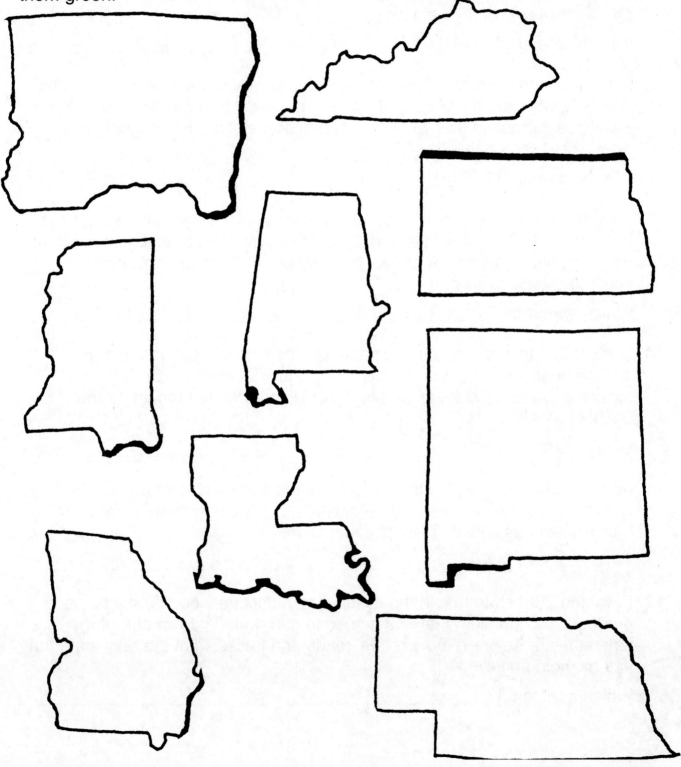

Name _____   Date _____

Flag Match

Directions: Write the number of the flag next to the state to which it belongs. Color the flags correctly.

1.

4.

2.

5.

3.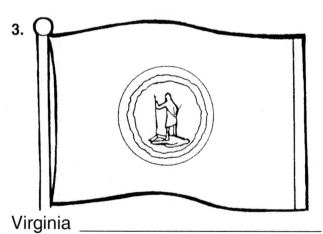

6.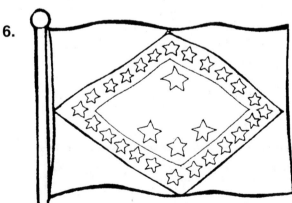

Virginia _____   Louisiana _____

Mississippi _____   Kentucky _____

Arkansas _____   West Virginia _____

Name _____   Date _____

Flag Match *(cont.)*

Directions: Write the number of the flag next to the state to which it belongs. Color the flags correctly.

1.

4.

2.

5.

3.
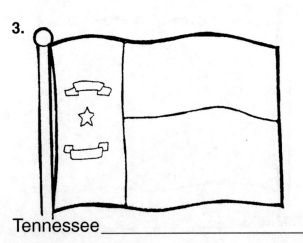

6.

Tennessee_____   South Carolina _____

North Carolina_____   Florida _____

Alabama _____   Georgia _____

Name _____   Date _____

City Match

Directions: Match the cities with their states by writing the numbers of the cities on the appropriate lines.

1. Pine Bluff
2. Hattiesburg
3. Savannah
4. Little Rock

5. Columbus
6. Baton Rouge
7. Lake Charles
8. Biloxi

9. Atlanta
10. Fort Smith
11. New Orleans
12. Laurel

Georgia

Louisiana

_____

_____

Mississippi

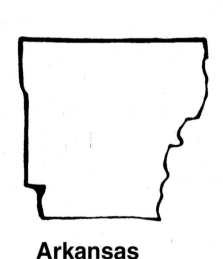

Arkansas

_____

_____

Name _____   Date _____

City Match *(cont.)*

Directions: Match the cities with their states by writing the numbers of the cities on the appropriate lines.

13. Mobile	17. Birmingham	21. Columbia
14. Montgomery	18. Virginia Beach	22. Tampa
15. Greenville	19. Jacksonville	23. Norfolk
16. Charleston	20. Miami	24. Richmond

South Carolina

_____

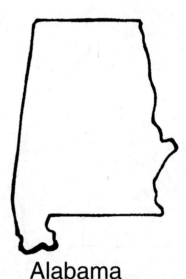

Alabama

_____

Florida

_____

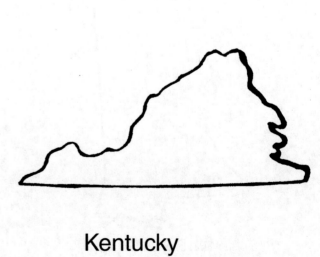

Kentucky

_____

Name _____   Date _____

How Far Is It?

Directions: Choose ten pairs of cities from the map below. Write their names in the blanks. Then use the map of the midwest and the scale on this page to find the distances between the cities you listed.

1. _____ to _____ = _____ mi./km

2. _____ to _____ = _____ mi./km

3. _____ to _____ = _____ mi./km

4. _____ to _____ = _____ mi./km

5. _____ to _____ = _____ mi./km

6. _____ to _____ = _____ mi./km

7. _____ to _____ = _____ mi./km

8. _____ to _____ = _____ mi./km

9. _____ to _____ = _____ mi./km

10. _____ to _____ = _____ mi./km

Name _____   Date _____

Comparing Areas of the Southeast

Directions: Record the area (sq. miles) of each state on the numbered lines. Round off these numbers to the nearest thousand. Write the rounded numbers on the lettered lines. Complete the bar graph using the rounded numbers.

Alabama	1. _____	a. _____
Arkansas	2. _____	b. _____
Florida	3. _____	c. _____
Georgia	4. _____	d. _____
Kentucky	5. _____	e. _____
Louisiana	6. _____	f. _____
Mississippi	7. _____	g. _____
North Carolina	8. _____	h. _____
South Carolina	9. _____	i. _____
Tennessee	10. _____	j. _____
Virginia	11. _____	k. _____
West Virginia	12. _____	l. _____

Area Comparisons

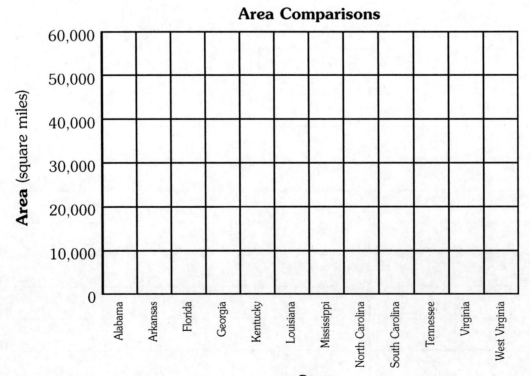

State

Name _____   Date _____

Admission Days

Directions: Complete the following exercises to learn more about when each of the southeastern states received statehood.

A. Research to find out when the southeast states below were granted statehood. Record their admission dates next to the states' names.

Name	Month	Day	Year
1. Alabama	_____	_____	_____
2. Arkansas	_____	_____	_____
3. Florida	_____	_____	_____
4. Georgia	_____	_____	_____
5. Kentucky	_____	_____	_____
6 Louisiana	_____	_____	_____
7. Mississippi	_____	_____	_____
8. North Carolina	_____	_____	_____
9. South Carolina	_____	_____	_____
10. Tennessee	_____	_____	_____
11. Virginia	_____	_____	_____
12. West Virginia	_____	_____	_____

B. The admission dates of the southeastern states can be plotted on a time line. Plot them on the time line below, making sure to label each one.

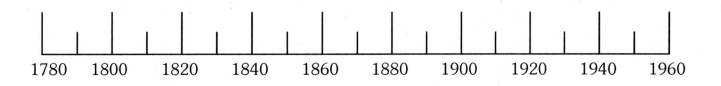

1780   1800   1820   1840   1860   1880   1900   1920   1940   1960

Name _____   Date _____

States Puzzler

Directions: Fill in the blanks with the correct words. Ring the words in the puzzle.

```
H  N  F  A  H  A  N  A  I  S  I  U  O  L  W
S  T  A  L  A  B  A  M  A  O  N  T  D  Y  S
N  U  S  K  O  A  T  E  W  L  W  E  T  I  H
N  O  G  E  O  R  G  I  A  Y  E  U  A  T  O
U  H  R  N  A  D  I  E  P  S  S  C  A  L  M
T  O  E  T  I  S  S  D  S  F  T  O  A  E  I
O  C  R  U  H  F  L  E  A  O  V  W  L  G  S
T  A  L  C  K  C  N  I  E  I  I  T  F  E  S
L  I  U  K  Y  N  A  U  E  A  R  T  N  R  I
U  Y  I  Y  E  E  S  R  K  S  G  H  Y  L  S
S  O  U  T  H  C  A  R  O  L  I  N  A  I  S
E  S  Y  N  C  C  M  O  T  L  N  E  O  K  I
I  T  H  V  E  T  V  I  R  G  I  N  I  A  P
H  Y  D  E  T  I  A  O  G  I  A  N  G  I  P
A  R  K  A  N  S  A  S  I  O  N  L  A  O  I
```

1. The capital of _____is Tallahassee.

2. The "Magnolia State" is _____ .

3. The flowering dogwood is the state flower of _____ .

4. _____is the "Heart of Dixie."

5. The eighth state was _____ .

6. The "Empire State of the South" is _____.

7. The capital of_____ is Nashville.

8. _____ was the fifteenth state.

9. The state tree of_____ is the sugar maple.

10. _____ is the "Old Dominion" state.

11. The state flower of _____ is the apple blossom.

12. The capital of _____ is Baton Rouge.

The Northeast

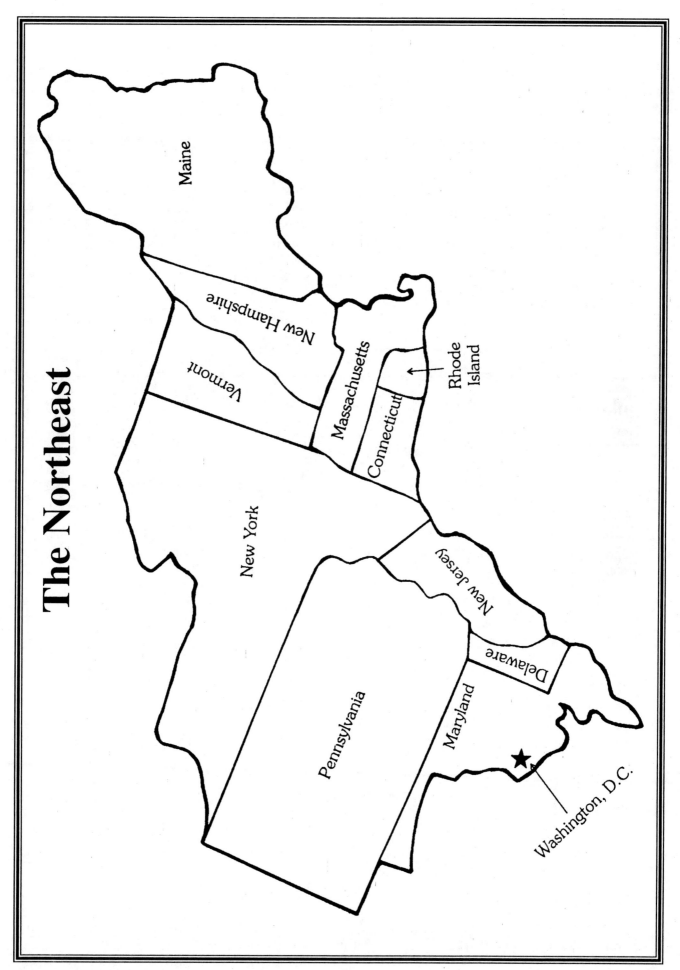

Maine

New Hampshire

Vermont

Massachusetts

Connecticut

Rhode Island

New York

New Jersey

Delaware

Pennsylvania

Maryland

Washington, D.C.

Connecticut
"The Constitution State"

Basic Facts

Capital: *Hartford*
Statehood: *January 9, 1788*
Admittance: *5th state*
Motto: *He Who Transplanted Still Sustains*
Song: *"Yankee Doodle"*
Bird: *Robin*
Flower: *Mountain laurel*
Tree: *White oak*
Abbreviation: *CT*

Area: *5,018 square miles (12,997 sq. km)*
Elevation: *(above sea level)*
   Highest: 2,380 ft. (725 m) – Mount Frissell
   Lowest: Sea level along coastline
Average Temperatures:
   July: 71°F. (22°C)
   January: 26°F. (-3°C)
Average Yearly Precipitation: *47 in. (119 cm)*

Population

How Many: *3,295,669 (1990 Census)*
Where They Live: *79% urban, 21% rural*
Largest Cities: *Bridgeport, Hartford, New Haven*

Connecticut State Flag

State Government

Governor: *4-year term*
Senators *(36): 4-year term*
Representatives *(151): 2-year term*
Towns: *169*

Federal Government

Senators *(2): 6-year term*
Representatives *(6): 2-year term*
Electoral Votes: *8*

Economy

Agriculture: *eggs, milk, greenhouse and nursery products, tobacco*
Fishing: *lobsters, oysters, clams*
Manufacturing: *chemicals, primary metals, transportation equipment, printed materials, food
           products*
Mining: *stone, sand, gravel*

Interesting Facts

- The Hartford Courant is the oldest continuously published newspaper. Publication began in 1764.
- The "tackling dummy," which is used during football practice, was invented by Amos Stagg while he was a student at Yale University in 1889.-

Interesting Connecticuter

- P.T. Barnum opened his first circus in 1871. Later he joined with James Bailey to create "The Greatest Show on Earth!" Phineas Taylor Barnum was born in Bethel.

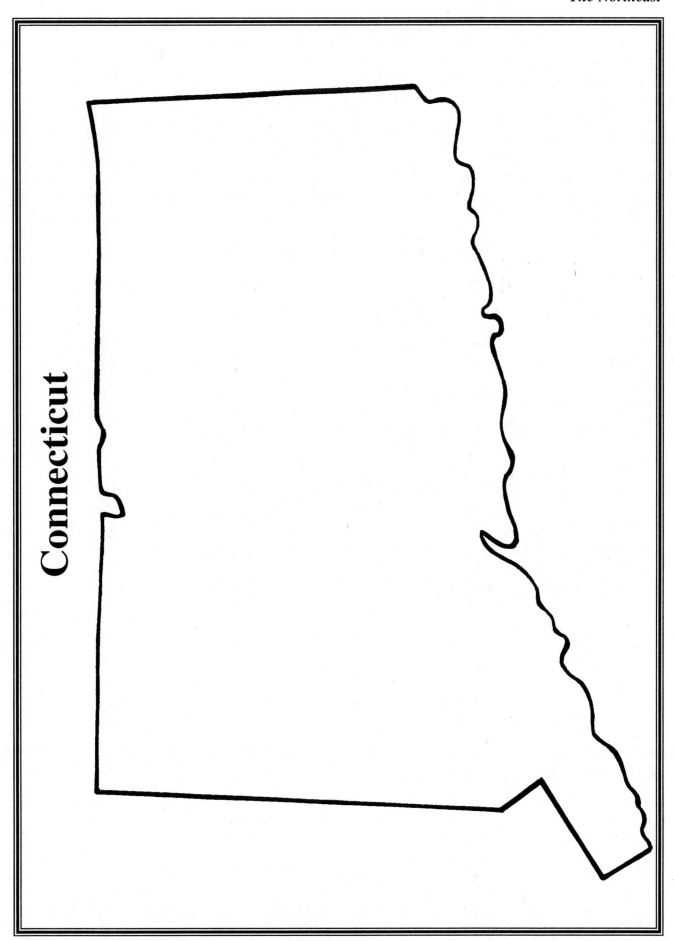

Connecticut

Connecticut: Mystic Seaport

The Marine Historical Association, founded in 1929, built Mystic Seaport as a museum. The Mystic Seaport lies on the Mystic River in Mystic, Connecticut. In the forty years following its construction, Mystic Seaport has become the state's number-one tourist attraction. This historical site is dedicated to the preservation of America's maritime heritage. It shows the growth of our national shipping, the fearlessness of our sea captains and sailors, and the skills that made their voyages possible. The museum includes parts of a 19th century seaport village. You can see waterfront buildings and shops typical of the mid-1800's where men and women are engaged in nautical occupations of a century ago. Some of the oldest American schooners and ships are docked at the Mystic Seaport. One of the finest collections of clipper ship models in America is housed at Mystic Seaport.

Activity: Hoist the Mainsail!

Ship building began to thrive in the Northeastern region as early as the 1600's. Ships were planned by master shipbuilders. Find books about the history of seaports and ship building in the Northeast. Share your information with classmates.

In the mid-1800's, clipper ships graced the seas with both their slender designs and increased speed capabilities. Locate information and pictures of clipper ships. Learn about the parts and the design of these sailing vessels. Then, label several of the parts of the clipper ship on page 69. Give your ship a name and write a short story about one of its voyages.

Mystic Seaport *(cont.)*

Clipper Ship Diagram

See page 68 for directions

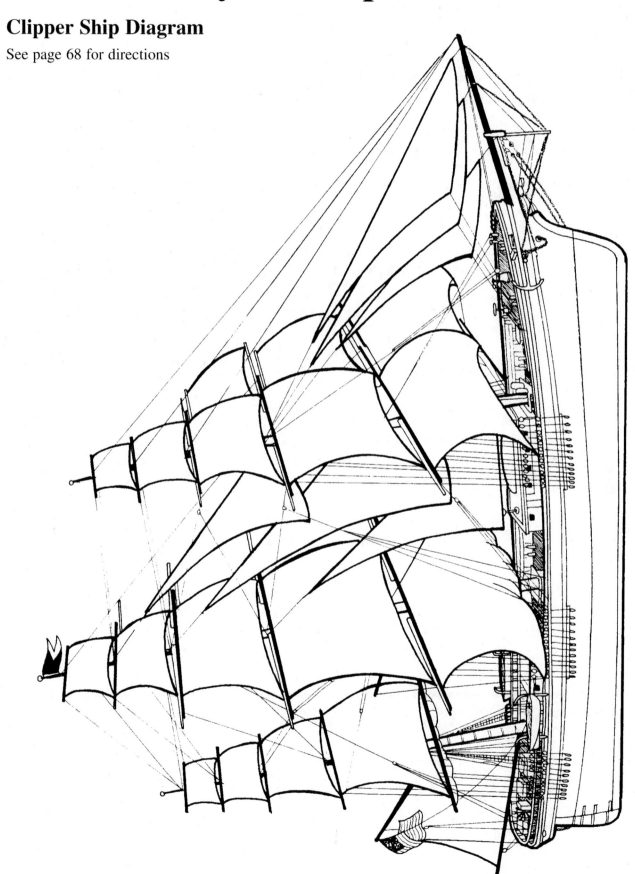

First Written Constitution

Connecticut is appropriately named "The Constitution State." Over a century before the War of Independence, the colony of Connecticut wrote and passed voting laws. As a result, Connecticut is often considered the state with the first written constitution.

Activity: "Get to Know" the Constitution

For this activity you will need a copy of the United States Constitution or a simplified document that explains the articles.

Work in a group to discover the answers to the questions below. Use the information provided in the articles of the Constitution to answer "yes" or "no" and explain your answer.

1. Mr. X was born in the United States. He has lived in the state of Maryland for twenty years. He is twenty-two years old, married, and the father of two children. Is he allowed to serve in the House of Representatives for his district in Maryland?

   Why or why not? _____

   What part of the Constitution gives you this information? _____

2. Miss Y is thirty-three years old. She has been a citizen of the United States for six years. Miss Y has lived in the state of Alabama for one year. Is she allowed to serve as one of Alabama's senators?

   Why or why not? _____

   What part of the Constitution gives you this information? _____

3. Mrs. W is a mother of four. She was born in France, but her parents are citizens of the United States. She has lived in foreign countries, but returned to live in the United States four years ago. She is fifty-five years old. Can she run for President?

   Why or why not? _____

   What part of the Constitution gives you this information? _____

4. Can the number of congressmen and congresswomen from a state be reduced?

   Why or why not? _____

   What part of the Constitution gives you this information? _____

Delaware

"The First State"

Basic Facts

Capital: *Dover*
Statehood: *December 7, 1787*
Admittance: *1st state*
Motto: *Liberty and Independence*
Song: *"Our Delaware"*
Bird: *Blue hen chicken*
Flower: *Peach blossom*
Tree: *American holly*
Abbreviation: *DE*

Area: *2,044 square miles (5,295 sq. km)*
Elevation: *(above sea level)*
  Highest: 442 ft. (135 m) – Ebright Road
  Lowest: Sea level along the coastline
Average Temperatures:
  July: 76°F. (24°C)
  January: 350F. (2°C)
Average Yearly Precipitation: *45 in. (114 cm)*

Population

How Many: *668,696 (1990 Census)*
Where They Live: *71% urban, 29% rural*
Largest Cities: *Wilmington, Newark, Dover*

State Government

Governor: *4-year term*
Senators *(21): 4-year term*
Representatives *(41): 2-year term*
Counties: *3*

Federal Government

Senators *(2): 6-year term*
Representatives *(1): 2-year term*
Electoral Votes: *3*

Delaware State Flag

DECEMBER 7, 1787

Economy

Agriculture: *broiler chickens, soybeans, corn, milk*
Fishing: *crabs, clams*
Manufacturing: *automobiles, paper products, chemicals, rubber and plastic products, metal products*
Mining: *magnesium, sand, gravel*

Interesting Facts

• The first beauty contest was held at Rehoboth Beach in 1880. It was called the "Miss United States" pageant. Thomas Edison was one of the three judges.

• Swedish immigrants settled in southern Delaware in 1683. They introduced a new kind of house called a "log cabin."

Interesting Delawarean

• E.I. du Pont, developer of the world's largest chemical manufacturing plant, was born in this state.

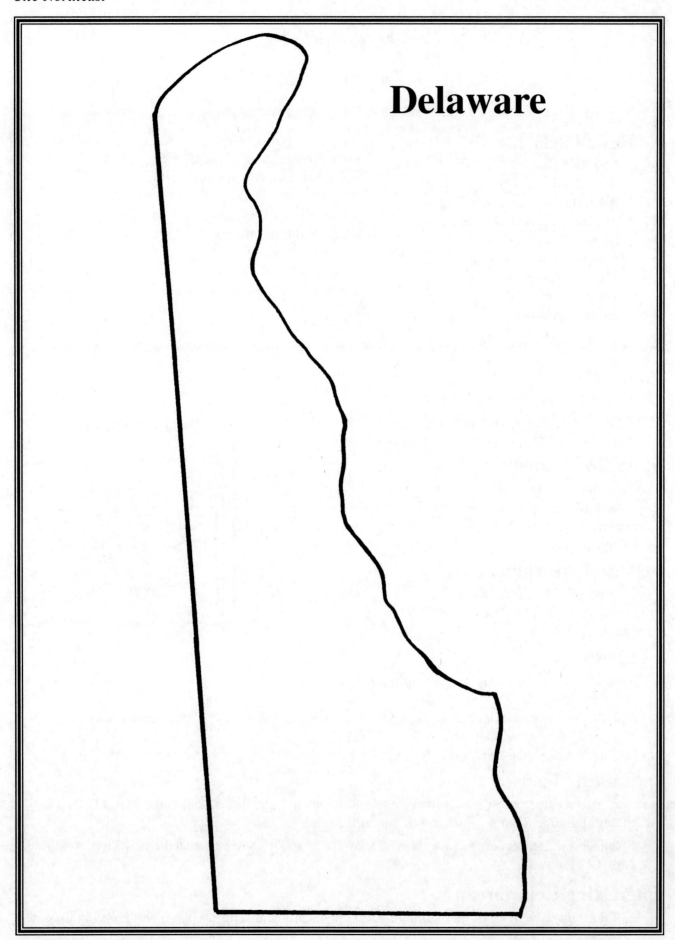

Delaware

Early Colonial Days

In the Beginning

People in Europe had learned about America from an explorer named Christopher Columbus. Columbus was sent to find a water route from Europe to Asia and unexpectedly landed in America. After Columbus, other explorers like John Cabot of England, also landed in America. These explorers claimed large parts of this "New World."

Colonial Life in Delaware

When the colonists first landed in Delaware, immediate shelter was needed. Cabins were often built out of rough logs. Moss and clay were mixed together to fill in between the logs. These houses were quickly replaced by houses made of brick or stone. However, the Swedish made their homes of sturdy wood.

The kitchen was the most important room in a colonist's house, and sometimes the only room. For breakfast, waffles and maple syrup were common. White toast was also a staple food for breakfast. For dinner, deer stew bubbled in a pot over the fire, and next to the fire was a broiler. Here, rabbits were cooked slowly. The majority of the dinner was not eaten with silverware, but was eaten with the colonist's hands. Forks were not used and only a few spoons were available. Items made from corn, such as corn-on-the cob and cornmeal, were eaten at least once a day.

Colonists would hang their clothes from wooden pegs because there were no closets in the early colonial home. Bedding and linen were stored in a large chest in the corner of the room.

In colonial Delaware, children did not attend school. It was difficult without schoolhouses or teachers, and no formalized school books. The first schools were called "dame schools." Here housewives were the teachers and their homes were the schools. The books used in these "dame schools" were called hornbooks. A hornbook was a flat wooden board, shaped like a paddle with the Lord's prayer printed on it. On the board was pasted a sheet of paper. Printed on the paper were usually the alphabet, the Lord's Prayer, and the Roman numerals.

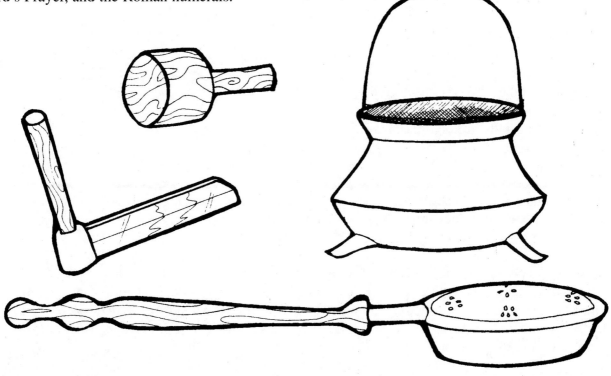

Early Colonial Days *(cont.)*

Candle making was a necessary part of the daily activities for the women and children. Pounds of beef fat and mutton fat were saved year round. This fat was boiled in large pots and turned into tallow. As the fat was boiling, the children would tie wicks to the candlerods. Once the fat was turned into tallow, the children would dip the rods into the tallow until the candles were of proper size. Two chairs were set back to back at a distance with two rods laying across the tops of the chairs. The chairs and rods were used to dry the candles. Soon candle molds were invented, which made the process much more simple.

Activity: Make Your Own Homemade Candles

Essentials

- box of paraffin wax
- 2 coffee cans
- hot plate or stove
- candle wicking or string
- crayon bits for color
- pot larger than coffee cans
- water
- potholders or oven mitts
- dowels or long pencils

Preparation

Heat water on the stove in large pot. The water level should be lower than the top of a coffee can. Put a slab of paraffin into the empty coffee can. Carefully place the can into a pot of hot water. Allow the wax to melt. Prepare the wick by cutting a length of string twice the depth of the can (about 12"/30 cm for a double candle and 6"/15 cm for a single candle). Fill the second coffee can with ice water.

Directions

Use a dowel to hold the wick for the double candle in the center, dipping the wick into hot wax and then into cold water. Straighten the wick after each cold water dip. Alternate back and forth between the hot wax and cold water until your candle grows to the size you desire. If making a single candle, tie the wick to a pencil or stick before dipping it.

When the candles reach the desired thickness, hang them from a coat hanger to cool and harden. (Wicks of the double candles can be hung over the bottom of wire hangers; single candles can be attached by the wicks using clothespins.) Cut the double candles apart.

Caution: This activity should be conducted only with adult supervision. Only adults should handle hot paraffin and should use potholders or oven mitts when doing so. Paraffin is dangerous. Never boil, overheat, or mix with water. It should only be melted. Wax can ignite and smoke. Always use a double boiler. Warm wax makes a better candle than hot wax. Wax fires must be smothered. Treat hot wax just as you would hot oil.

Maine

"The Pine Tree State"

Basic Facts

Capital: *Augusta*
Statehood: *March 15, 1820*
Admittance: *23rd state*
Motto: *I Direct or I Guide*
Song: *"State of Maine Song"*
Bird: *Chickadee*
Flower: *White pine cone and tassel*
Tree: *White pine*
Abbreviation: *ME*

Area: *33,625 square miles (86,156 sq. km)*
Elevation: *(above sea level)*
    Highest: 5,268 ft. (1,606 m) – Mount Katahdin
    Lowest: Sea level along coastline
Average Temperatures:
    July: 67°F. (19°C)
    January: 15°F. (-9°C)
Average Yearly Precipitation: *41 in. (104 cm)*

Population

How Many: *1,233,223 (1990 Census)*
Where They Live: *52% urban, 48% rural*
Largest Cities: *Portland, Lewiston, Bangor*

State Government

Governor: *4-year term*
Senators *(35): 4-year term*
Representatives *(151): 2-year term*
Counties: *16*

Federal Government

Senators *(2): 6-year term*
Representatives *(2): 2-year term*
Electoral Votes: *4*

Maine State Flag

Economy

Agriculture: *milk, eggs, potatoes, hay, beef cattle, apples*
Fishing: *lobsters, clams*
Manufacturing: *paper products, leather products, electric machinery, textiles, transportation equipment*
Mining: *stone, garnet*

Interesting Facts

• The first earmuffs were patented by Chester Greenwood of Farmington in 1877. He invented his first pair when he was 15.

• More toothpicks are produced in Maine than anywhere else in the United States. They are made from the white birch tree.

Interesting Mainer

• Henry Wadsworth Longfellow was one of the most widely published and famous American poets of the 1880's. Many of his poems are based on early American history.

Maine

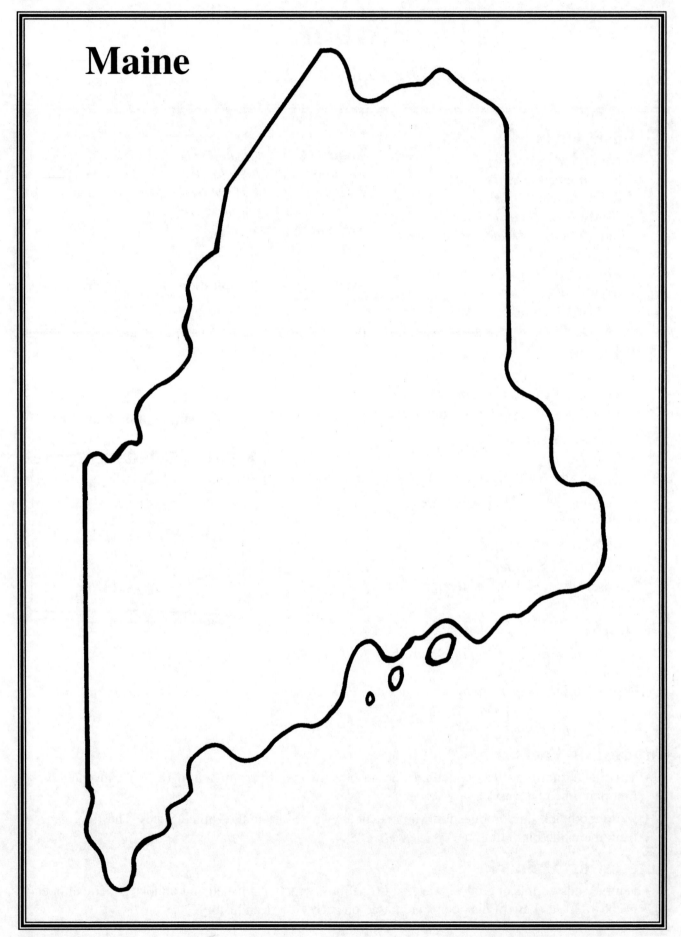

The Catch of the Day

Maine leads all other states in lobster fishing. The common lobsters found in Maine are called American lobsters. They measure from 12 to 24 inches (30-61 cm) long and weigh anywhere from 1 to 20 pounds (.5-9 kg). Lobsters live on the bottom of the ocean near the shore at depths of 6 to 120 feet (2-36 m). They hide in holes or near rocks. Lobsters eat crabs, snails, small fish, and other lobsters. Lobsters are caught in cages called "pots." A lobster will enter the pot for bait and will not be able to get out. The trap must be emptied daily because lobsters will fight and injure or kill each other if not separated.

A yearly lobster catch in Maine will weigh approximately 22 million pounds (9.9 million kilograms). At one time so many lobsters were caught that they were in danger of dying out. Laws were then made to protect lobsters, and the lobsters were grown where it was prohibited to lobster fish. Maine holds an outstanding annual event called the Maine Lobster Festival. It is held in the city of Rockland during the first week in August.

The state of Maine is also known for its many offshore islands, called continental islands, because they were once connected to a continent. Some of these islands were disconnected by a rise in the sea level. Other islands were disconnected due to the erosion of a former link with the mainland. Streams, rivers, and ocean waves, over many years, wear away at the land that connected the island to the continent. These offshore islands have plant and animal life similar to Maine. However, because of the isolation of these animals or plants they may evolve into a separate species not found on the mainland of Maine.

Activity 1: Make a Pie Plate Island

Essentials

- large pie plate
- heavy-duty aluminum foil
- dirt, sand, grass, twigs, rocks, and leaves
- blue tissue paper
- yarn
- blue construction paper

Directions

- Research the islands off Maine. Line a pie plate with heavy-duty foil. Remove the foil from the pie plate and reform the foil to create bays, inlets, etc.

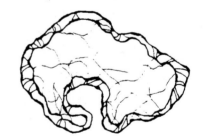

- To make your island, put dirt and sand inside the foil. Create mountains by raising some areas. Vary the terrain by adding rocks, twigs, leaves, grass, and bits of plants to simulate forests, grasslands, mountains, etc. Use a toothpick or pencil to "carve" in rivers and lakes. Add bits of blue tissue paper or yarn to add color to the "water." Give your island a name and write a description of it.

The Catch of the Day *(cont.)*

Activity 2: Marine-Life Web

Although the lobster is found in great quantities in Maine, it is certainly not alone in the vast Atlantic ocean. The waters around Maine and its islands are full of marine life.

Find out about some of the marine life in the waters around Maine and its islands. Then complete the following "Marine-Life Web."

Essentials

- books and magazines on ocean animals
- pencils or crayons

Directions

- Choose a marine animal that can be found in the waters surrounding the coast of Maine. Draw a picture of the animal in the square below. Next, write interesting facts about your chosen animal in the web. Decorate the page further if you wish. Share your web with the class.

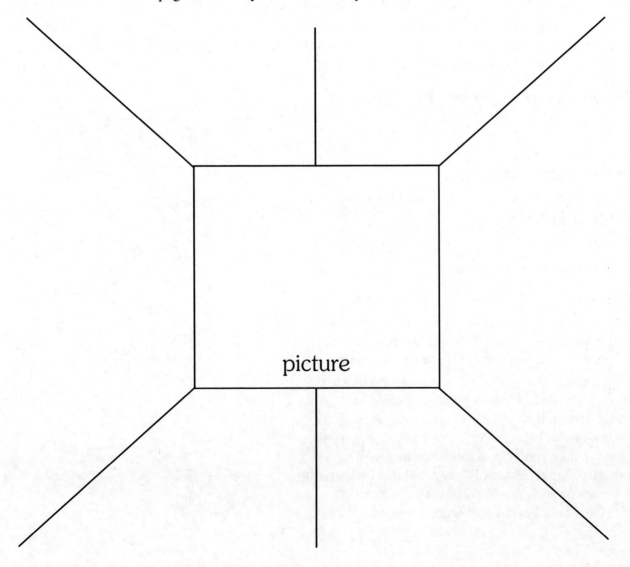

picture

Maryland
"The Old Line State"

Basic Facts

Capital: *Annapolis*
Statehood: *April 28, 1788*
Admittance: *7th state*
Motto: *Manly Deeds, Womanly Words*
Song: *"Maryland, My Maryland"*
Bird: *Baltimore oriole*
Flower: *Black-eyed susan*
Tree: *White oak*
Abbreviation: *MD*

Area: *10,460 square miles (27,092 sq. km)*
Elevation: *(above sea level)*
  Highest: 3,360 ft. (1,024 m) – Backbone Mt.
  Lowest: Sea level along the coastline
Average Temperatures:
  July: 75°F. (24°C)
  January: 33°F. (1°C)
Average Yearly Precipitation: *43 in. (109 cm)*

Population

How Many: *4, 798,622 (1990 Census)*
Where They Live: *80% urban, 20% rural*
Largest Cities: *Baltimore, Silver Spring, Dundalk*

State Government

Governor: *4-year term*
Senators *(47): 4-year term*
Representatives *(141): 4-year term*
Counties: *23*

Federal Government

Senators *(2): 6-year term*
Representatives *(8): 2-year term*
Electoral Votes: *10*

Maryland State Flag

Economy

Agriculture: *broiler chickens, milk, corn, soybeans, beef cattle, tobacco*
Fishing: *oysters, clams, crabs*
Manufacturing: *electric machinery and equipment, food products, chemicals, primary metals, nonelectric machinery*
Mining: *coal, stone, clay*

Interesting Facts

- Jousting, fighting on horseback with lances, is the official state sport.
- Francis Scott Key wrote "The Star-Spangled Banner" in Baltimore during the War of 1812.

Interesting Marylander

- Benjamin Banneker was born in Baltimore in 1731. He was one of America's earliest African American scientists. He specialized in astronomy.

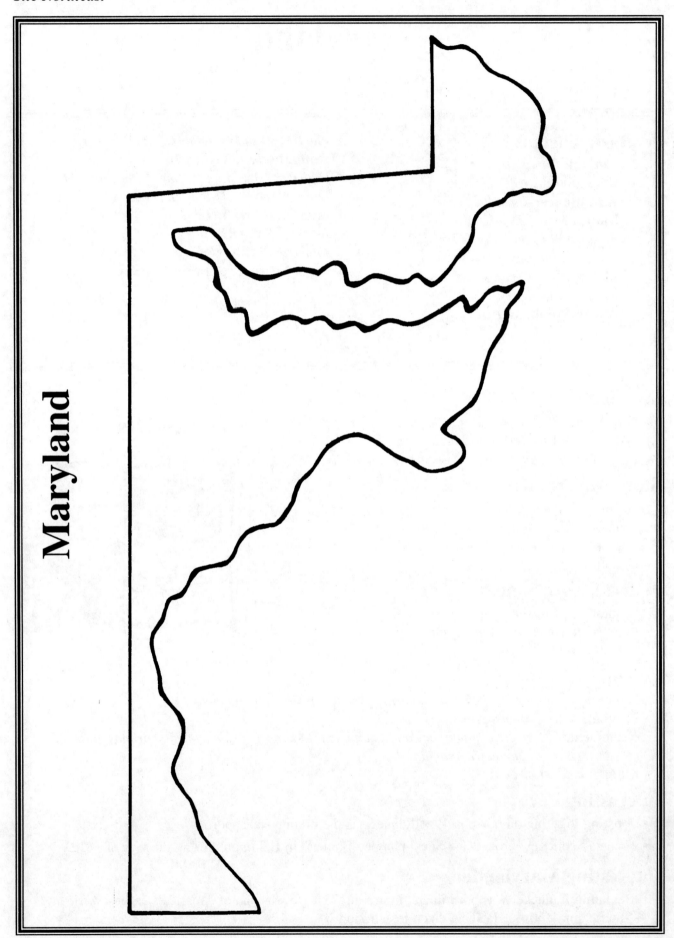

Maryland

"Our Flag Was Still There"

While it may be a well known fact that on the night of September 13, 1814, Francis Scott Key was inspired to write "The Star Spangled Banner" aboard a boat in the Chesapeake Bay while watching the shelling of a Baltimore fort, the story of the flag that inspired him is not widely known.

At that time, the United States had fifteen states. Congress ordered the flag to be changed to include fifteen stars and fifteen stripes. Since the start of the War of 1812, the British had been threatening to attack Fort McHenry, which guarded the inner harbor of Baltimore. The commander of this fort wished to have "a flag so large that the British will have no difficulty in seeing it from a distance."

A young widow named Mary Pickersgill was given the enormous task of making a flag to measure thirty feet by forty-two feet (9 m x 13 m). After months of spinning, weaving, and sewing by hand, the flag was ready.

The huge flag flew over Fort McHenry and withstood a twenty-five-hour bombardment by the British. As the smoke and mist cleared early the next morning after the attack, Francis Scott Key was so overjoyed to see the flag still waving that he quickly began writing the first of the four verses of "The Star Spangled Banner" on some old paper he had in his pocket.

The song became popular immediately, especially among the military, but it was not until 1931 that it was officially made the national anthem of the United States.

Today, the original flag is on display at the Smithsonian Institution's National Museum of American History in Washington, D.C. It is only lowered for viewing for two minutes every hour to protect it from light and dust. Mary Pickersgill's home is also open to visitors. It is called the Star-Spangled Banner Flag House and is located in Baltimore.

Activities: Our Flag a Star Spangled Banner

- Locate a copy of "The Star Spangled Banner." In a small group, read the words and think about its message. How do the verses reflect what Francis Scott Key might have seen after the bombardment at Fort McHenry?

- Design a new flag for our country, your state, your school, or your classroom. Display your flag in the classroom and tell why you decided to design it as you did.

- What do you suppose a flag with fifty stars and fifty stripes would look like? Find out why the Continental Congress reduced the number of stripes to thirteen and ordered that it should stay that way. Report your findings to the class.

Massachusetts
"The Bay State"

Basic Facts

Capital: *Boston*
Statehood: *February 6, 1788*
Admittance: *6th state*
Motto: *By the Sword We Seek Peace, but Peace Only Under Liberty*
Song: *"All Hail to Massachusetts"*
Bird: *Chickadee*
Flower: *Mayflower*
Tree: *American elm*

Abbreviation: *MA*
Area: *8,284 square miles (21,456 sq. km)*
Elevation: *(above sea level)*
   Highest: 3,491 ft. (1,064 m) – Mt. Greylock
   Lowest: Sea level along the coastline
Average Temperatures:
   July: 71°F. (220C)
   January: 25°F. (-4°C)
Average Yearly Precipitation: *45 in. (114 cm)*

Population

How Many: *6,029,051 (1990 Census)*
Where They Live: *84% urban, 16% rural*
Largest Cities: *Boston, Worcester, Springfield*

State Government

Governor: *4-year term*
Senators *(40): 2-year term*
Representatives *(160): 2-year term*
Counties: *14*

Federal Government

Senators *(2): 6-year term*
Representatives *(10): 2-year term*
Electoral Votes: *12*

Massachusetts State Flag

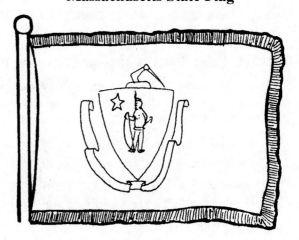

Economy

Agriculture: *greenhouse and nursery products, cranberries, eggs, milk*
Fishing: *scallops, flounder, cod, lobster, haddock*
Manufacturing: *printed materials, transportation equipment, fabricated metal products, electric machinery*
Mining: *stone, sand*

Interesting Facts

• The Pilgrims first settled near Plymouth Rock in 1620.

• Baseball's first World Series was played in Boston from October 1 to October 13, 1903.

Interesting Massachusettsan

• Elias Howe is known as the inventor of the sewing machine. He was born in Spencer and learned his trade as a machine maker in Cambridge.

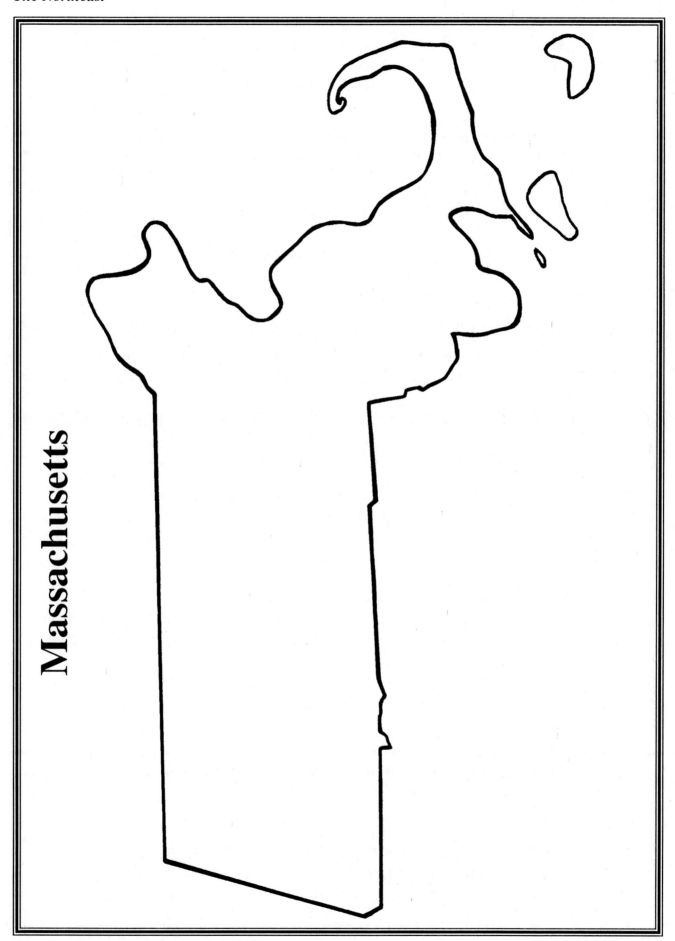

Massachusetts

Famous Facts, Folks, and Firsts

Plymouth, Massachusetts, is one of the most significant and well-known historical sites in America. It was here that the Pilgrims landed in 1620 to found the first New England colony.

In the early 1600's, a group of people called Separatists, set sail for America. The Separatists, whose purpose in coming to America was to worship God in their own way, sailed from Plymouth, England, on the Mayflower.

Activity 1: Facts About Colonial Massachusetts

There are many wonderful books about Pilgrims. Read a book about one of the following subjects: Pilgrims, Plymouth Rock, The Mayflower Compact, The First New England Thanksgiving in 1621, The Massachusetts Bay Colony, Separatists. Then, form a discussion group to share information about the books. Your group may wish to role play some of the information you discovered about the Pilgrims.

Activity 2: Famous Folks and Famous Firsts

Using additional references and the information below, work in a small group to make a Big Book of "Famous Folks" or "Famous Firsts" about Massachusetts.

Did You Know?

- Massachusetts has produced three famous U.S presidents: John Adams (17351826), a signer of the Declaration of Independence; his son, John Quincy Adams (1767-1848); and John Fitzgerald Kennedy (1913-1963).

- Among other historic colonial and state leaders were John Winthrop, a founder of Massachusetts and longtime governor, William Bradford, a founder of Plymouth; and Paul Revere, the Patriot's silversmith courier.

- The state of Massachusetts is responsible for the following "Famous Firsts":

  —The first American post office was established in Boston in 1639.

  —Alexander Graham Bell first demonstrated the telephone in 1876 in Boston.

  —The first book published in the English colonies was in Cambridge in 1640. The first regularly issued American newspaper, the *Boston News Letter* was published in 1704. Massachusetts is also a book publishing center, with more than 25 publishing houses.

New Hampshire
"The Granite State"

Basic Facts

Capital: *Concord*
Statehood: *June 21, 1788*
Admittance: *9th state*
Motto: *Live Free or Die*
Song: *"Old New Hampshire"*
Bird: *Purple finch*
Flower: *Purple lilac*
Tree: *White birch*
Abbreviation: *NH*

Area: *9,297 square miles (24,219 sq. km)*
Elevation: *(above sea level)*
  Highest: 6,288 ft. (1,917 m) – Mt. Washington
  Lowest: Sea level along the coastline
Average Temperatures:
  July: 68°F. (20°C)
  January: 19°F. (-7°C)
Average Yearly Precipitation: *42 in. (107 cm)*

Population

How Many: *1,113,915 (1990 Census)*
Where They Live: *52% urban, 48% rural*
Largest Cities: *Manchester, Nashua, Concord*

State Government

Governor: *2-year term*
Senators *(24): 2-year term*
Representatives *(400): 2-year term*
Counties: *10*

Federal Government

Senators *(2): 6-year term*
Representatives *(2): 2-year term*
Electoral Votes: *4*

New Hampshire State Flag

Economy

Agriculture: *milk, hay*
Fishing: *lobsters, cod*
Manufacturing: *paper products, nonelectric machinery and equipment, rubber and plastic products, leather products*
Mining: *granite, sand, gravel*

Interesting Facts

• The Brattle Organ, which is said to be the oldest organ in the United States is located in St. John's Episcopal Church in Portsmouth.

• Mount Washington is the highest mountain in the Northeastern United States.

Interesting New Hampshirite

• Horace Greeley, a politician and publisher, was born in Amherst. He founded and edited the New York Tribune and was a leader in the antislavery movement.

New Hampshire

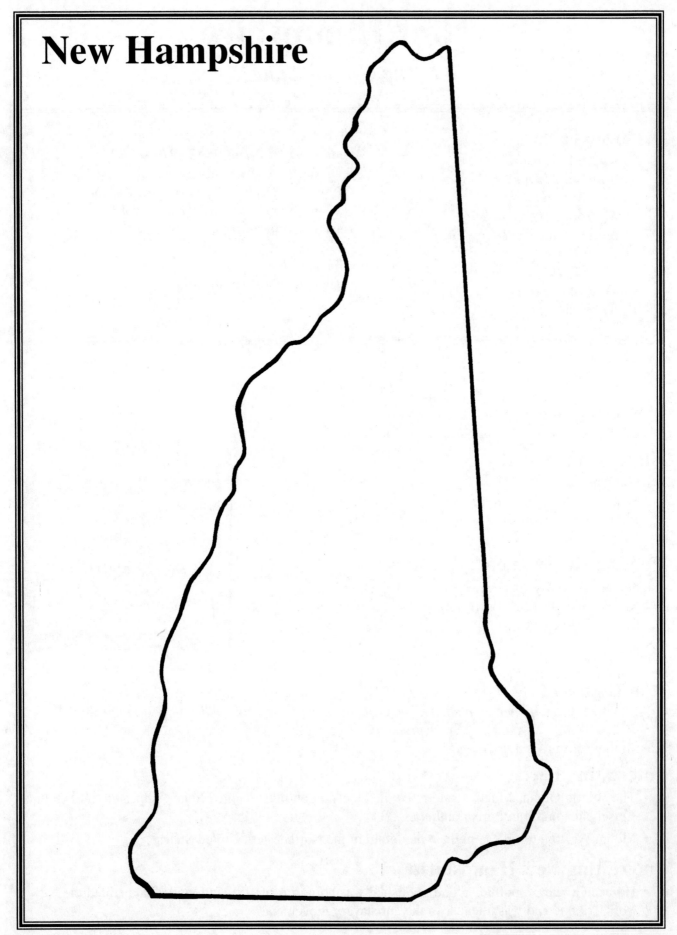

The Land of Spectacular Colors

New Hampshire, like other New England states, draws many spectators each year to view the spectacular colors of autumn. Have you wondered why the leaves on trees change their colors many times throughout the year? Chlorophyll, a green pigment found in leaves, is the tree's main food source. It is an important part of the process of food making called photosynthesis. Chlorophyll absorbs energy from sunlight and turns water and minerals from the soil into a food for the tree.

During the summer months, the sunlight causes the leaves to make food. As the hours of sunlight decrease, the leaves slow down their food-making process until the process stops completely. The chlorophyll is no longer needed and slowly vanishes. This is when you see the brilliant colors of autumn: reds, yellows, purples, oranges, and browns.

Where do these colors come from? Actually, the colors are always there; they are just hidden by the strong green color produced in the presence of chlorophyll. As the leaves change color, the tree draws the leftover food out of the leaves in order to survive the winter. The brilliance of the colors depends upon the fall weather conditions. Cloudy, rainy weather produces dull shades of red. Warm, humid conditions produce brightly colored but speckled leaves. Dry, sunny, fall weather produces the prettiest colors of all.

Activity: Leaf Experiment

Essentials

- healthy potted plant
- aluminum foil (cut 6"/15 cm square pieces)
- 2 tablespoons (30 mL) petroleum jelly
- 1 magnifying glass

Directions

- Put the potted plant in a well lighted area.
- Cover one of the leaves completely with aluminum. Next, cover another leaf with petroleum jelly. Leave the petroleum jelly and the foil on the leaves for ten days. Uncover the leaf with foil. Has anything happened? What happened to the leaf that was covered with petroleum jelly?
- After ten days the leaf that was covered in aluminum foil turned a yellowish brown. It is essential for the leaves of green plants to receive sunlight in order to complete the photosynthesis process. Without sunlight the leaves will be unable to produce a food supply to keep the plant alive.
- Now use a magnifying glass to examine the leaf that was covered in petroleum jelly. This leaf also turned yellowish-brown. The petroleum jelly kept the air from coming into contact with the leaf. A plant needs carbon dioxide from the air and energy from sunlight to carry on the photosynthesis process and make food. When this process is interrupted, the plant's leaves will no longer be green.

New Jersey

"The Garden State"

Basic Facts

Capital: *Trenton*
Statehood: *December 18, 1787*
Admittance: *3rd state*
Motto: *Liberty and Prosperity*
Song: *None*
Bird: *Eastern goldfinch*
Flower: *Purple violet*
Tree: *Red oak*
Abbreviation: *NJ*

Area: *7,787 square miles (20,169 sq. km)*
Elevation: *(above sea level)*
Highest: 1,803 ft. (550 m) – High Point
Lowest: Sea level along coastline
Average Temperatures:
July: 75°F. (24°C)
January: 31°F. (-1°C)
Average Yearly Precipitation: *45 in. (114 cm)*

Population

How Many: *7,748,634 (1990 Census)*
Where They Live: *89% urban, 11% rural*
Largest Cities: *Newark, New Jersey, Paterson*

New Jersey State Flag

State Government

Governor: *4-year term*
Senators *(40): 2-or-4-year term*
Representatives *(80): 2-year term*
Counties: *21*

Federal Government

Senators *(2): 6-year term*
Representatives *(13): 2-year term*
Electoral Votes: *15*

Economy

Agriculture: *greenhouse and nursery products, milk, tomatoes*
Fishing: *clams, menhaden, flounder*
Manufacturing: *chemicals, food products, electric machinery and equipment, transportation
equipment, rubber and plastic products*
Mining: *stone, zinc, sand, and gravel*

Interesting Facts

• New Jersey is the most densely populated state.

• The first drive-in-movie theater was opened on June 6, 1933, on Crescent Boulevard outside Camden.

Interesting New Jerseyite

• Thomas Edison invented the electric light bulb and the phonograph in his laboratory in Menlo Park.

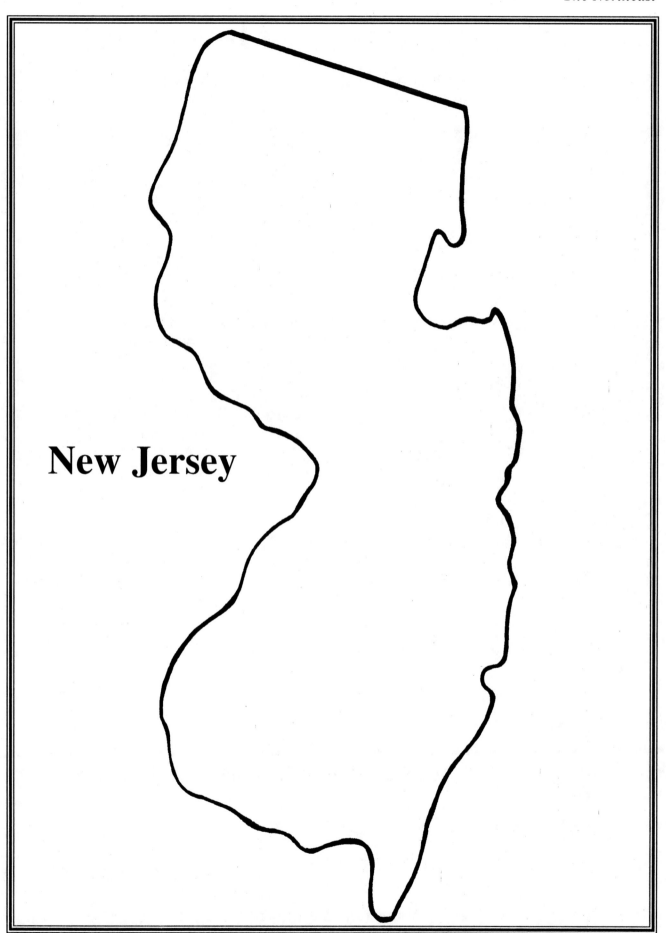

New Jersey

The Inventor of All Inventors!

Thomas Edison was a man of many questions, his favorite question being, "Why?" He was born on February 11, 1847. At that time there were no telephones, automobiles, movies, or radios.

Edison's first laboratory was in his bedroom; from there, he graduated to the cellar and then to a baggage car on a train. Finally, Tom bought a piece of land called Menlo Park, New Jersey. He constructed a plain wooden building which he called the "Invention Factory." One of his first inventions was the phonograph, completed in 1877. But Thomas Edison's most miraculous invention was the electric light bulb, completed on October 19, 1879.

When Tom's wife died, he decided to leave Menlo Park. His new laboratory was in West Orange, New Jersey. This laboratory was much bigger than Menlo Park and was the birthplace of another one of Tom's inventions, motion pictures. Today, you can see many of Thomas Edison's inventions in his West Orange laboratory. Five buildings have been turned into a museum. Almost everything Thomas wrote about or made is there.

Activity: Other Inventive Inventors

Below is a list of famous American inventors. Choose one to research. On a separate piece of paper, list the person's name, the state in which the inventor was born, and information about the invention(s) and the impact they made on the world.

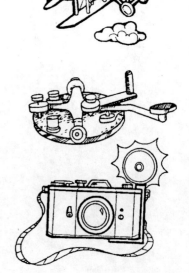

Orville and Wilbur Wright
Benjamin Franklin
George Eastman
Vincent Bendix
Robert Fulton
Samuel Morse
George Washington Carver
George Westinghouse
Elijah McCoy
Levi Strauss
Eli Whitney
Alexander Graham Bell

New York
"The Empire State"

Basic Facts

Capital: *Albany*
Statehood: *July 26, 1788*
Admittance: *11th state*
Motto: *Ever Upward*
Song: *"I Love New York"*
Bird: *Bluebird*
Flower: *Rose*
Tree: *Sugar maple*
Abbreviation: *NY*

Area: *49,108 square miles (127,189 sq. km)*
Elevation: *(above sea level)*
  Highest: 5,344 ft. (1,629 m) – Mount Marcy
  Lowest: Sea level along the coastline
Average Temperatures:
  July: 69°F. (21°C)
  January: 21°F. (-60 C)
Average Yearly Precipitation: *39 in. (99 cm)*

Population

How Many: *18,044,505 (1990 Census)*
Where They Live: *85% urban, 15% rural*
Largest Cities: *New York City, Buffalo, Rochester*

State Government

Governor: *4-year term*
Senators *(61): 2-year term*
Representatives *(150): 2-year term*
Counties: *62*

Federal Government

Senators *(2): 6-year term*
Representatives *(31): 2-year term*
Electoral Votes: *33*

New York State Flag

Economy

Agriculture: *milk*
Fishing: *clams, oysters*
Manufacturing: *printed materials, scientific instruments, electric equipment, machinery, chemicals*
Mining: *crushed stone, salt, petroleum*

Interesting Facts

- The World Trade Center, located in New York City, is so large that each of the twin towers has separate zip codes.

Interesting New Yorker

- Franklin D. Roosevelt was the 32nd President of the United States. He was born in the state of New York. He was the fifth cousin to another President, Theodore Roosevelt, the 26th President of the United States.

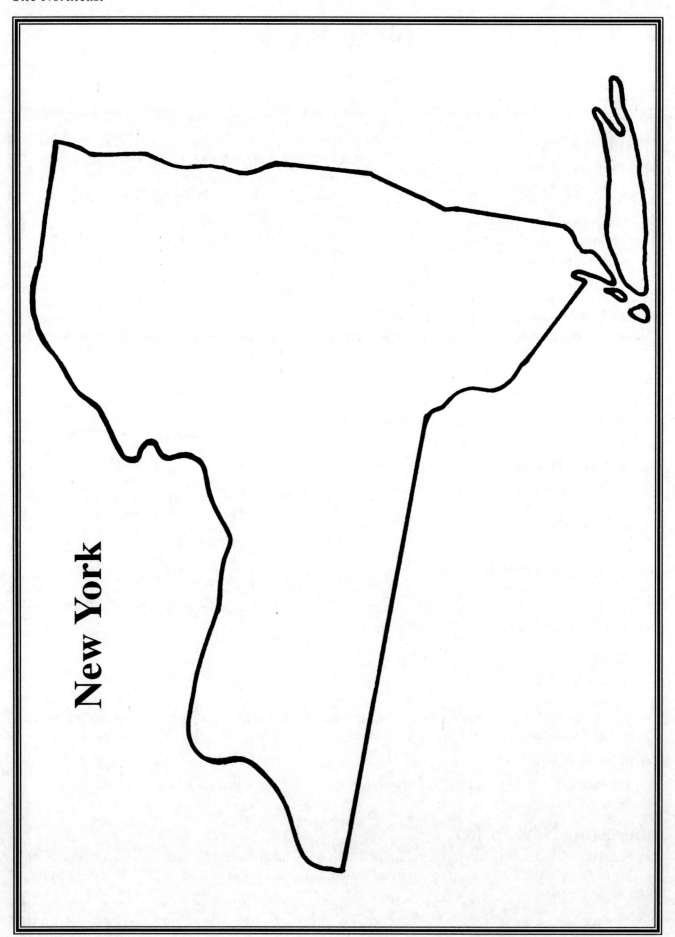

New York

Give Us Your Tired...

Ellis Island, located in Upper New York Bay, was the nation's chief immigration station from 1892 to 1952. During that time, over 12 million immigrants entered the United States through Ellis Island and were sent onward to an uncertain future. Since the early 1800's, New York has been, and still is, the primary port of entry for Europeans coming to the U.S.

Today, more than four out of every ten American people can trace their roots to an ancestor who entered America through Ellis Island.

Activity: What Was It Like?

Read the following information about the processing of immigrants as they entered the United States. Find a partner and simulate the arrival of a group of immigrants to Ellis Island using the questions below. (You can add questions of your own.) You and your partner can trade off role playing the immigrant and the questioner.

General Information

Once the immigrants stepped off their boats, large numbered tags were tied to their clothing. They were taken to the registry hall where, after waiting in long lines, they were examined by doctors. Many were delayed or sent home for medical reasons. Those who made it past the medical inspection were questioned by a government inspector. If all tests were passed, the average stay on Ellis Island was about five hours.

Questions

- *What is your name?*
- *How old are you?*
- *What is your occupation? Can you read or write?*
- *Where are you from?*
- *Where are you going in the United States ? How will you get there?*
- *Did you pay for your passage? If not, who did?*
- *Have you ever been to prison?*
- *How is your health?*

Discussion

If an immigrant seemed unsure of an answer, he or she might be sent to a special inquiry board. How did each of you answer your questions?

As a challenge, your class could appoint a panel of five students who will listen to your answers and vote to determine whether you will be allowed to remain in the United States.

Pennsylvania

"The Keystone State"

Basic Facts

Capital: *Harrisburg*
Statehood: *December 12, 1787*
Admittance: *2nd state*
Motto: *Virtue, Liberty, and Independence*
Song: *None*
Bird: *Ruffled grouse*
Flower: *Mountain laurel*
Tree: *Hemlock*
Abbreviation: *PA*

Area: *45,308 square miles (117,348 sq. km)*
Elevation: *(above sea level)*
   Highest: 3,213 ft. (979 m) -Mt. Davis
   Lowest: Sea level along Delaware River
Average Temperatures:
   July: 71°F. (22°C)
   January: 27°F. (-3°C)
Average Yearly Precipitation: *41 in. (104 cm)*

Population

How Many: *11,924,710 (1990 Census)*
Where They Live: *69% urban, 31% rural*
Largest Cities: *Philadelphia, Pittsburgh, Erie*

State Government

Governor: *4-year term*
Senators *(50): 4-year term*
Representatives *(203): 2-year term*
Counties: *67*

Federal Government

Senators *(2): 6-year term*
Representatives *(21): 2-year term*
Electoral Votes: *23*

Economy

Agriculture: *milk, greenhouse and nursery products, hay, beef cattle, eggs, corn*
Manufacturing: *food products, chemicals, machinery, metal products, printed materials, transportation equipment*
Mining: *coal, limestone*

Pennsylvania State Flag

Interesting Facts

- The world's largest chocolate factory is located in Hershey.
- The first magazine in the American Colonies was published in Philadelphia. It was called *The American Magazine* and lasted only three months.

Interesting Pennsylvanian
- Marian Anderson, born in Philadelphia, was the first black soloist to sing with the Metropolitan Opera. She also served as a United States delegate to the United Nations.

94

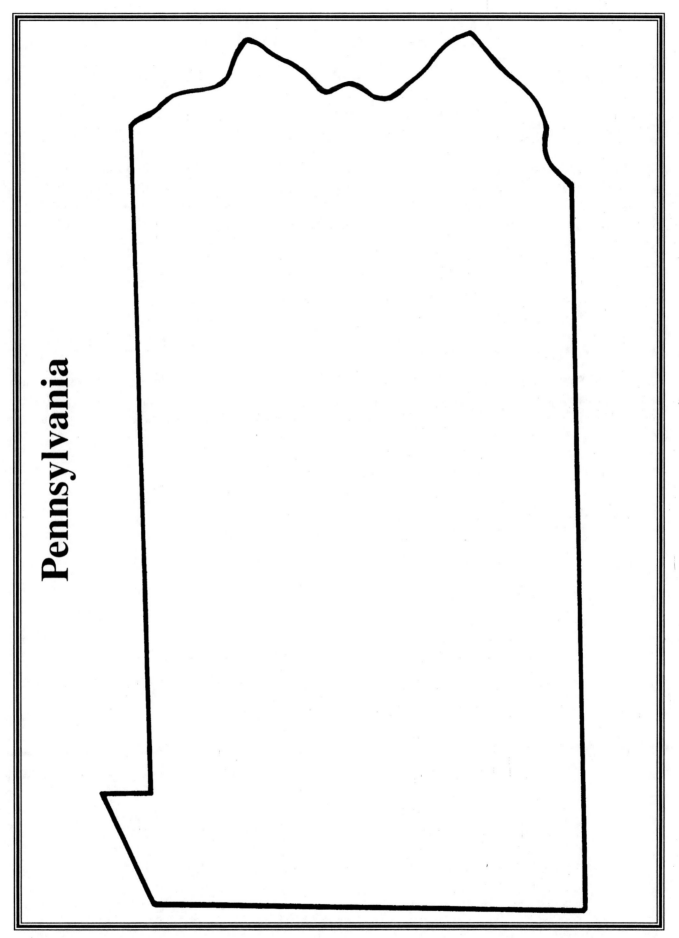

Pennsylvania

Symbols of Pride

A symbol is a picture or a thing that stands for something else. Different symbols stand for many different things. A symbol can be used alone or with other symbols. Individuals often pick symbols to stand for something special about their country. Pennsylvania is one state related to a couple of very important American symbols.

The Liberty Bell is the symbol of American independence. The Liberty Bell was rung on July 8, 1776, to announce the adoption of the Declaration of Independence. Today the bell hangs in Liberty Bell Pavilion, just north of Independence Hall in Philadelphia. Another important symbol, and probably the best-known, is the United States flag. In Philadelphia, Pennsylvania on June 14, 1777, the Continental Congress decided that the flag of the United States should have 13 stripes, alternating red and white, and that "the Union be 13 stars white in a blue field representing a new constellation." The United States flag was created to symbolize the land, the people, the government, and the ideals of the United States. It is important to protect and preserve our symbols because these are the special things that remind us of important ideas and beliefs of our country.

Activity: Respect For Our Flag

The United States flag is a symbol to be treated with honor and respect. Examples of ways to honor our flag are illustrated on page 97. Color the pictures. Some rules for displaying the flag are written in the boxes below. Cut out the boxes and glue them under the appropriate pictures on page 97.

Do not display the flag if the weather could damage it.	Do not let the flag touch the ground.
Display the flag from sunrise to sunset.	Carefully fold the flag when it is not being displayed.
Do not hang the flag upside down. That signals a serious emergency.	The flag of the United States may not be used for clothing. Use the colors, not the flag.

Symbols of Pride *(cont.)*

See page 96 for directions.

Rhode Island
"The Ocean State"

Basic Facts

Capital: *Providence*
Statehood: *May 29, 1790*
Admittance: *13th state*
Motto: *Hope*
Song: *"Rhode Island"*
Bird: *Rhode Island red*
Flower: *Violet*
Tree: *Red maple*
Abbreviation: *RI*

Area: *1,212 square miles (3,140 sq. km)*
Elevation: *(above sea level)*
  Highest: 812 ft. (247 m) – Jerimoth Hill
  Lowest: Sea level along coastline
Average Temperatures:
  July: 71°F. (22°C)
  January: 290F. (-2°C)
Average Yearly Precipitation: *44 in. (112 cm)*

Population

How Many: *1,005,984 (1990 Census)*
Where They Live: *87% urban, 13% rural*
Largest Cities: *Providence, Warwick, Cranston*

State Government

Governor: *2-year term*
Senators *(50): 2-year term*
Representatives *(100): 2-year term*
Cities and Towns with Local Governments: 39

Federal Government

Senators *(2): 6-year term*
Representatives *(2): 2-year term*
Electoral Votes: *4*

Economy

Agriculture: *greenhouse and nursery products, milk*
Fishing: *clams, flounder, lobsters*
Manufacturing: *jewelry and silverware, metal products, electric equipment*
Mining: *sand, gravestone*

Rhode Island State Flag

Interesting Facts

• Rhode Island, the smallest state, has the longest official name: State of Rhode Island and Providence Plantations.

• Rhode Island was the first colony to claim independence from Britain in May of 1776.

Interesting Rhode Islander

• George M. Cohan, born in Providence, wrote many plays and musicals. His popular patriotic songs include "Over There," "You're a Grand Old Flag," and "I'm a Yankee Doodle Dandy."

Rhode Island

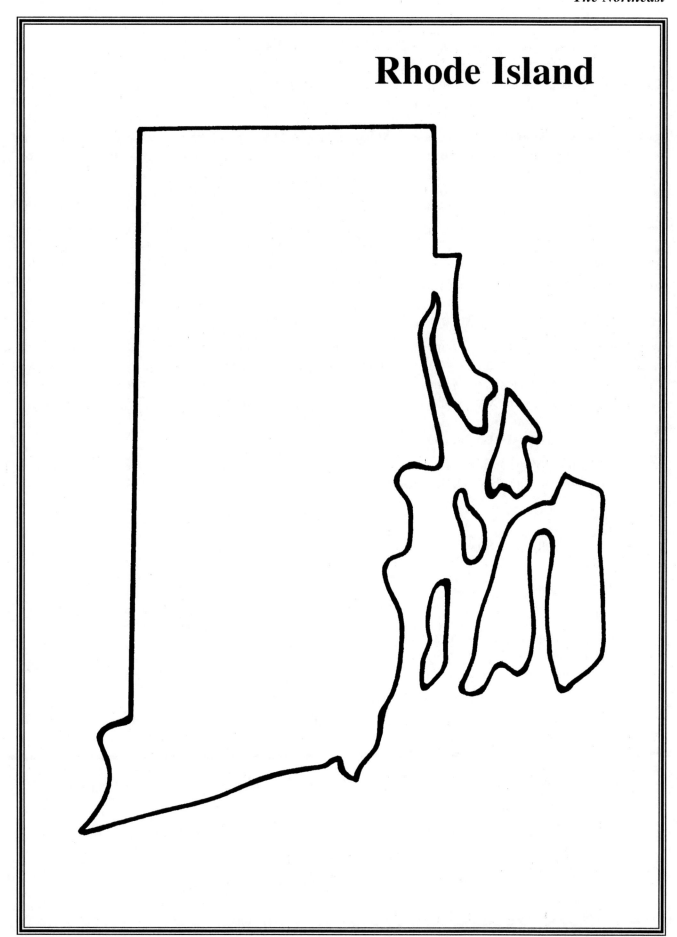

Small in Size—Big on Sails

Tiny Rhode Island is sometimes called "Little Rhody," and is the smallest of the fifty states. Five-hundred Rhode Islands can fit into Alaska, the largest of the United States.

Although Rhode Island is the smallest state, it is not an island. There is a bay, however, that does contain many small islands. Some historians believe that the Italian sea captain Giovanni da Verrazano, who named Rhode Island, named it after the Isle of Rhodes in the Aegean Sea.

This state claims to be the sailing capital of the world. The city of Newport is host to a number of yacht races and regattas. Large numbers of people are drawn to Newport every summer for these exhilarating sailing races. From 1930 to 1983, Newport was the home of America's Cup race, the most prestigious of all international sailing competitions. Americans took first place for an incredible 132 years! This has been called the longest winning streak in sporting history.

Activity 1: A "Sail Tale"

Working in a small group or by yourself, create a story about a sailing adventure. Brainstorm ideas that will help you write your "Sail Tale." You could imagine yourself sailing in a big race like the America's Cup. You and your friends could write an adventure on the high seas on your way to a distant island. When you are ready, write your story in the sail on page 101. Share your "Sail Tale" with classmates.

Activity 2: Miniature Sailboats

Make one or more of these miniature sailboats. When you are done, enjoy a regatta of your own by racing your sailboat with those made by your classmates.

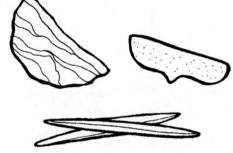

Essentials

- walnut shell half or acorn cap
- toothpick
- play clay (see page 165)
- scissors
- paper (any color)
- pan of water

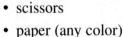

Directions

1. Prepare play clay (or use a commercial brand). Press the clay into the walnut shell.

2. Make a sail by cutting a triangle out of colored paper. Be sure that the size of the sail is appropriate for the walnut shell.

3. Insert a toothpick into the triangular sail, as shown.

4. Attach the sail to the walnut shell by pushing the toothpick with its sail into the clay.

5. Place your miniature sailboat into the pan of water. Blow gently on the sail and watch your boat sail away!

Small in Size—Big on Sails *(cont.)*

(Title)

by _____

Vermont

"The Green Mountain State"

Basic Facts

Capital: *Montpelier*
Statehood: *March 4, 1791*
Admittance: *14th state*
Motto: *Freedom and Unity*
Song: *"Hail, Vermont!"*
Bird: *Hermit thrush*
Flower: *Red clover*
Tree: *Sugar maple*
Abbreviation: *VT*

Area: *9,614 square miles (24,900 sq. km)*
Elevation: *(above sea level)*
   Highest: 4,393 ft. (1,339 m) – Mount Mansfield
   Lowest: 95 ft. (29 m) – Franklin County
Average Temperatures:
   July: 68°F. (20°C)
   January: 17°F. (-8°C)
Average Yearly Precipitation: *39 in. (99 cm)*

Population

How Many: *564,964 (1990 Census)*
Where They Live: *66% urban, 34% rural*
Largest Cities: *Burlington, Rutland, South Burlington*

Vermont State Flag

State Government

Governor: *4-year term*
Senators *(30): 4-year term*
Representatives *(150): 2-year term*
Towns: 237

Federal Government

Senators *(2): 6-year term*
Representatives *(1): 2-year term*
Electoral Votes: *3*

Economy

Agriculture: *milk, beef cattle, eggs, maple products, apples*
Manufacturing: *electric equipment, fabricated metal products, printed materials, paper products,*
   machinery, food products, transportation equipment
Mining: *granite, asbestos*

Interesting Facts

- Vermont produces more maple syrup than any other state.
- Vermont was the first state that allowed all men to vote, not just men who owned land.

Interesting Vermonter

- In 1823, Reverend Samuel Read Hall opened the first academy (school) established solely for training school teachers.

Vermont

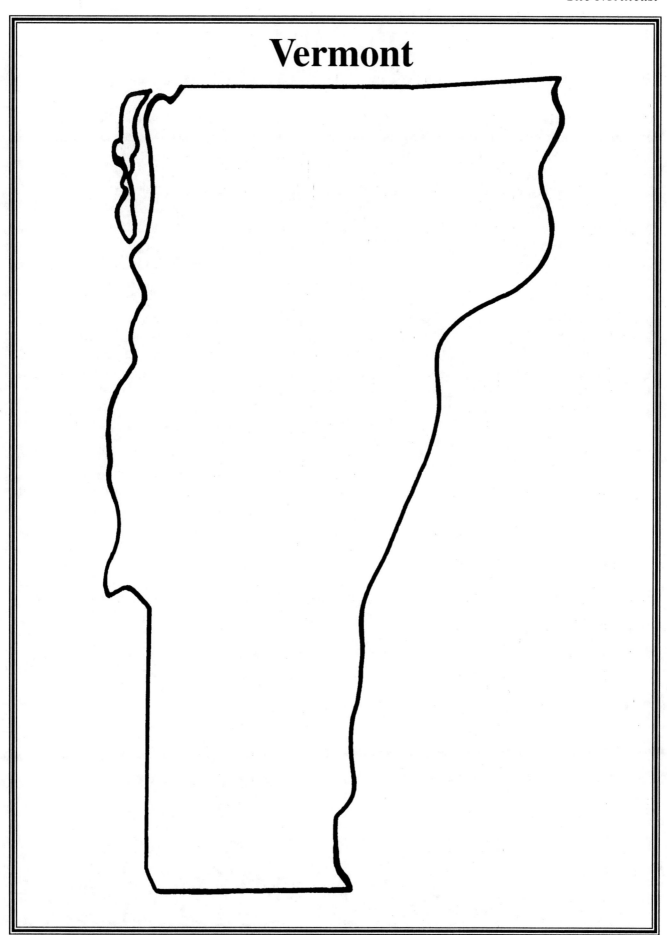

Maple Madness

Spring is maple sugar season in Vermont. Vermont is the largest producer of maple syrup in the U.S.

Maple sugar tree growers require the magic potion of warm nights and cool days. The difference in temperature starts the sap to flow in the trunks of the maple trees. There is no fast way to make or produce syrup. There are two different methods of making maple syrup.

The first method is the slower, older method, and is still in service today. First, holes are drilled into the maple trees and a metal spout is driven into each hole. Under the spout, the producer hooks up small buckets. After the buckets are filled, the producer empties the contents into a larger bucket. From there the bucket is taken by sled or wagon to a building called the sugar house. In the second method holes are drilled into the maple trees and a plastic spout is inserted into each hole. The sap runs through tubes connected to the spouts and into a pipeline system. This system carries the sap to a sugarhouse.

When the sap first gets to the sugarhouse it is a colorless, watery solution. At the sugarhouse the sap is boiled in a long, shallow pan called the evaporator, which evaporates the water content, leaving the maple sugar behind. It is during this process that the maple taste and golden brown color develop. Approximately 40 gallons (152 liters) of sap must boil away to leave one gallon (3.8 liters) of maple syrup. In Vermont, you can visit sugarhouses to watch the syrup being made.

Activity: Taste-Test Syrups

Have you ever tasted genuine maple syrup or maple sugar candy? Do you think that if you compared real maple syrup to other sugar-based syrups you could tell the difference? Try it and see!

Sample various brands of pancake syrup, including those made from genuine maple syrup.

Check the labels for ingredients to see which products use maple syrup and which use other sweeteners. Then taste unmarked samples of each product on your favorite kind of pancake or waffle. Identify the sample(s) you think contain maple syrup.

Northeastern Clip Art

Connecticut

Yale University

Charter Oak

Mystic Seaport

Delaware

beach resorts

fruits & vegetables

farming

Northeastern Clip Art *(cont.)*

Maine

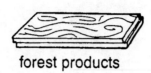
forest products

Portland
Head
Light

potatoes

lobsters

Maryland

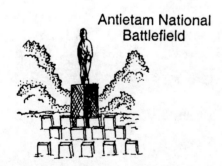
Antietam National
Battlefield

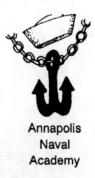
Annapolis
Naval
Academy

Northeastern Clip Art *(cont.)*

Massachusetts

corn

Bunker Hill
Monument

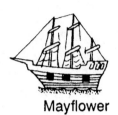

Mayflower

Birthplace of
John F. Kennedy
(Brookline)

Martha's Vineyard

New Hampshire

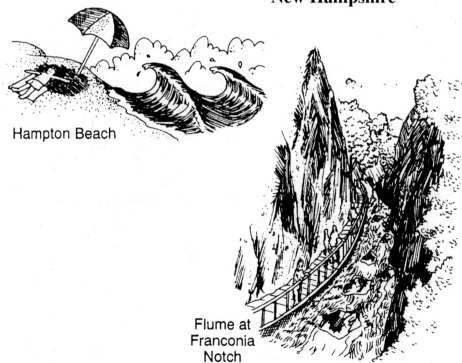

Hampton Beach

Flume at
Franconia
Notch

Old Man
of the
Mountains

Northeastern Clip Art *(cont.)*

New Jersey

First organized
baseball game

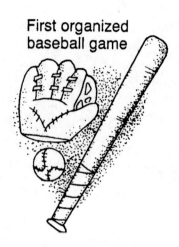

Barnegat
Lighthouse

Miss America
Pageant

New York

Niagara Falls

West Point,
United States
Military Academy

Manhattan

Northeastern Clip Art *(cont.)*

Pennsylvania

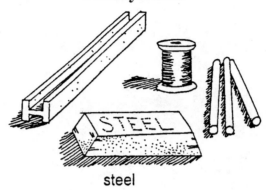

steel

Battle of Gettysburg

Pine Creek Gorge

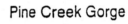

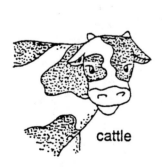

cattle

Independence Hall

Northeastern Clip Art *(cont.)*

Rhode Island

Slater Mill

silver industry

recreational boating

poultry

Stone
Lighthouse

Northeastern Clip Art *(cont.)*

Vermont

marble quarry

Bennington
Battle
Monument

maple syrup

Name _____ Date _____

Which State Am I?

Directions: Identify the state described. Write its name on the line.

1. I was one of the first thirteen states. I am mostly a manufacturing state, although I do produce eggs, milk, and even some tobacco. From the Atlantic Ocean to the south I get lobsters, oysters, and clams. I have the first written constitution in the United States.

   Which state am I? _____

2. I joined the Union with the other original thirteen states. From the large bay next to me, people find oysters, clams, and crabs. On my farms I produce chickens, dairy products, corn, and tobacco. I even have some coal mines. "The Star-Spangled Banner" was written here. You might recognize me because of my odd shape.

   Which state am I? _____

3. Because I was the first of the thirteen original states, people might think I am too proud. Actually, I am thought of as number one by many other than myself, even if I am rather small. Still, with the mighty Atlantic Ocean on my shore and other Northeastern states around me, I am content.

   Which state am I? _____

4. I was one of the first colonies to set up my own government. My climate and soil are not very good for farming, so much of my economy is tied to manufacturing instruments, rubber and plastic products, as well as leather goods. Three northeastern states border me, as does Canada and the Atlantic Ocean.

   Which state am I? _____

5. I was among the first 30 states to enter the union. People in my state can see the sun rise before anyone else in the United States. I am also proud to say that I have the largest lobster catch of any state. My wood-processing industry forms the backbone of my economy.

   Which state am I? _____

6. I was also one of the first thirteen states. Manufactured goods, such as books, electric machinery, and metal products, come from me. My fishermen bring in scallops, cod, and haddock. The Pilgrims first settled on my shores.

   Which state am I? _____

Name _____ Date _____

Which State Am I? *(cont.)*

7. I, too, was one of the thirteen original states. Some would say that I am the key to the Northeastern states. I should be very popular for several reasons, such as my coal, metal, and dairy products. Or perhaps people like me because I have the world's largest chocolate factory. Most importantly, you could call me the birthplace of the United States.

   Which state am I? _____

8. I was one of the first thirteen states. Because of my small size, I do not produce many agricultural products. Of those I do produce, many are grown in greenhouses. I am proud of being the smallest state in the United States. The Atlantic Ocean borders me like other New England states, but in my case it is to the south.

   Which state am I? _____

9. I became a state in a spring month. I was among the first fifteen states to join the Union. People admire my green mountains. Some of the goods I produce are apples, electric equipment, maple syrup, and eggs. I am a landlocked state, unlike my neighbors.

   Which state am I? _____

10. I know you have heard this before, but I was also one of the thirteen original states. I am famous for having the largest city in the United States and for producing printed materials and all forms of entertainment. i have the biggest and busiest port. To my north is Canada, to the west is a great lake, and to the east is an ocean.

    Which state am I? _____

11. I was one of the thirteen original states. To the east of me are the waters of the Atlantic Ocean. To the north, west, and south I am bordered by other northeastern states. Even though my nickname makes it sound like I am an agricultural state, I am mostly known for manufacturing. The first professional baseball game in the world was played here.

    Which state am I? _____

Name _____   Date _____

Identifying Northeastern States

Directions: Outlines of the states in the northeast region of the United States are mixed up with those of other regions. Identify the northeastern states by coloring them red.

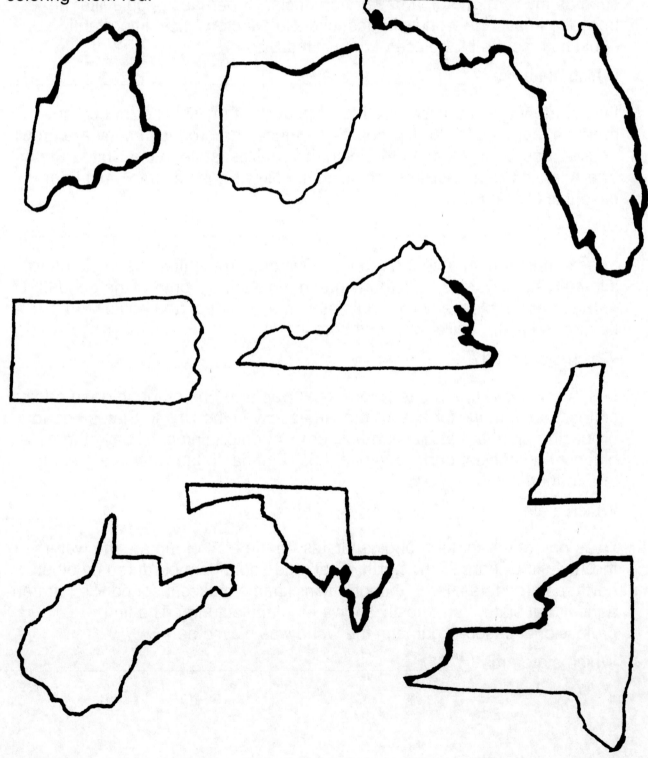

Flag Match *(cont.)*

Directions: Write the number of the flag next to the state to which it belongs. Color the flags correctly.

1.

4.

2.

5.

3.

6.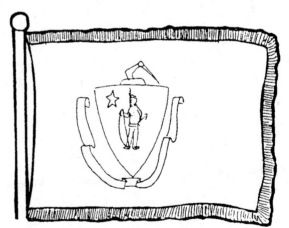

Pennsylvania _____

New York _____

Massachusetts _____

New Jersey _____

Delaware _____

Maine _____

Name _____   Date _____

Flag Match *(cont.)*

Directions: Write the number of the flag next to the state to which it belongs. Color the flags correctly.

1.

4.

2.

5.

3.

6.

New Hampshire_____   Maryland _____

Rhode Island_____   Connecticut _____

Vermont_____

Name _____   Date _____

City Match

Directions: Match the cities with their states by writing the numbers of the cities on the appropriate lines.

1. Worcester
2. Rochester
3. Waterville
4. Albany

5. Syracuse
6. Augusta
7. Bangor
8. Annapolis

9. Baltimore
10. Springfield
11. Fitchburg
12. Washington, D.C.

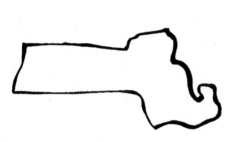

Massachusetts

Maine

_____

New York

_____

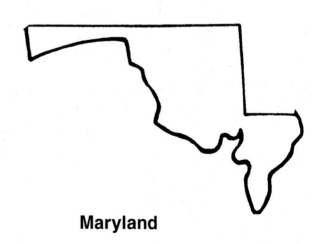

Maryland

_____

Name _____   Date _____

City Match *(cont.)*

13. Warwick   17. Bridgeport   21. Providence

14. Pittsburgh   18. Dover   22. Milford

15. Newport   19. Philadelphia   23. Manchester

16. Hartford   20. Reading   24. Wilmington

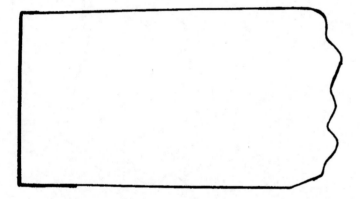

Pennsylvania

Rhode Island

_____   _____

Connecticut

Delaware

_____   _____

Name _____   Date _____

How Far Is It?

Directions: Choose ten pairs of cities from the map below. Write their names in the blanks. Then use the map of the northeast and the scale on this page to find the distances between the cities you listed.

1. _____ to _____ = _____ mi./km
2. _____ to _____ = _____ mi./km
3. _____ to _____ = _____ mi./km
4. _____ to _____ = _____ mi./km
5. _____ to _____ = _____ mi./km
6. _____ to _____ = _____ mi./km
7. _____ to _____ = _____ mi./km
8. _____ to _____ = _____ mi./km
9. _____ to _____ = _____ mi./km
10. _____ to _____ = _____ mi./km

Name _____   Date _____

Comparing Population

Directions: Record the population of each state on the numbered lines. Round these numbers to the nearest 100,000. Write the rounded numbers on the lettered lines. Complete the bar graph using the rounded numbers.

Connecticut	1. _____	a. _____
Delaware	2. _____	b. _____
Maine	3. _____	c. _____
Maryland	4. _____	d. _____
Massachusetts	5. _____	e. _____
New Hampshire	6. _____	f. _____
New Jersey	7. _____	g. _____
New York	8. _____	h. _____
Pennsylvania	9. _____	i. _____
Rhode Island	10. _____	j. _____
Vermont	11. _____	k. _____

State Populations

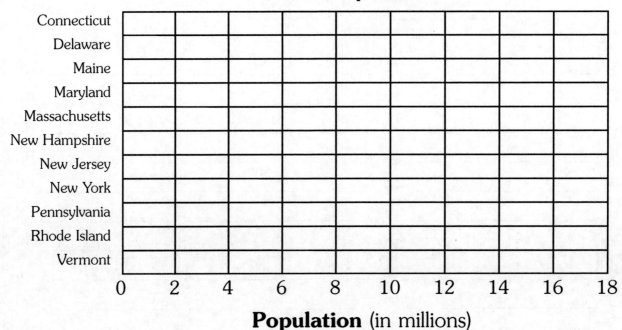

Population (in millions)

Name _____ Date _____

Admission Days

Directions: Complete the following exercises to learn more about when each of the northeastern states received statehood.

A. When were the states in the northeast granted statehood? Record their admission dates next to the states' names.

Name	**Month**	**Day**	**Year**
1. Connecticut	_____	_____	_____
2. Delaware	_____	_____	_____
3. Maine	_____	_____	_____
4. Maryland	_____	_____	_____
5. Massachusetts	_____	_____	_____
6. New Hampshire	_____	_____	_____
7. New Jersey	_____	_____	_____
8. New York	_____	_____	_____
9. Pennsylvania	_____	_____	_____
10. Rhode Island	_____	_____	_____
11. Vermont	_____	_____	_____

B. The admission dates of the northeastern states can be plotted on a time line. Plot them on the time line below, making sure to label each one.

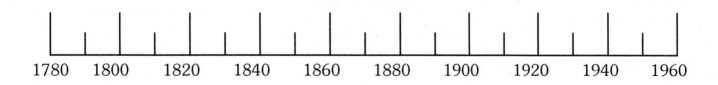

1780   1800   1820   1840   1860   1880   1900   1920   1940   1960

Name _____   Date _____

States Puzzler

Directions: Use the clues to help you complete the puzzle. When you have filled in the circles, read the vertical word formed by the dark circles. Write the word on the line at the bottom of the page.

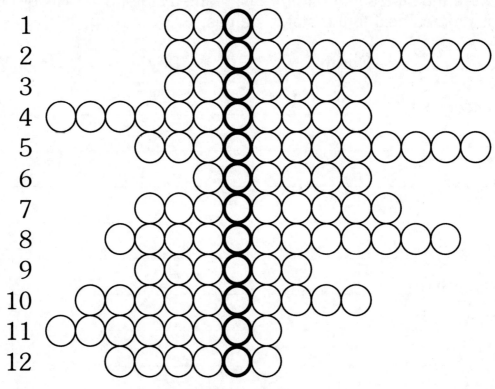

1. "The Pine Tree State"
2. "The Ocean State"
3. "The Green Mountain State"
4. "The Constitution State"
5. "The Granite State"
6. New Jersey's largest city
7. Maryland's Capital
8. "The Keystone State"
9. Capital of Massachusetts
10. Vermont's Capital
11. "The First State"
12. New York's Capital

Puzzler Word: _____

The Midwest

Illinois

"The Prairie State"

Basic Facts

Capital: *Springfield*
Statehood: *December 3, 1818*
Admittance: *21st state*
Motto: *State Sovereignty,*
National Union
Song: *"Illinois"*
Bird: *Cardinal*
Flower: *Native Violet*
Tree: *White Oak*
Abbreviation: *IL*

Area: *56,345 square miles (145,934 sq. km)*
Elevation: *(above sea level)*
Highest: 1,235 ft. (376 m) – Charles Mound
Lowest: 279 ft. (85 m) -Alexander County
Average Temperatures:
July: 76°F. (24°C)
January: 260F. (-3°C)
Average Yearly Precipitation: *38 in. (97 cm)*

Population

How Many: *11,466,682 (1990 Census)*
Where They Live: *83% urban, 17% rural*
Largest Cities: *Chicago, Rockford, Peoria*

State Government

Governor: *4-year term*
Senators *(59): 4-year term*
Representatives *(118): 2 or 4 year term*
Counties: *102*

Federal Government

Senators *(2): 6-year term*
Representatives *(20): 2-year term*
Electoral Votes: *22*

Illinois State Flag

Economy

Agriculture: *corn, soybeans, hogs, beef cattle, milk*
Manufacturing: *nonelectric machinery, food products, chemicals, fabricated metal products,*
transportation equipment
Mining: *coal, petroleum, stone*

Interesting Facts

• Chicago's Sears Tower is the tallest building in the world. It is 1,454 feet (436 m) tall.

• Joseph Glidden became famous for inventing a machine that could make barbed wire in 1874. Interesting Illinoisan

• Abraham Lincoln became famous for his stand against slavery in his debates with Stephen Douglas in Illinois. He was practicing law in Springfield when elected President in 1860.

Illinois

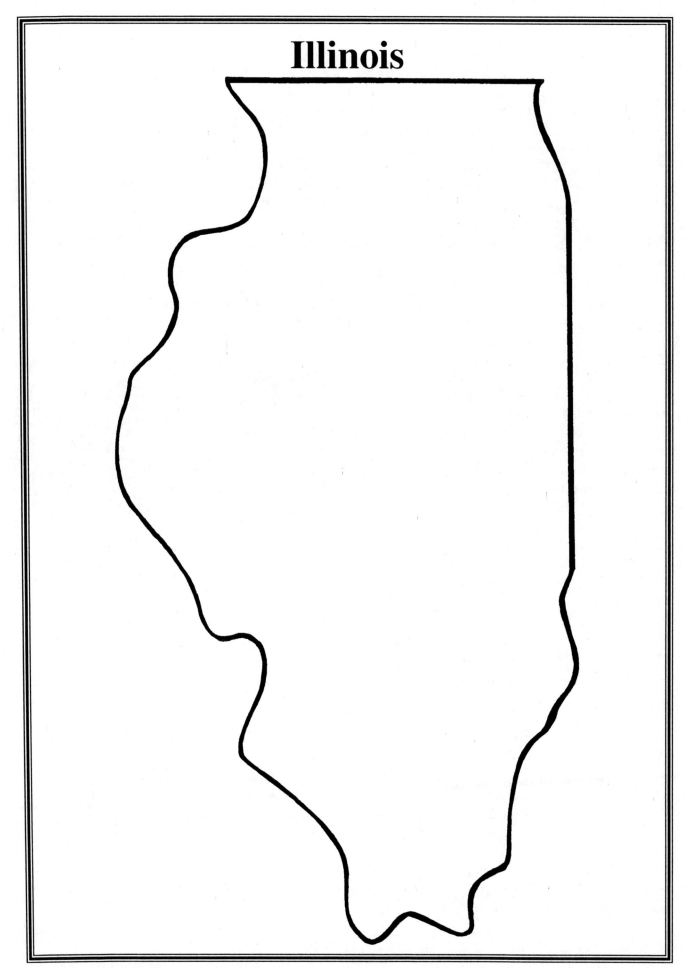

The Land of Lincoln

Illinois got its name from the French word, "Iliniwek," which means "tribe of superior men." The name is appropriate when describing one of its most famous residents, Abraham Lincoln. Lincoln was important to the political life of Illinois. He was nominated for the presidency in 1860 at a Republican convention held in Chicago. In 1861, he was elected the 16th President of the United States, and is credited with freeing the slaves and fighting to keep our country together during the Civil War. Abraham Lincoln was assassinated on April 14, 1865, by John Wilkes Booth.

Activity 1: Make a Log Cabin

Abraham Lincoln, like many people living in the United States at the time, began his life in a log cabin. In fact, one of the shelters he built with his father, Thomas, consisted of a three-sided log structure known as a "half-faced camp."

Make a simple log cabin model by gluing straight pretzels to the sides and top of a clean, pint-sized milk container. Cut out a door and window from construction paper and glue them on the log cabin. You can also create your own free-standing cabins using toothpicks, craft sticks, pretzels, or rolled-up newspaper or construction paper. Cut the "logs" (construction material you have chosen) to the lengths you need for the sides and roof of the log cabin. Glue the "logs" together. Cut out a door and window and add them to the log cabin.

Activity 2: Have a Debate

Use your school or local library to find materials about the Lincoln-Douglas debates. Conduct a debate in class. Subjects to debate could include which of two states is more interesting, who was the better of two presidents, or any pertinent issue that has two sides to be argued.

Activity 3: The Great Fire

Log cabins and other flimsy shacks provided shelter for many Illinois pioneers. Later, the balloon frame house, much cheaper to build than traditional houses, became a trademark of the "Prairie State." That ended when a third of Chicago's wooden houses burned in the Great Fire of 1871. When the city rebuilt, its predominate dwelling then became the three to five story brick apartment house.

Find out more about the fire that nearly destroyed Illinois' largest city. What farm animal was believed to have started it? Invite a firefighter to your class to talk about fire safety. Learn about changes in housing over time in your city or town.

A Booming City

Between 1845 and 1870, Chicago grew from a small city to one of the largest cities in the country. It became a major steel manufacturer and the largest center for meat packing and food processing in the world. Today, this third largest city in the United States is one of the world's leading transportation and industrial centers.

Why did it happen in Chicago? Look at the map below. It provides you with some clues that will help you discover why Chicago became such a booming city in the late 1800's. Brainstorm your ideas with a partner. Then write them on the lines below the map.

_____

_____

_____

_____

_____

Indiana

"The Hoosier State"

Basic Facts

Capital: *Indianapolis*
Statehood: *December 11, 1816*
Admittance: *19th state*
Motto: *The Crossroads of America*
Song: *"On the Banks of the Wabash FarAway"*
Bird: *Cardinal*
Flower: *Peony*
Tree: *Tulip tree*
Abbreviation: *IN*

Area: *36,185 square miles (93,720 sq. km)*
Elevation: *(above sea level)-*
 Highest: 1,257 ft. (383 m) – Wayne County
 Lowest: 320 ft. (17 m) – Posey County
Average Temperatures:
 July: 75°F. (24°C)
 January: 28°F. (-2°C)
Average Yearly Precipitation: *40 in. (102 cm)*

Population

How Many: *5,564,228 (1990 Census)*
Where They Live: *64% urban, 36% rural*
Largest Cities: *Indianapolis, Fort Wayne, Gary*

State Government

Governor: *4-year term*
Senators *(50): 4-year term*
Representatives *(100): 2-year term*
Counties: *92*

Federal Government

Senators *(2): 6-year term*
Representatives *(10): 2-year term*
Electoral Votes: *12*

Economy

Agriculture: *corn, soybeans, hogs*
Manufacturing: *primary metals, transportation equipment, electric machinery and equipment, chemicals*
Mining: *coal, stone*

Indiana State Flag

Interesting Facts

• In 1826, New Harmony became the first city to teach girls and boys in the same classes.

• The rapid-fire machine gun was invented by Richard J. Gatling in Indianapolis in 1862. The first gun fired 250 shots in one minute.

Interesting Hoosier

• Larry Bird is one on the most famous basketball players in the history of the sport. He played on the Boston Celtics team for many years.

Indiana

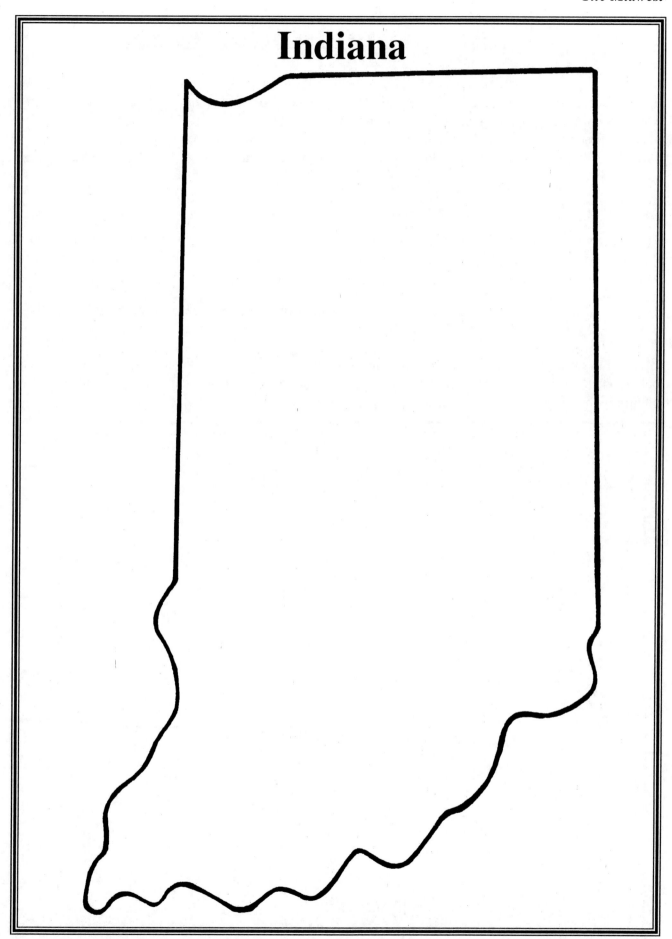

Home of the Studebaker

In 1852, a man named Clement Studebaker, and his brother Henry started a blacksmith and wagon shop in South Bend, Indiana. By the 1890's the Studebaker brothers decided to try their luck making carriages with self-propelling engines, better known as "horseless carriages." The Studebaker family made its first electric-powered car in 1902 and began producing gasoline-powered automobiles by 1904. They became quite a success, having produced over three hundred and fifty thousand Studebaker cars by 1917.

Activity: The Car of the Future

The Studebaker brothers, like inventors and business people with new and unique ideas, saw the need for a new form of transportation. They decided to explore their new ideas in order to build a "horseless carriage."

Think about what the "car of the future" might look like. How would it perform? What kind of "self-propelling engine" would it have?

Brainstorm ideas about what you think the "car of the future" will be like. Write your ideas in the space below. Then, on a large piece of drawing paper, make a sketch of your new car. Share your ideas and picture with others.

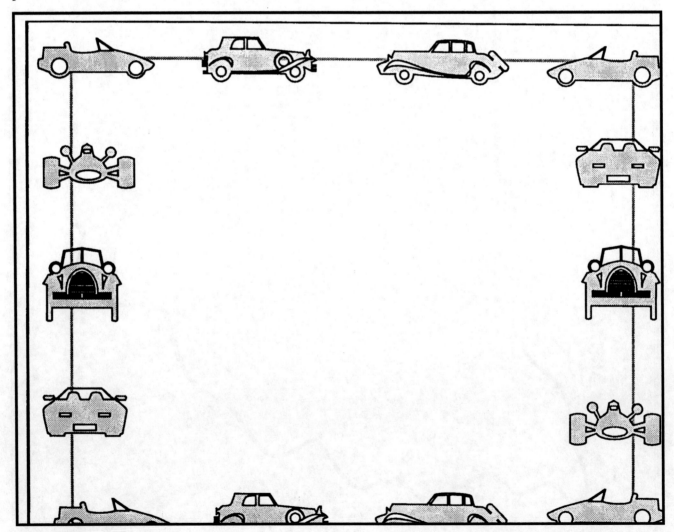

Iowa
"The Hawkeye State"

Basic Facts

Capital: *Des Moines*
Statehood: *December 28, 1846*
Admittance: *29th state*
Motto: *Our Liberties We Prize and Our Rights We Will Maintain*
Song: *"The Song of Iowa"*
Bird: *Eastern goldfinch*
Flower: *Wild rose*
Tree: *Oak*
Abbreviation: *IA*

Area: *56,275 square miles (146,753 sq. km)*
Elevation: *(above sea level)*
  Highest: 1,670 ft. (509 m) – Ocheyedan Mound
  Lowest: 480 ft. (146 m) – Lee County
Average Temperatures:
  July: 75°F. (24°C)
  January: 19°F. (-7°C)
Average Yearly Precipitation: *32 in. (81 cm)*

Population

How Many: *2,787,424 (1990 Census)*
Where They Live: *62% urban, 38% rural*
Largest Cities: *Des Moines, Cedar Rapids, Davenport*

Iowa State Flag

State Government

Governor: *4-year term* Senators *(50): 4-year term*
Representatives *(100): 2-year term*
Counties: *99*

Federal Government

Senators *(2): 6-year term*
Representatives *(5): 2-year term*
Electoral Votes: *7*

Economy

Agriculture: *corn, beef cattle, hogs, soybeans, milk, eggs*
Manufacturing: *nonelectric machinery, food products, electric machinery and equipment, chemicals, printed materials*
Mining: *stone, sand, and gravel*

Interesting Facts

• The famous red delicious apple was developed in an orchard in East Peru in the 1880's.

• The Effigy Mounds National monument, near Marquette, is made of earthen mounds built by prehistoric people. The mounds are more than 300 feet (90 m) long and resemble animals.

Interesting Iowan

• Grant Wood is an American artist known for his paintings of the Midwest. His famous work, American Gothic, shows a farm couple. He was born near Anamosa.

Iowa

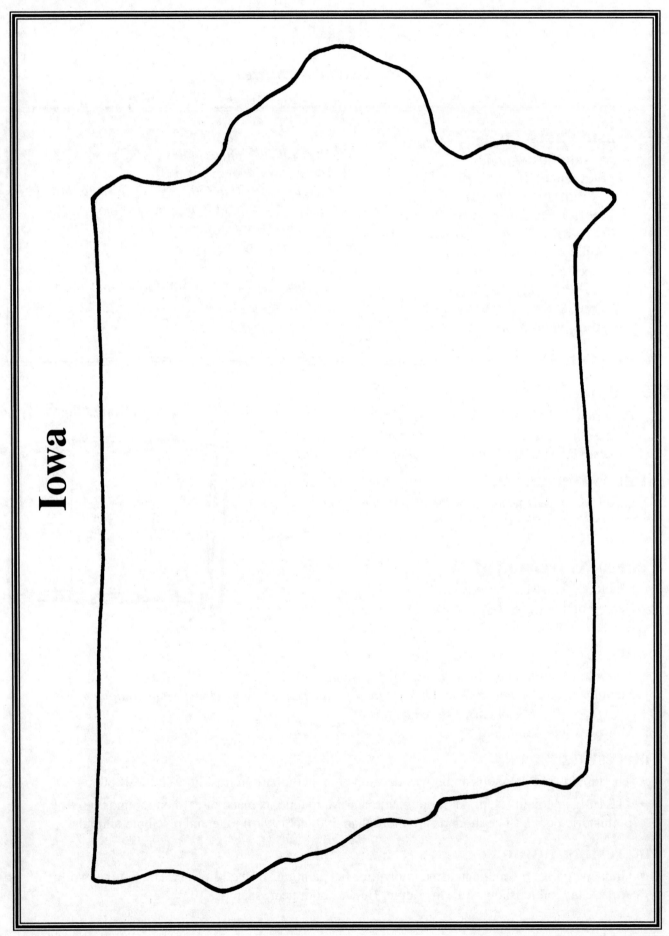

Where the Tall Corn Grows

It is rumored that on a quiet Iowa summer night, you can actually hear the corn growing. Robert Frost once said of Iowa's rich black soil, "It looks good enough to eat without putting it through Yegetables."

In the mid 1800's, farmers from all over the country rushed to the fertile soil of the Iowa prairie. Today, 93 percent of the land in Iowa is used for farming, and corn is the leading source of farm income. Each year, Iowa and Illinois compete to be the number-one corn producer in the nation.

Corn is related to rice, wheat, oats, and barley. This cereal grass was first used about 10,000 years ago. The farmland region of the Midwest is known as the Corn Belt. In addition to its value as a food product, corn is also used to manufacture industrial products such as ceramics, metal molds, paper goods, textiles, and construction materials.

Activity: Cornhusk dolls

The part of the corn plant that protects the ear of corn is called the husk. Collect corn husks and make cornhusk dolls using the directions below.

Essentials

- cornhusks (can be purchased in grocery stores in Mexican food sections)
- string or yellow yarn
- water colors
- scissors
- paper towels
- bucket or pan for soaking cornhusks
- cloth or sponge
- fabric

Directions

Soak the cornhusks in warm water until soft. This may take up to an hour. Drain them on paper towels. Keep the husks damp with a cloth or sponge while working with them.

1. Put 6 cornhusks together and tie a string around the middle for a waist. Tie another piece of string about 2" (5 cm) below the first for the body. Fold the ends of the husks down from the top and hold them down by tying them in place with another string placed on top of the first string that you tied in the middle.

2. Put two husks together and tie them near the ends with strings for the arms and hands. Roll and slip the arms through the opening in the top of the body near the neck, or tie the arms to the body by wrapping string around them at the neck.

3. To make a girl doll, keep the bottom of the dress as is. To make a boy doll, divide or cut the husks below the waist. Roll into trouser legs and tie with string at the bottom of each foot.

4. Use the fabric or paint to add clothes and features to the dolls.

Popcorn Magic

Popcorn is one of the oldest types of corn. It was grown thousands of years ago by Native Americans. The popcorn kernel has a very hard section called the endosperm which encases a soft, moist center. Heating a popcorn kernel causes steam to form in the center. Pressure builds up within the kernel, until it explodes, or pops. Try the following experiments and discover the magic of popcorn!

Activity 1: Which Pops the Most?

There are various ways to pop popcorn. Hot air poppers, metal pots on a stove, standard poppers, and microwave bags are among the most popular methods. Which do you think pops the most popcorn flakes? Conduct an experiment. Begin by writing down your predictions for the number of kernels you think will pop using three different methods.

- Count out 400 kernels (approximately ¼ cup/60 mL).
- Pop the popcorn as directed for each method.
- After the kernels stop popping and cool down, count the number of popped flakes and old maids (unpopped kernels). Use this information to fill in a chart showing your results. How close was your prediction to the actual count? Which method seemed to produce the best results? Share your information with the class.

Activity 2: How Can That Be?

If you drop popcorn kernels in water, they sink. If you drop popcorn flakes in water they float. This is because the puffed flakes are less dense, or not as compact as the kernels. The flakes are "lighter" than the water so they float, while the kernels are "heavier" than water and will sink.

But did you know you can still make kernels float? Follow the directions below to see for yourself.

1. Fill a glass with soda water. Place a few popcorn kernels in the glass.

2. After a few moments, the kernels will begin to rise to the surface, then go back down, only to rise up again. Look carefully at the surface of the kernels to help you predict why this happens. Then read the explanation below. How close was your prediction?

Explanation: The kernels rise and fall because the soda water contains a gaseous element, and the "gas" is attracted to the kernels. When enough gas bubbles form around the kernel, it "lifts" to the surface. The gas is then released into the air and the kernel sinks back down. The process starts all over again.

Kansas

"The Sunflower State"

Basic Facts

Capital: *Topeka*
Statehood: *January 29, 1861*
Admittance: *34th state*
Motto: *To The Stars Through Difficulties*
Song: *"Home on the Range "*
Bird: *Western Meadowlark*
Flower: *Sunflower*
Tree: *Cottonwood*
Abbreviation: *KS*

Area: *82,277 square miles (213,098 sq. km)*
Elevation: *(above sea level)*
  Highest: 4,039 ft. (1,231 m) – Mount Sunflower
  Lowest: 680 ft. (204 m) – Montgomery Co.
Average Temperatures:
  July: 780F. (26°C)
  January: 30°F. (-1°C)
Average Yearly Precipitation: *27 in. (69 cm)*

Population

How Many: *2,485,600 (1990 Census)*
Where They Live: *67% urban, 33% rural*
Largest Cities: *Wichita, Kansas City, Topeka*

State Government

Governor: *4-year term*
Senators *(40): 4-year term*
Representatives *(125): 2-year term*
Counties: *105*

Federal Government

Senators *(2): 6-year term*
Representatives *(4): 2-year term*
Electoral Votes: *6*

Kansas State Flag

Economy

Agriculture: *beef cattle, wheat, sorghum grain, hogs, corn, soybeans*
Manufacturing: *transportation equipment, chemicals, stone, clay, glass and coal products*
Mining: *petroleum, natural gas*

Interesting Facts

• The first woman mayor in the United States, Susanna Salter, was elected in Argonia in 1887.

• Helium, the gas used to inflate balloons, was first discovered in natural gas in 1905 by University of Kansas scientists.

Interesting Kansasan

• Amelia Earhart, born in Atchison, was the first woman pilot to fly an airplane solo across the Atlantic Ocean. Her historic flight took place in 1932.

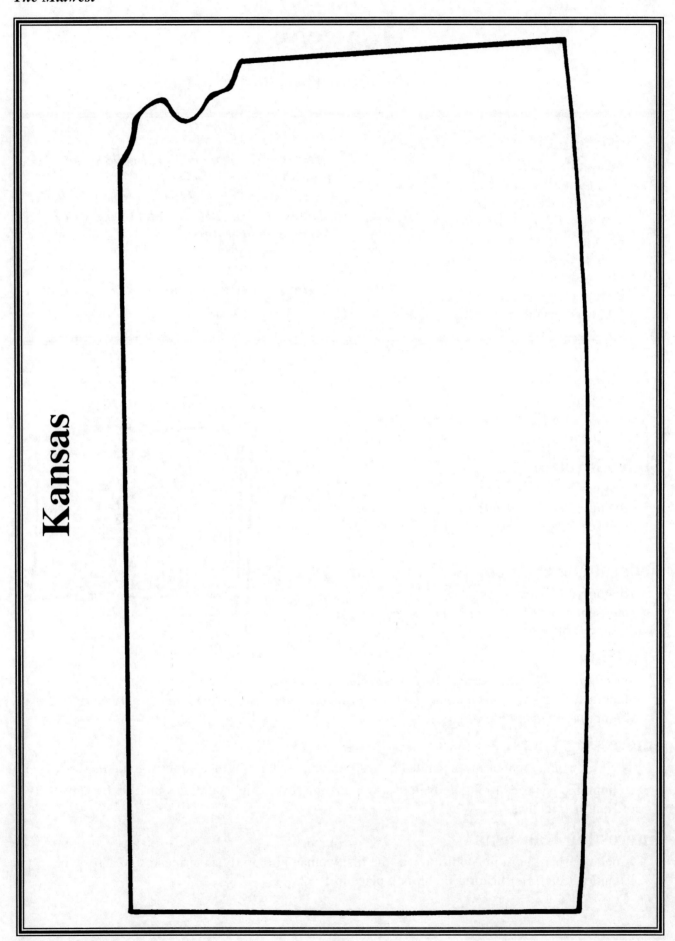

Kansas

Hurray for the Harvey House!

By the late 1800's, the face of America was changed by the railroads. The trains replaced covered wagons as a means of transporting homesteaders to the plains and Pacific Coast. The railroad system moved mail, factory goods, lumber, cattle, and other materials.

The trains were responsible for a great deal of progress, but comfort was definitely not a strong point. They had long, uncomfortable wooden seats and windows that let in cinders and ashes. The ride was bumpy, there was no place to sleep, and animals were allowed on board with the passengers. One of the worst problems was finding something to eat. The trains did not yet have dining cars, so that left passengers with few choices—either bring a lunch on board (these often spoiled, and uneaten food littered the train) or join the hundreds of other passengers trying to get a meal in the unappetizing station lunchrooms during the quick stopovers.

Frederick Henry Harvey, a freight agent who had had some restaurant experience, wanted to change this. He thought about starting a comfortable sit-down restaurant where a passenger could get a good, hot meal at a reasonable price. The conductor could get a count of how many passengers would want to eat there, and the food would be ready and waiting when the train pulled in. He presented his idea to some of the larger railroads, and his idea was greeted with laughter. They jokingly suggested he try his idea in Kansas. He did, and in 1876 in Topeka, the first Harvey House restaurant was opened. He carefully chose his waitresses, known as Harvey girls, and their jobs became prestigious. The popularity of these restaurants continued until the 1920's.

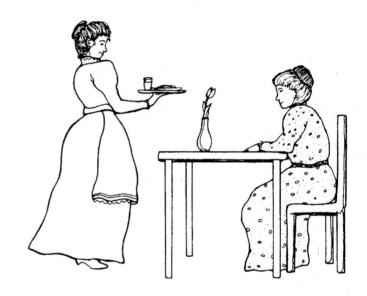

Activity: Cup Codes

Harvey girls were famous for their "cup codes." After asking a customer for his or her choice of beverage (coffee, hot tea, iced tea, or milk) the Harvey Girl would rearrange the customer's cup. Soon a "drink girl" would arrive with the proper drink without even asking. The cup's position was the key. Right side up meant coffee. Upside down was hot tea. Upside down and tilted meant iced tea. Upside down and away from the saucer signaled milk.

Directions

In groups of three, role play a drink order. One person will be the passenger, one the Harvey girl or boy, and one the drink girl or boy.

Design a similar system for food orders using the placement of silverware. Use the placemat pattern on page 138 to illustrate your arrangement. Beneath the placemat, write a short explanation about the position of items on the illustration.

Hurray for the Harvey House *(cont.)*

Michigan

"The Wolverine State"

Basic Facts

Capital: *Lansing*
Statehood: *January 26, 1837*
Admittance: *26th state*
Motto: *If You Seek a Pleasant Peninsula Look About You*
Song: *"Michigan, My Michigan"*
Bird: *Robin*
Flower: *Apple blossom*
Tree: *White Pine*

Abbreviation: *MI*
Area: *58,527 square miles (151,586 sq. km)*
Elevation: *(above sea level)*
  Highest: 1,980 ft. (604 m) – Mount Curwood
  Lowest: 572 ft. (174 m) – Lake Erie
Average Temperatures:
  July: 69°F. (21°C)
  January: 20°F. (-7°C)
Average Yearly Precipitation: *32 in. (81 cm)*

Population

How Many: *9,328,784 (1990 Census)*
Where They Live: *71% urban, 29% rural*
Largest Cities: *Detroit, Grand Rapids, Warren*

Michigan State Flag

State Government

Governor: *4-year term*
Senators *(38): 4-year term*
Representatives *(110): 2-year term*
Counties: *83*

Federal Government

Senators *(2): 6-year term*
Representatives *(16): 2-year term*
Electoral Votes: *18*

Economy

Agriculture: *milk, corn, beef cattle, soybeans, greenhouse and nursery products*
Fishing: *whitefish, chubs*
Manufacturing: *transportation equipment, nonelectric machinery, metal products, food products, chemicals*
Mining: *petroleum, iron ore, natural gas*

Interesting Facts

- Battle Creek is known as the Cereal Bowl of America. This city produces more breakfast cereal than anywhere else in the world.

- Michigan produces more automobiles than anywhere else in the United States.

Interesting Michiganlander

- Charles Lindbergh was the first pilot to fly non-stop across the Atlantic Ocean in a plane. His historic night began in St. Louis, Missouri, and ended when he landed near Paris, France. The flight lasted 33½ hours.

Michigan

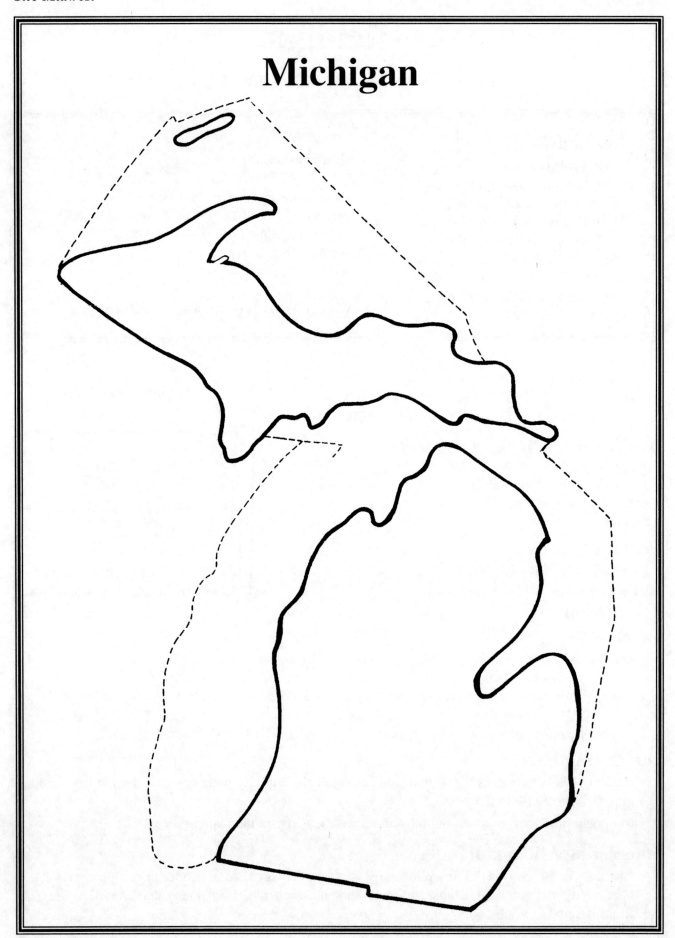

140

It's Time for an Assembly Line!

In the last years of the 1800's, automobile companies grew in the Midwest.

In 1896, a man from Lansing, Michigan, named Ranson Olds built one of the first cars in the United States. The average cost of a Ranson Olds' car was over $1,000 dollars—a price far too high for the average person at that time.

In Detroit, at about the same time, Henry Ford was trying to build a cheaper, better, gasoline-powered car. He thought of using assembly lines, an idea he got from watching the methods of a meat-packing industry in Chicago. By using assembly lines where unfinished cars travel on a moving belt past workers and machines, Ford succeeded in lowering the cost of making a car and began manufacturing cars much quicker. This allowed many families to buy and enjoy automobiles. A trip that had taken three hours by horse now took only one hour by car.

Activity: Your Own Assembly Line

Find out if an assembly line really does save time.

Essentials

- bread
- peanut butter
- jelly

- plastic knives
- sandwich bags
- paper towels for work area/clean-up

Directions

1. Divide the class into two parts: individual workers and assembly line teams (with no more than five members per assembly-line team).

2. The individual workers will be responsible for making their sandwiches by themselves. The assembly-line workers will each have a small job in making the sandwiches (e.g., one worker can place the bread, a second worker can spread the jelly, etc.). Use the directions for making peanut butter sandwiches on page 142.

3. Allow enough time to get completely set up. Have the assembly-line workers sit in the order of their jobs. They will do their jobs and pass the materials to the next person.

4. Stop the activity after 15 minutes. Find out who made more sandwiches, the assembly-line workers or the individual workers. Use the lines provided on page 142 to write your feelings about performing the job using the different methods of production.

5. Enjoy the sandwiches!

It's Time for an Assembly Line! *(cont.)*

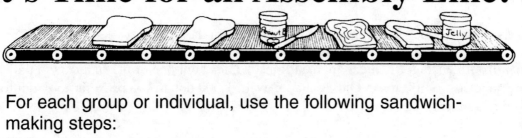

For each group or individual, use the following sandwich-making steps:

1. Take two slices of bread from the bag.
2. Spread peanut butter on the bread.
3. Spread jelly on the bread.
4. Put the slices together and cut the sandwich in half.
5. Put the halves in a sandwich bag.

Student Name _____

Method Used _____

My feelings about performing the job using this method (for example, how effective you were, how quickly you got the job done, how satisfied you are with the finished product, etc.).

_____

_____

_____

_____

_____

_____

_____

America's Cereal Capital

Battle Creek is known as the "Cereal Bowl of America." This city produces more breakfast cereal than anywhere else in the world.

Activity: What's in It for Me?

There are many brands and types of cereal on the market today—high fiber, vitamin-supplemented, hot and cold cereals, pre-sweetened, all natural, etc.

Use the following ideas to learn more about breakfast cereals:

- Which cereal is your favorite? Conduct a class survey to discover the top five cereals among your classmates.
- Make a classroom collection of cereal boxes and read the nutritional information on the boxes. Then compare the nutritional value of the cereals you collected with the information in the chart below. It contains some of the nutrients (food ingredients) your body needs to stay healthy. How nutritious do you think your cereal samples are?

Proteins help build and repair your body. When you scrape or cut yourself, proteins help to repair your skin. Some foods with protein are meat, milk, nuts, beans, and eggs.

Carbohydrates give your body fuel for energy. When you eat carbohydrates, you have more energy to run, work, and play for a longer time. There are two types of carbohydrates—starch and sugar. Some foods with starch are bread, cereal, and rice. Fruits with sugar include oranges and apples.

Minerals help you grow, you use your food more efficiently, and make your blood healthy. Some important minerals are calcium, phosphorus, and iron. Calcium helps your bones and teeth. Iron makes your blood healthy. Some foods containing these minerals are milk, eggs, grains, and fish.

Vitamins help you grow and help you use your food. Some foods with vitamins are vegetables, whole grain breads and cereals, nuts, fruit, and eggs.

Minnesota
"The Gopher State"

Basic Facts

Capital: *St. Paul*
Statehood: *May 11, 1858*
Admittance: *32nd state*
Motto: *The Star of the North*
Song: *"Hail! Minnesota "*
Bird: *Common loon*
Flower: *Pink and white lady's slipper*
Tree: *Norway pine*
Abbreviation: *MN*

Area: *84,402 square miles (218,601 sq. km)*
Elevation: *(above sea level)*
 Highest: 2,301 ft. (701 m) – Eagle Mountain
 Lowest: 602 ft. (183 m) – Lake Superior
Average Temperatures:
 July: 70°F. (21°C)
 January: 8°F. (-13°C)
Average Yearly Precipitation: *26 in. (66 cm)*

Population

How Many: *4,387,029 (1990 Census)*
Where They Live: *67% urban, 33% rural*
Largest Cities: *Minneapolis, St. Paul, Bloomington*

State Government

Governor: *4-year term* Senators *(67): 4-year term*
Representatives *(134): 2-year term*
Counties: *87*

Federal Government

Senators *(2): 6-year term*
Representatives *(8): 2-year term*
Electoral Votes: *10*

Minnesota State Flag

Economy

Agriculture: *corn, milk, soybeans, hogs, beef cattle, hay, wheat*
Fishing: *catfish, walleye, carp*
Manufacturing: *paper products, chemicals, food products, electric machinery and equipment*
Mining: *iron ore, sand, gravel, stone*

Interesting Facts

• Duluth is the busiest freshwater port in the United States.

• Cellophane tape was invented and patented in St. Paul in 1930.

Interesting Minnesotan

• Alfred M. Butz invented and manufactured the thermostat in 1885. A thermostat regulates the
 heating of your house.

Minnesota

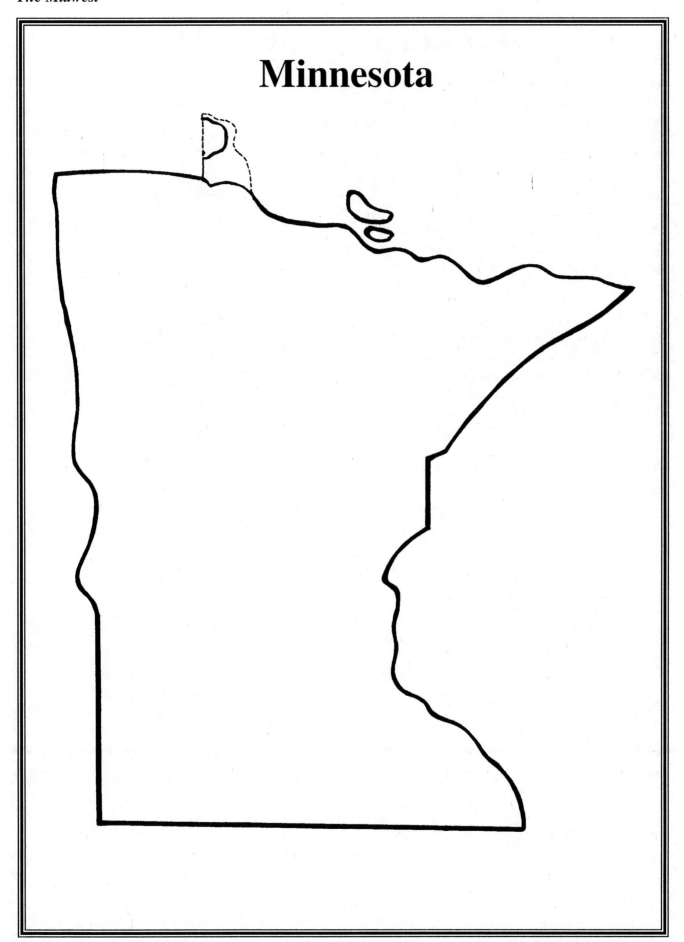

Tantalizing Tall Tales

Many years ago, lumberjacks enjoyed sitting around campfires at the end of a hard day's work. Not only did they enjoy the warmth of the fire, but they loved to hear and tell outrageous tall tales. A favorite among these stories was a tall tale about Paul Bunyan and Babe.

A tall tale is a story based on a fact, but told in a highly exaggerated and humorous way. Exaggeration plays a major role in the telling of the tale.

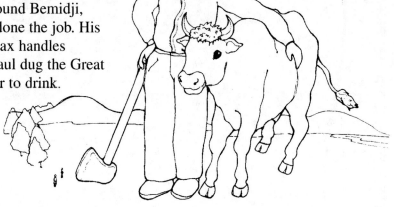

In the 1900's, so much lumber was cut around Bemidji, Minnesota, that Paul Bunyan might have done the job. His ox, Babe, at full size, measured forty-two ax handles between the eyes. Some people say that Paul dug the Great Lakes so that Babe would have fresh water to drink.

Today, on Lake Bemidji, stands the statues of Minnesota's two very famous characters. Paul stands tall and strong, and the lovable Babe's eyes light up. Babe's eyes are constructed from automobile headlights.

Activity: Write Your Own Tall Tale

Read the tall tales of Paul Bunyan. Then, write your own.

- Organize your thoughts on a piece of paper folded into three columns. Label the columns Character, Setting, and Exaggeration.
- Fill in the columns by using your imagination and creating ideas about the who, when, where, and how of your tall tale.

CHARACTER	SETTING	EXAGGERATION
Muscle-bound Max	Thunderbolt Mountain	Tamed the mighty mountain with his bare hands.

- Next, write a story based on your ideas. Remember to use lots of imagination. Some ideas for stories include:

    The Boy Who Drank Up the Ocean

    The Girl Who Could Communicate with the Sun and the Moon

    The Ant Who Stilled the Forest

    The Grasshopper Who Conquered the Prairie

You may wish to illustrate your story as well.

"The Bread and Butter State"

In the late 1800's, thousands of immigrants from Norway, Sweden, and Germany came to Minnesota. They became millers, grew wheat, and raised dairy cattle. As a result, the land was used for farming and the nickname, "The Gopher State," was replaced with a new nickname—"The Bread and Butter State."

Play the following game to explain the farm-to-table process that turns wheat into bread.

Preparation

Make copies of the "Farm-to-Table Game Board" on pages 148-149 and the spinner below. Mount the game board on the inside of a file folder. Glue the directions at the bottom of this page to the front of the folder. Use beans, seeds, unpopped popcorn, etc. for game markers.

Spinner

Cut out the spinner and arrow. Punch a hole in the center of the spinner and arrow. Attach the arrow to the spinner with a brad fastener. If the arrow does not spin freely, loosen the fastener a little.

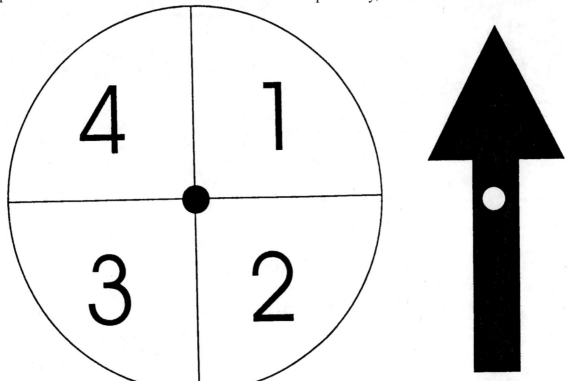

Directions

Each player spins the spinner. The player with the highest number goes first. Player 1 spins the spinner. He/she must name a word from the game board (or other chosen list of words) that begins with one of the blends or digraphs on page 149. To find the blend or digraph to be used in a word, match the spinner number to the number indicated on the game board. (For example, if a player spins a 3, he/she must name a word that begins with Br.) If correct, the player moves his/her marker the number of spaces indicated by a spin of the spinner. The first player to reach the bread is the winner.

Farm-to-Table

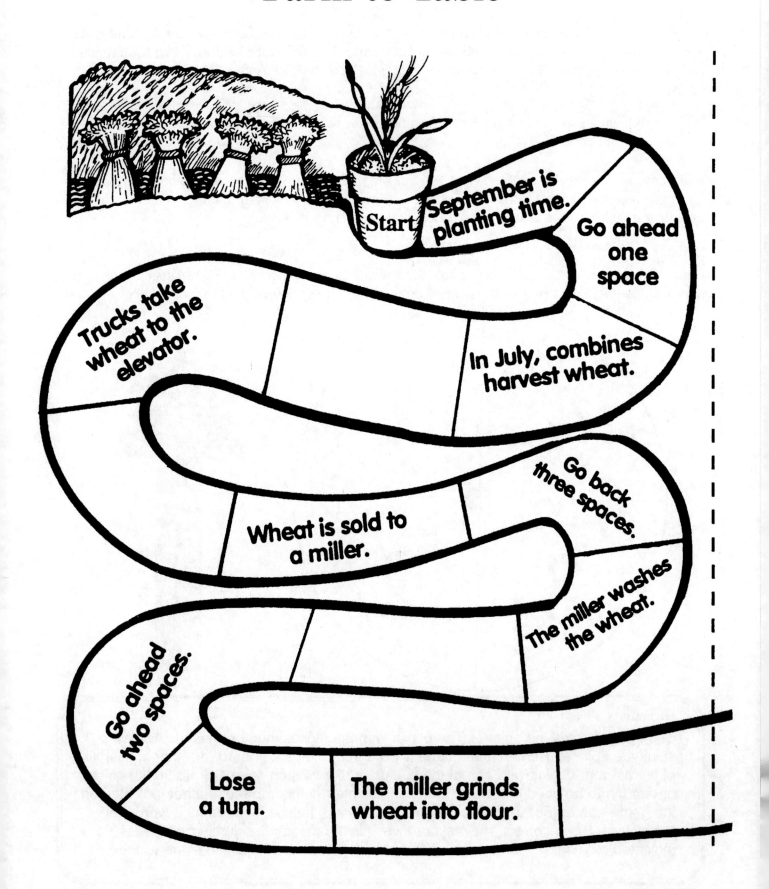

Start — September is planting time.

Go ahead one space

In July, combines harvest wheat.

Trucks take wheat to the elevator.

Go back three spaces.

Wheat is sold to a miller.

The miller washes the wheat.

Go ahead two spaces.

Lose a turn.

The miller grinds wheat into flour.

Game Board

Spin 1—Fl   Spin2—Tr   Spin3—Br   Spin 4—Wh

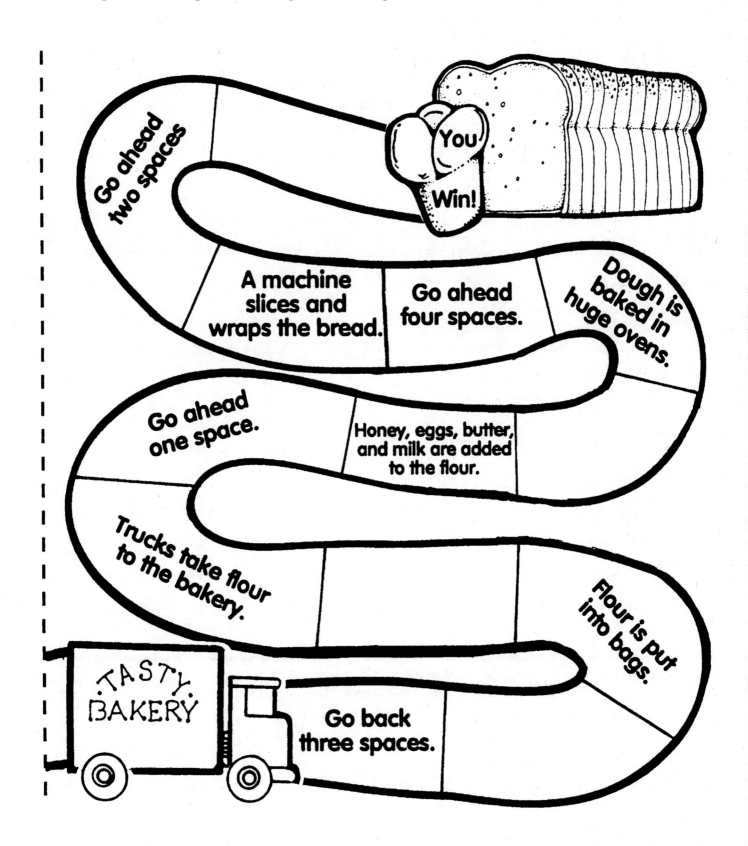

Go ahead two spaces

You Win!

A machine slices and wraps the bread.

Go ahead four spaces.

Dough is baked in huge ovens.

Go ahead one space.

Honey, eggs, butter, and milk are added to the flour.

Trucks take flour to the bakery.

Flour is put into bags.

TASTY BAKERY

Go back three spaces.

Missouri

"The Show Me State"

Basic Facts

Capital: *Jefferson City*
Statehood: *August 10, 1821*
Admittance: *24th state*
Motto: The Welfare of the People
Shall Be The Supreme Law
Song: *"Missouri Waltz"*
Bird: *Bluebird*
Flower: *Hawthorn*
Tree: *Flowering dogwood*

Abbreviation: *MO*
Area: *69,697 square miles (180,516 sq. km)*
Elevation: *(above sea level)*
  Highest: 1,772 ft. (540 m) – Taum Sauk Mt.
  Lowest: 230 ft. (17 m) – near Cardwell
Average Temperatures:
  July: 78°F. (26°C)
  January: 30°F. (-1°C)
Average Yearly Precipitation: *40 in. (102 cm)*

Population

How Many: *5,137,804 (1990 Census)*
Where They Live: *68% urban, 32% rural*
Largest Cities: *St. Louis, Kansas City, Springfield*

Missouri State Flag

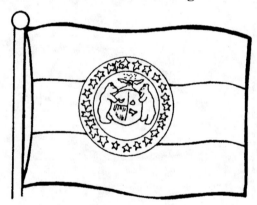

State Government

Governor: *4-year term*
Senators *(34): 4-year term*
Representatives *(163): 2-year term*
Counties: *114 Federal*

Government

Senators *(2): 6-year term*
Representatives *(9): 2-year term*
Electoral Votes: *11*

Economy

Agriculture: *beef cattle, soybeans, hogs, milk*
Manufacturing: *food products, chemicals, electric machinery, printed materials, transportation equipment*
Mining: *lead, stone*

Interesting Facts

- Ice cream cones were first served at the 1904 World's Fair in St. Louis.
- The first parachute jump was made on March 1, 1912, by Captain Alfred Berry in St. Louis. He jumped 1,500 feet (450 m).

Interesting Missourian

- Harry S. Truman was the 33rd president of the United States. He was born in Lamar and lived in Independence when he was elected president.

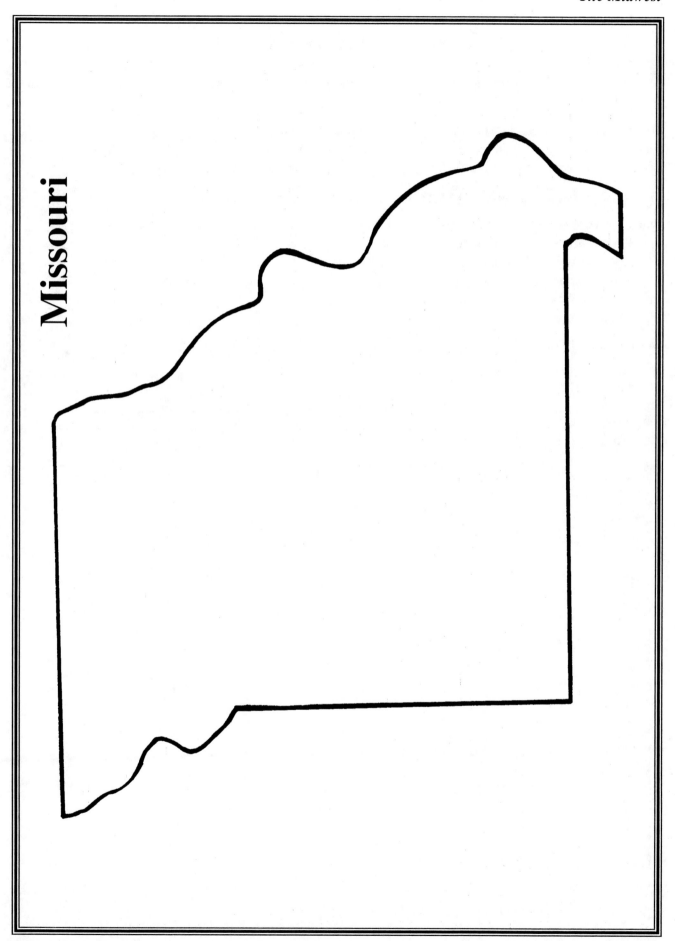

Missouri

What's in a Name?

The Show Me State's name originates from the Iliniwek Indian word "missouri," meaning "owners of big canoes."

Its nickname, "The Show Me State," can be traced to a speech given in Philadelphia by Missouri Congressman William Vandiver in 1899, where he was quoted as saying "...frothy eloquence neither convinces nor satisfies me. I am from Missouri. You have got to show me."

Activity: "Show Me" Riddles

Make up your own "Show Me" riddles. Begin the riddles with the words "Show me" and end with two rhyming words. For example: "Show me a kitty that eats too much and I'll show you a fat cat," or "Show me an insect in a blanket and I'll show you a snug bug."

Write some of your riddles on the lines below.

Share your riddles with the class by stating the first part ("Show me a _____ and I'll show you a _____), and asking other students to complete the riddle.

"Show Me" Historic Missouri

Celebrate some of the history of Missouri by learning about the following famous people.

Activity 1: Mark Twain Read-a-Thon

Mark Twain, the great American author of such classics as The Adventures of Tom Sawyer and The Adventures of Huckleberry Finn, was born in 1835 in Florida, Missouri. He grew up in Hannibal, Missouri.

Have a Mark Twain read-a-thon. Break up the reading with events such as a frog jumping contest (real or paper frogs), fence painting, and charades of scenes from his books.

Activity 2: Explore with Lewis and Clark

Lewis and Clark began their famous journey to the Pacific Northwest near St. Louis in 1804. They were to explore the western two-thirds of the American continent. At the time of their expedition, much of the land explored still belonged to Spain or England.

Use encyclopedias or other reference materials to find out more about this expedition. Trace Lewis and Clark's route on the map below.

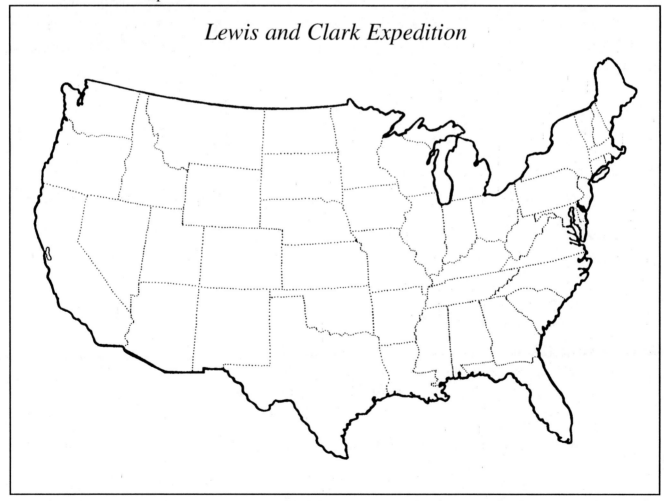

Lewis and Clark Expedition

Write a journal from the point-of-view of either Lewis or Clark describing the journey.

Nebraska

"The Cornhusker State"

Basic Facts

Capital: *Lincoln*
Statehood: *March 1, 1867*
Admittance: *37th state*
Motto: *Equality Before the Law*
Song: *"Beautiful Nebraska"*
Bird: *Western meadowlark*
Flower: *Goldenrod*
Tree: *Cottonwood*
Abbreviation: *NE*

Area: *77,355 square miles (200,350 sq. km)*
Elevation: *(above sea level)*
 Highest: 5,426 ft. (1,654 m) – Kimball County
 Lowest: 840 ft. (256 m) – Richardson County
Average Temperatures:
 July: 76°F. (24°C)
 January: 23°F. (-5°C)
Average Yearly Precipitation: *22 in. (56 cm)*

Population

How Many: *1,584,617 (1990 Census)*
Where They Live: *63% urban, 37% rural*
Largest Cities: *Omaha, Lincoln, Grand Island*

Nebraska State Flag

State Government

Governor: *4-year term*
One House Legislature
Senators *(49): 4-year term*
Counties: *93*

Federal Government

Senators *(2): 6-year term*
Representatives *(3): 2-year term*
Electoral Votes: *5*

Economy

Agriculture: *corn, beef cattle, hogs, hay, soybeans, wheat, sorghum grain, milk*
Manufacturing: *food products, chemicals, electric machinery, fabricated metal products*
Mining: *petroleum, sand and gravel*

Interesting Facts

• Farms make up 95% of the land area, more than any other state.

• The largest mammoth fossil was unearthed near Wellfleet in 1922.

Interesting Nebraskan

• Henry Fonda was born in Grand Island. He was a famous actor of both stage and screen. One of his most famous movies is Young Mr. Lincoln.

154

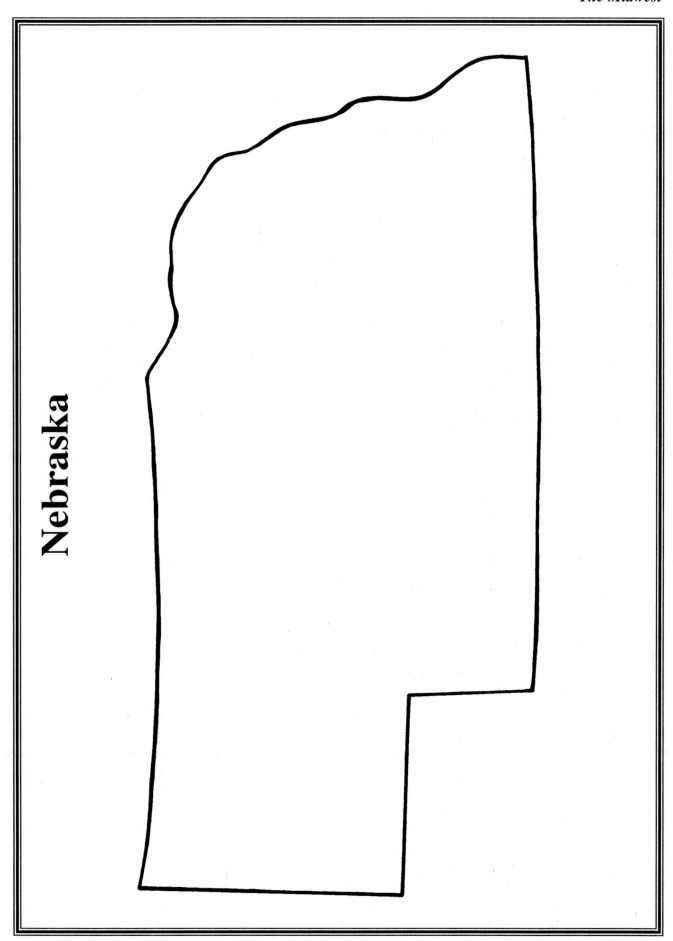

Nebraska

Noteworthy Nebraskans

Nebraska is the home of many famous and interesting individuals. Learn more about some noteworthy Nebraskans by reading about them and completing the activities below.

Activity 1: A Thing As Lovely As a Tree

Arbor Day has its "roots" in Nebraska. Arbor refers to trees. Julius Sterling Morton, a Nebraska journalist and statesman, realized that trees would enrich the soil and conserve the moisture in it, and bring welcome shade in the summer. Through much effort, April 10, 1872, was set aside as Nebraska's first Arbor Day; over a million trees were planted on that day. After Morton died, the Nebraska legislature made Arbor Day a legal holiday and changed the date to April 22, Morton's birthday. People may visit Morton's former home, now a tourist attraction called Arbor Lodge in Nebraska City.

Today most states in the United States, as well as most Canadian provinces, celebrate Arbor Day.

Read some of the following books about trees:

> *The Great Kapok Tree* by Cherry Lynne (HBJ, 1990)
>
> *The Lorax* by Dr. Seuss (Random House, 1971)
>
> *One Day in the Tropical Rain Forest* by Jean-Craighead George (Crowell, 1990)
>
> *Once There Was a Tree* by Natalia Romanova (Dial Books, 1985)
>
> *Keeper of the Earth* by Michael J. Caudato and Joseph Bruchac (Fulcrum, Inc., 1988)

Find out the date your state celebrates Arbor Day. With permission, plan a ceremony to include poems, songs, and the planting of a tree in your local community or on the school grounds.

Activity 2: Class Big Book

Make a Class Big Book that includes stories and illustrations about some of the following "Noteworthy Nebraskans." You may wish to choose from the following list, or research to find other famous Nebraskans for your big book. Share your Class Big Book with other classes as you tell them about the state and people of Nebraska.

- Gerald R. Ford, former United States president, was born in Nebraska.
- Native American leaders important in Nebraska's history include chiefs Red Cloud (1822-1909) and Crazy Horse (1849-1877).
- Another famous Nebraskan was Father Edward Joseph Flanagan (Ireland, 1886-1948), the founder of Boys Town, a home for underprivileged youth.
- Nebraskans important in entertainment include Fred Astair, Henry Fonda, Robert Taylor, Marlon Brando, Sandy Dennis, Johnny Carson, Dick Cavett, and motion picture producer Daryl F. Zanuck.

North Dakota
"The Flickertail State"

Basic Facts

Capital: *Bismarck*
Statehood: *November 2, 1889*
Admittance: *39th state*
Motto: *Liberty and Union, Now and Forever, One and Inseparable*
Song: *"North Dakota Hymn"*
Bird: *Western meadowlark*
Flower: *Wild prairie rose*
Tree: *American elm*
Abbreviation: *ND*

Area: *70,702 square miles (183,119 sq. km)*
Elevation: *(above sea level)*
 Highest: 3,506 ft. (1,069 m)—White Butte
 Lowest: 750 ft. (229 m)—Pembina County
Average Temperatures:
 July: 70°F. (21°C)
 January: 7°F. (-14°C)
Average Yearly Precipitation: *17 in. (43 cm)*

Population

How Many: *641,364 (1990 Census)*
Where They Live: *51% urban, 49% rural*
Largest Cities: *Fargo, Bismarck, Grand Forks*

State Government

Governor: *4-year term*
Senators *(53): 4-year term*
Representatives *(106): 2-year term*
Counties: *53*

Federal Government

Senators *(2): 6-year term*
Representatives *(1): 2-year term*
Electoral Votes: *3*

North Dakota State Flag

Economy

Agriculture: *wheat, beef cattle, barley, hay, sunflower seeds*
Manufacturing: *food products, nonelectrical machinery, printed material, stone, clay, glass products*
Mining: *petrolems, coal, natural gas*

Interesting Facts

- The geographic center of North America is near the town of Rugby, North Dakota.
- An international golf course can be found in Portal. Half of the course is in the United States, the other half is in Canada.

Interesting North Dakotan

- Louis L'Amour was a famous American author who wrote many western novels about life on the American frontier. He was born in Jamestown.

North Dakota

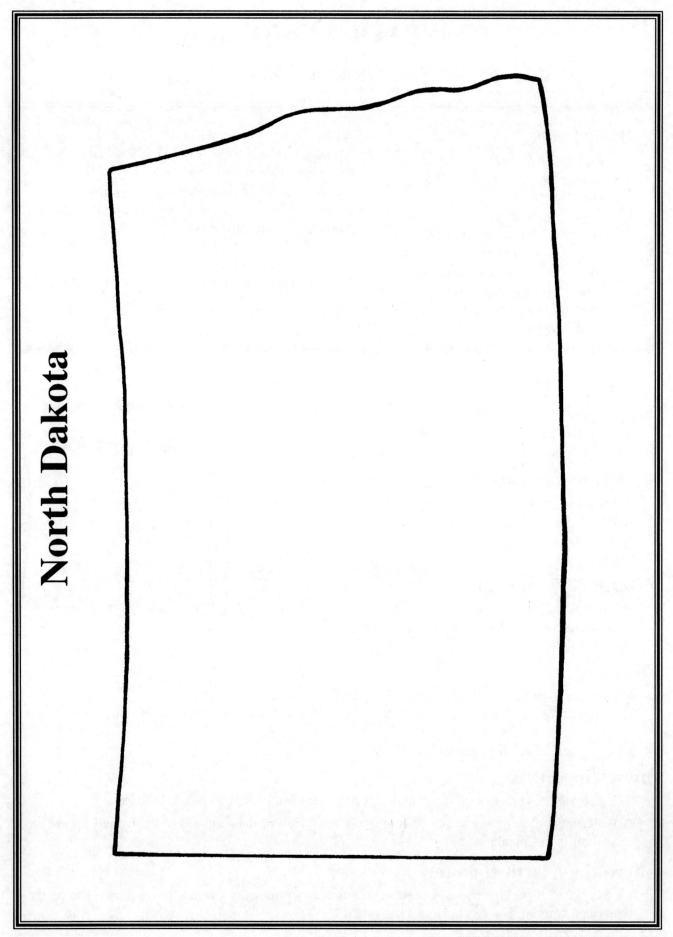

The "Bird Woman" of North Dakota

Sacagawea was a Shoshone Indian woman 16 years of age who accompanied the Lewis and Clark expedition in 1805 and 1806. The name Sacagawea means "Bird Woman." Sacagawea joined this expedition in what is now known as North Dakota.

Lewis and Clark hired Sacagawea's husband, Toussaint Charbonneau, as an interpreter for their expedition. Lewis and Clark were told that Charbonneau's wife was a Shoshone Indian, and that Sacagawea's presence on the journey into Shoshone territory would be beneficial to the expedition.

Sacagawea eased the communication between the Shoshones and the explorers. She also helped secure horses from the tribe for the explorers. In addition, she cooked meals for the explorers and found wild plants for them to eat and use for medicine. If not for the contributions of Sacagawea, Lewis and Clark's historic expedition might have failed.

Activity: Tribal Tribute

One of Lewis and Clark's jobs on the expedition was to establish communication with Native Americans while gathering information about the various tribes. Learn more about Native Americans by researching a tribe from the following list and preparing a display of the tribe you have chosen.

Area	Tribe
Northwest Coastal	Hupa, Yurok, Kwakiutl, Tsimshian, Salish
Plateau	Nez Perce, Yakima, Flathead, Spokan
Great Basin	Commanche, Ute, Klamath, Washo
California	Modoc, Pomo, Yana, Chumash
Plains and Prairie	Arapaho, Pawnee, Crow, Sioux
Eastern Woodlands	Eari, Huron, Mohawk, Iroquois
Southwest	Navajo, Pueblo, Hopi, Apache

Essentials

- 3 sheets of poster board or cardboard (for stand-up display)
- research books on Native Americans
- crayons, pencils, markers, glue, tape, and scissors to decorate the display
- manila folders to write, store, and present information

Directions

Work in a small group for this activity. Together, decide on a Native American tribe to research from each of five or six areas listed above. From the following list, choose several topics to research: food, shelter, religion, transportation, clothing, communication/language.

When your group has completed its research, use the information gathered to create a visual display. Include such items as a map, illustrations, a report, and helpful reference materials. Share your display with the class.

Ohio
"The Buckeye State"

Basic Facts

Capital: *Columbus*
Statehood: *March 1, 1803*
Admittance: *17th state*
Motto: *With God, All Things Are Possible*
Song: *"Beautiful Ohio"*
Bird: *Cardinal*
Flower: *Scarlet carnation*
Tree: *Buckeye*
Abbreviation: *OH*

Area: *41,330 square miles (107,044 sq. km)*
Elevation: *(above sea level)*
 Highest: 1,550 ft. (472 m) – Campbell Hill
 Lowest: 433 ft. (132 m) – Hamilton County
Average Temperatures:
 July: 73°F. (23°C)
 January: 28°F. (-2°C)
Average Yearly Precipitation: *38 in. (97 cm)*

Population

How Many: *10,887,325 (1990 Census)*
Where They Live: *73% urban, 27% rural*
Largest Cities: *Cleveland, Columbus, Cincinnati*

State Government

Governor: *4-year term*
Senators *(33): 4-year term*
Representatives *(99): 2-year term*
Counties: *88*

Federal Government

Senators *(2): 6-year term*
Representatives *(19): 2-year term*
Electoral Votes: *21*

Ohio State Flag

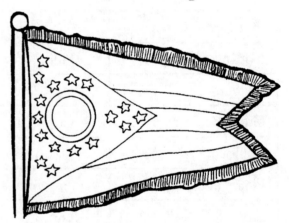

Economy

Agriculture: *corn, soybeans, milk, hogs, beef cattle, hay*
Fishing: *yellow perch, white bass*
Manufacturing: *transportation equipment, metal products, food products, chemicals*
Mining: *coal, natural gas, petroleum*

Interesting Facts

• Eight United States presidents have come from Ohio: Grant, Garfield, Hayes, McKinley, Harding, Taft, William Harrison, and Benjamin Harrison.

• The first electric traffic light signals were invented by James Hoge in Cleveland.

Interesting Ohioan

• Neil Armstrong was the first person to set foot on the moon during the Apollo 11 lunar landing mission. He was born in Wapakoneta

Ohio

Johnny Appleseed

When you think of apples, what name often comes to mind? Johnny Appleseed! Although considered by many to be a legend, Johnny Appleseed really did exist. His real name was John Chapman. So you see, the only thing made up about Johnny was his last name. Johnny Appleseed was more than a nature lover—nature was Johnny's life. He grew up to be a nurseryman, he knew about herbs and flowers, but most of all he was devoted to growing apples. Johnny gathered his seeds from cider mills. For 50 years, Johnny Appleseed planted these apple seeds in the Ohio Valley. He would often give them to settlers and pioneers, showing them how to care for the apple trees that would someday be carried westward.

Today, the apple trees of Ohio and many other states are a tribute to Johnny Appleseed. Many of the apple trees in Indiana, Illinois, and Pennsylvania are descended from Johnny's trees.

Activity: "Apple a Day" Treats

You may have heard the expression, "An apple a day keeps the doctor away." Apples are one of the most popular and nutritionally valuable fruits that grow on trees. They provide us with necessary water and contain vitamins A and C, pectin, potassium, and fiber, all of which our bodies need to grow strong and remain healthy. Try some of the following recipes and enjoy the delicious taste of apples while you take good care of your body.

Apple Smiles

Essentials

For each sandwich you will need:
- apples
- peanut butter
- paring knife
- miniature marshmallows

Directions

Core and slice an apple. Spread peanut butter on one side of each apple slice. Place four tiny marshmallows on top of the peanut butter. Top with another apple slice, peanut butter side down. Gently squeeze the "smile" together. Enjoy!

Essentials
- two slices of bread (Whole wheat or raisin bread is especially tasty!)
- cheddar cheese slices
- apple slices (thin)
- butter

Apple-Cheddar Grilled Sandwich

Directions

Melt a pat of butter in a frying pan. (An electric fry pan works well.) Spread butter on one side of each slice of bread. Place one slice of bread, butter side down, in the pan. Put cheddar cheese slices on top and cover with apple slices. Lay the second piece of bread on top, butter side up. Cook until cheese begins to melt. Turn sandwich over; cook until the other side of bread is browned.

South Dakota

"The Sunshine State"

Basic Facts

Capital: *Pierre*
Statehood: *November 2, 1889*
Admittance: *40th state*
Motto: *Under God the People Rule*
Song: *"Hail, South Dakota"*
Bird: *Ring-necked pheasant*
Flower: *Pasqueflower*
Tree: *Black Hills spruce*
Abbreviation: *SD*

Area: *77,116 square miles (199,730 sq. km)*
Elevation: *(above sea level)*
 Highest: 7,242 ft. (2,207 m) – Harney Peak
 Lowest: 962 ft. (293 m) – Big Stone Lake
Average Temperatures:
 July: 74°F. (23°C)
 January: 16°F. (-9°C)
Average Yearly Precipitation: *18 in. (46 cm)*

Population

How Many: *699, 999 (1990 Census)*
Where They Live: *54% urban, 46% rural*
Largest Cities: *Sioux Falls, Rapid City, Aberdeen*

State Government

Governor: *4-year term*
Senators *(35): 2-year term*
Representatives *(70): 2-year term*
Counties: *66*

Federal Government

Senators *(2): 6-year term*
Representative *(1): 2-year term*
Electoral Votes: *3*

South Dakota State Flag

Economy

Agriculture: *beef cattle, hogs, corn, hay, milk, soybeans*
Manufacturing: *food products, machinery, medical equipment*
Mining: *gold, stone*

Interesting Facts

- The Homestake Mine is the oldest continuously working gold mine in the world. It was opened in 1876.
- The largest buffalo herd in the United States lives at the Standing Butte Ranch near Pierre.

Interesting South Dakotan

- Sitting Bull was a medicine man and leader of the Hunkpapa Sioux Indians. He was involved in the battle of Little Bighorn.

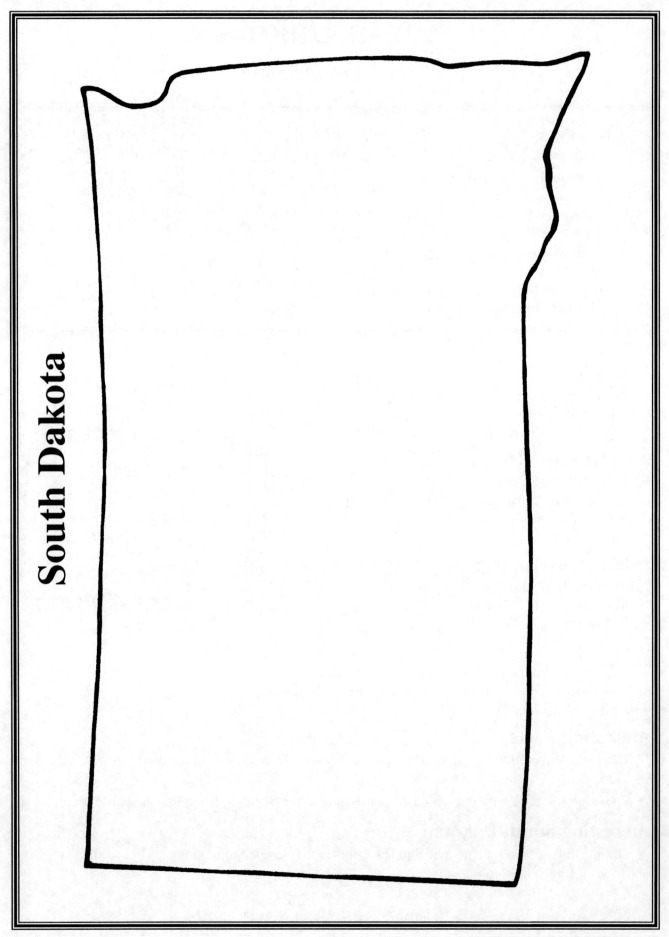

South Dakota

The Mighty Mount Rushmore

In 1927, Gutzon Borglum began work on Mount Rushmore National Memorial, an enormous carving situated on a granite cliff in the Black Hills of South Dakota. Sculptor Gutzon Borglum and his son carved the faces of Washington, Jefferson, Roosevelt, and Lincoln out of mountains of granite.

Activity 1: Is That a Fact!

Use the facts below to answer the questions that follow.

- Mount Rushmore National Memorial rises 5,725 feet (1,745 meters) above sea level.
- Each face is as tall as a five-story building (approximately 60 feet, or 18 meters high).
- The memorial rises more than 500 feet (150 meters) above the valley.
- Mount Rushmore National Memorial was begun in 1927 and completed by 1941.

Questions:

1. About how many miles (kilometers) high above sea level is the memorial?

2. How many years did it take to complete Mount Rushmore National Memorial?

3. According to the facts, about how high is a one-story building?

4. About how many feet (meters) above sea level is the valley? (round to nearest hundred)

Activity 2: "Famous People" Clay Figures

Work in groups of four. Model your own clay figures after those of the four presidents on Mount Rushmore. In your group, choose four famous people from the past or present. Use library and classroom resources to find out about the people you have chosen. Then use modeling clay or the play clay recipe below to make the figures.

Play Clay Recipe

Essentials

- 2 ¼ cups (530 mL) flour
- 1 cup (240 mL) salt
- 1 tsp. (15 mL) powdered alum *(available at drug stores)*
- 4 tbsp. (60 mL) vegetable oil
- 1 ½ cups (350 mL) boiling water
- food coloring or dry tempera paint to color clay

Directions

Mix flour, salt, alum, and food coloring together. Carefully stir in water and oil. When the mixture is smooth, knead it until it feels firm.

When each group member is finished with his/her figure, place the clay figures next to each other. Title your creation and write a few sentences about each famous person. Display your project in the classroom.

Wisconsin

"The Badger State"

Basic Facts

Capital: *Madison*
Statehood: *May 29, 1848*
Admittance: *30th state*
Motto: *Forward*
Song: *"On, Wisconsin!"*
Bird: *Robin*
Flower: *Wood violet*
Tree: *Sugar maple*

Abbreviation: *Wl*
Area: *56,153 square miles (145,436 sq. km)*
Elevation: *(above sea level)*
  Highest: 1,952 ft. (595 m) – 7imms Hill
  Lowest: 581 ft. (9177 m) – Lake Michigan
Average Temperatures:
  July: 70°F. (21 °C)
  January: 14°F. (-10°C)
Average Yearly Precipitation: *31 in. (79 cm)*

Population

How Many: *4,906,745 (1990 Census)*
Where They Live: *64% urban, 36% rural*
Largest Cities: *Milwaukee, Madison, Green Bay*

Wisconsin State Flag

State Government

Governor: *4-year term*
Senators *(33): 4-year term*
Representatives *(99): 2-year term*
Counties: *72*

Federal Government

Senators *(2): 6-year term*
Representatives *(9): 2-year term*
Electoral Votes: *11*

Economy

Agriculture: *chickens, beef cattle, eggs, soybeans, peanuts, cotton*
Manufacturing: *paper products, chemicals, rubber and plastic products, textiles, metals, transportation equipment*

Interesting Facts

• Malted milk was invented by William Horlick in 1887 in Racine.

• The first United States kindergarten was opened in Watertown, Wisconsin in 1856.

Interesting Wisconsinite

• Vinnie Ream, of Madison, was the first woman to be commissioned by Congress to create a sculpture. She created a statue of Abraham Lincoln which still stands in the U.S. Capitol Building rotunda.

Wisconsin

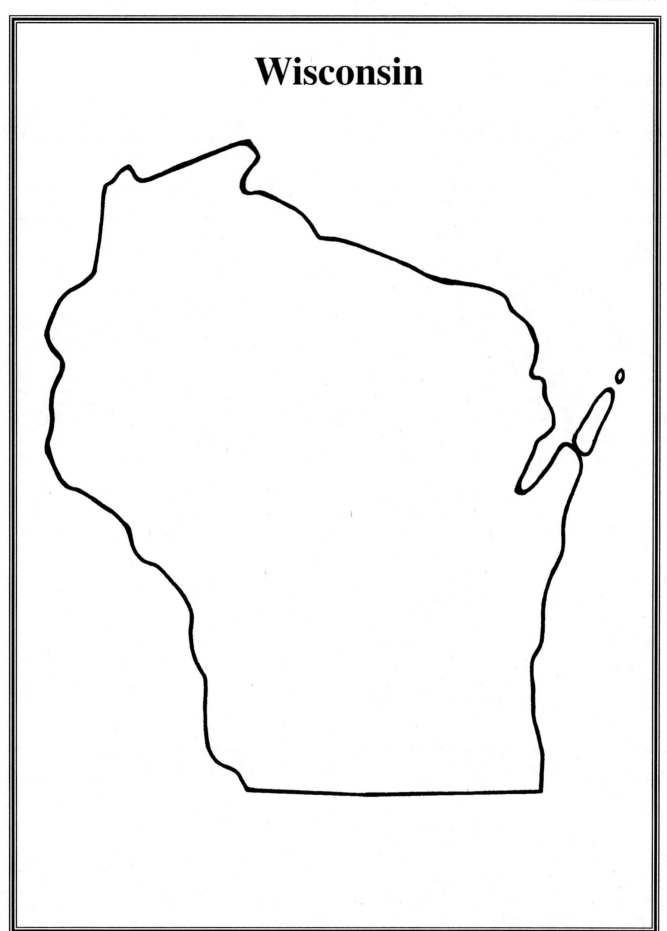

It's a Circus!

While circus-type acts and performers date back thousands of years, the world's largest and most famous Ringling Brothers and Barnum and Bailey has its roots in Baraboo, Wisconsin. The five Ringling Brothers had opened a variety show in Baraboo in 1882 and a circus in 1884. They then bought the Barnum and Bailey show in 1907, joining the two in 1919, and from that moment on the Ringling Brothers Barnum and Bailey Circus has been delighting children of all ages.

Today, a wonderful assortment of early circus equipment has been collected and is on display at the Circus World Museum in Wisconsin. One of the main attractions includes a trapeze similar to one in which Harry Houdini got his start before turning to magic and fame as a world-renowned escape artist.

Activity 1: Draw a Clown

Clowns are a very important part of the fun and magic of the circus. Learn how to draw a clown using the directions on page 169. Make several different kinds of clowns and decorate the classroom with them. Have a contest and vote on the clown drawings that are the funniest, happiest, strangest looking, silliest, etc.

Activity 2: Make Your Own Circus

As a group, make a list of events you would like to include. Some possibilities are:

- tumbling or other gymnastics
- juggling
- magic tricks
- pet tricks
- balloon shapes
- clowns

Determine who will participate in what activities. Remember, in addition to performers, you will also need advertising directors, a ring leader or circus master, ticket taker, refreshments, etc.

Drawing Clowns

Follow the steps to draw a clown. Practice drawing different clowns on another piece of paper. You may want to change the hair or costume. Draw, color, and decorate a clown in the large box below.

Draw your clown here.

Midwestern Clip Art

Illinois

Birthplace of
atomic energy
(U. of Chicago)

Brookfield Zoo

farm
equipment
manufacturing

Indiana

corn

oil

steel plant

Holiday World

Midwestern Clip Art *(cont.)*

Iowa
First center for
child development
research
(Iowa City)

Pella Tulip Festival

corn

Birthplace of
Herbert Hoover
(West Branch)

hogs

Kansas

Pony Express Station

Sunflower State

wheat

Dodge City

Midwestern Clip Art *(cont.)*

Michigan

Tahquamenon Falls

Holland

forest products

Detroit
(automobile
capital of the world)

iron ore

Minnesota

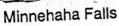

Minnehaha Falls

Paul Bunyan
& Babe

hogs

stone

fishing

Midwestern Clip Art *(cont.)*

Missouri

Gateway Arch

Boyhood home of
Mark Twain
(Hannibal)

Pony Express

Lake of the Ozarks

Nebraska

Chimney Rock

Buffalo Bill's Home

corn

hogs

Midwestern Clip Art *(cont.)*

North Dakota

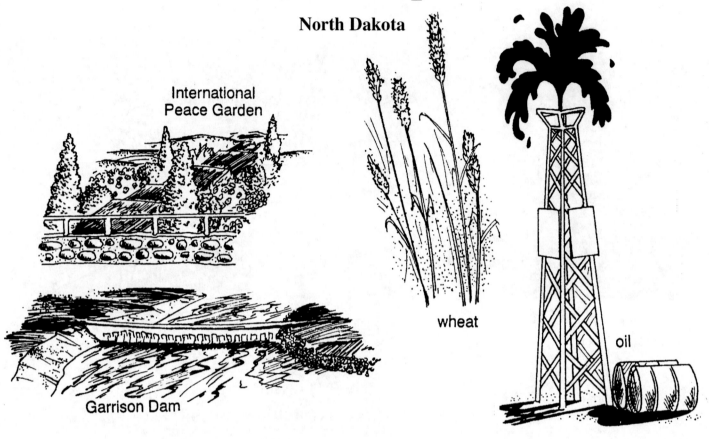

International
Peace Garden

wheat

oil

Garrison Dam

Ohio

Great Serpent Mound

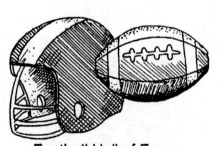

Football Hall of Fame

industry

174

Midwestern Clip Art *(cont.)*

South Dakota

Badlands

Mount Rushmore

Corn Palace

Sioux
Indians

dairy farming

Wisconsin

Circus World
Museum

Two Rivers
(First ice cream
sundae)

First
kindergarten

Name _____ Date _____

Which State Am I?

Directions: Identify the state described. Write its name on the line.

1. I was one of the last 15 states admitted to the Union. I am known mostly as an agricultural state, producing beef cattle, corn, and soybeans, among other things. I am home to the oldest continuously working gold mine in the world.

   Which state am I? _____

2. I was one of the first 30 states to enter the Union. I am a famous manufacturing state, mostly known for producing transportation equipment. If you like breakfast cereal, you probably eat one of my products. And if you visit me, you had better like water. I'm almost surrounded by it.

   Which state am I? _____

3. I was among the first 20 states of the United States. Each year I produce a huge amount of corn. I also produce manufactured goods, such as transportation equipment and chemicals. One of my cities was the first to teach girls and boys in the same classes.

   Which state am I? _____

4. I was also one of the first 20 states to join the Union. Each year I produce corn, hogs, beef cattle, and hay among other products. Hot dogs, ice cream cones, and crackerjacks were all thought up here. Natural resources such as petroleum, natural gas, and coal are found within my borders. I am bordered by five states, one lake, and an important river.

   Which state am I? _____

5. California became a state just before me. Corn, wheat, dairy and beef cattle, and hogs are important agricultural products of mine. I am very proud of the fact that I am an important producer of iron ore for the factories of America. One of my cities is the busiest freshwater port in the United States.

   Which state am I? _____

6. I was one of the first 30 states to enter the Union. The great midwestern corn belt has made me a rich state. I contain a river that flows backward, the Chicago River. I have the busiest airport in the world. I am bordered by five states and one lake.

   Which state am I? _____

Name _____   Date _____

Which State Am I? *(cont.)*

7. I was one of the first 30 states to enter the Union. I am one of the greatest farming states in the U.S.A. I am one of the largest corn producers in the nation. I also rank among the leading producers of beef cattle, milk, and oats. I have a beautiful state flower, the wild rose.

    Which state am I? _____

8. I was the 24th state to join the Union. My location and its two great rivers have made me a center of water, land, and air transportation. Mark Twain's boyhood home was located here. Vast fields of golden grain and green grasses cover my rolling plains in the north and west.

    Which state am I? _____

9. I was among the first 35 states to join the Union. My state flower is the beautiful sunflower, and I am known as the Sunflower State. Manufacturing and trade are my most important economic activities.

    Which state am I? _____

10. I was one of the first 40 states to join the Union. The geographic center of North America is located near one of my towns. Petroleum is my most valuable mineral resource.

    Which state am I? _____

11. I was the 37th state that joined the Union. Farms make up 95% of my land area. I am a leader in producing corn and beef cattle. I have very few trees on my lands, and therefore early settlers made their homes out of my sod. Such famous people as Henry Fonda and Chief Red Cloud lived here.

    Which state am I? _____

12. I became a state in a spring month. I was among one of the first 30 states to join the Union. I am famous for my dairy products. Manufacturing is my leading economic activity. Did you know that the Ringling brothers gave their first show here?

    Which state am I? _____

Name _____ Date _____

Identifying Midwestern States

Directions: Outlines of the states in the midwest region of the United States are mixed up with those of other regions. Identify the midwestern states by coloring them blue.

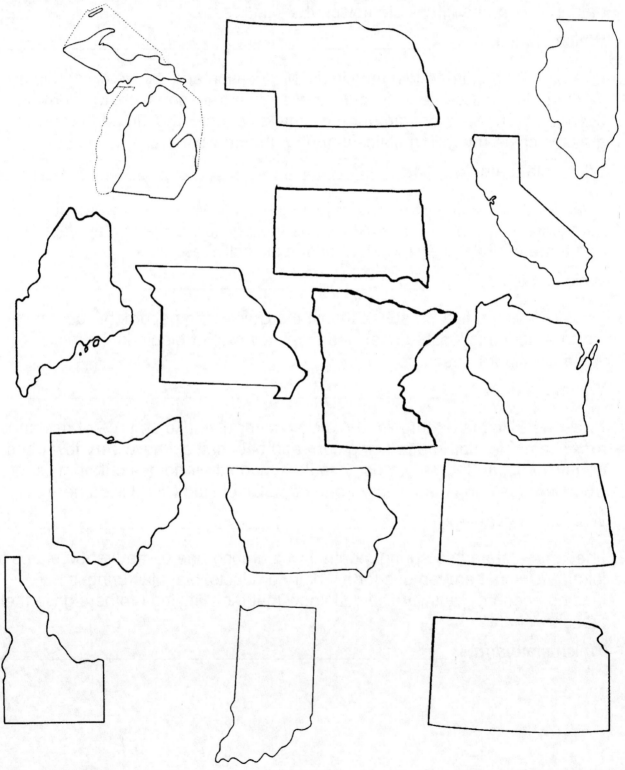

Name _____   Date _____

Flag Match

Directions: Write the number of the flag next to the state to which it belongs. Color the flags correctly.

1.

4.

2.
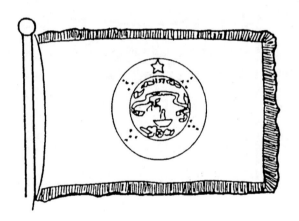

5.

3.
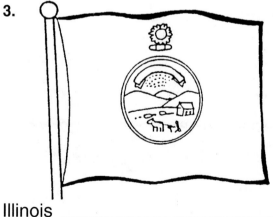

6.
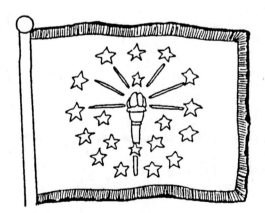

Illinois _____   Kansas _____

Indiana _____   Michigan _____

Iowa_____   Minnesota _____

Name _____   Date _____

Flag Match *(cont.)*

Directions: Write the number of the flag next to the state to which it belongs. Color the flags correctly.

1.

4.

2.

5.

3.

6.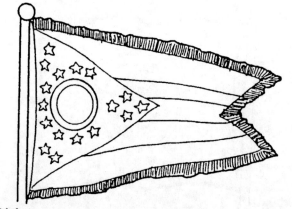

Missouri _____

Nebraska _____

North Dakota _____

Ohio _____

South Dakota _____

Wisconsin _____

Name _____   Date _____

City Match

Directions: Match the cities with their states by writing the numbers of the cities on the appropriate lines.

1. Cedar Rapids
2. Chicago
3. Davenport
4. Des Moines
5. Detroit
6. Duluth

7. Fort Wayne
8. Grand Forks
9. Grand Rapids
10. Indianapolis
11. Kansas City
12. Minneapolis

13. Peoria
14. Rockford
15. Saint Paul
16. Topeka
17. Warren
18. Wichita

Illinois

_____

Kansas

_____

Indiana

_____

Michigan

_____

Iowa

_____

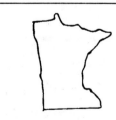

Minnesota

_____

Name _____   Date _____

City Match

Directions: Match the cities with their states by writing the numbers of the cities on the appropriate lines.

19. Aberdeen	25. Grand Forks	31. Milwaukee
20. Bismarck	26. Grand Island	32. Omaha
21. Cincinnati	27. Green Bay	33. Rapid City
22. Cleveland	28. Kansas City	34. Saint Louis
23. Columbus	29. Lincoln	35. Sioux Falls
24. Fargo	30. Madison	36. Springfield

Missouri

_____

Ohio

_____

Nebraska

_____

South Dakota

_____

North Dakota

_____

Wisconsin

_____

Name _____   Date _____

How Far Is It?

Directions: Choose ten pairs of cities from the map below. Write their names in the blanks. Then use the map of the midwest and the scale on this page to find the distances between the cities you listed.

1. _____ to _____ = _____ mi./km
2. _____ to _____ = _____ mi./km
3. _____ to _____ = _____ mi./km
4. _____ to _____ = _____ mi./km
5. _____ to _____ = _____ mi./km
6. _____ to _____ = _____ mi./km
7. _____ to _____ = _____ mi./km
8. _____ to _____ = _____ mi./km
9. _____ to _____ = _____ mi./km
10. _____ to _____ = _____ mi./km

Name _____   Date _____

Admission Days

Directions: Complete the following exercises to learn more about when each of the northeastern states received statehood.

A. Research to find out when the northeastern states below were granted
   statehood. Record their admission dates next to the states' names.

Name	**Month**	**Day**	**Year**
1. Illinois			
2. Indiana			
3. Iowa			
4. Kansas			
5. Michigan			
6. Minnesota			
7. Missouri			
8. Nebraska			
9. North Dakota			
10. Ohio			
11. South Dakota			
12. Wisconsin			

B. The admission dates of the northeastern states can be plotted on a time

1780   1800   1820   1840   1860   1880   1900   1920   1940   1960

Name _____   Date _____

States Puzzlers

Directions: Use the clues to help you complete the puzzle. When you have filled in the circles, read the vertical word formed by the dark circles. Write the word on the line at the bottom of the page.

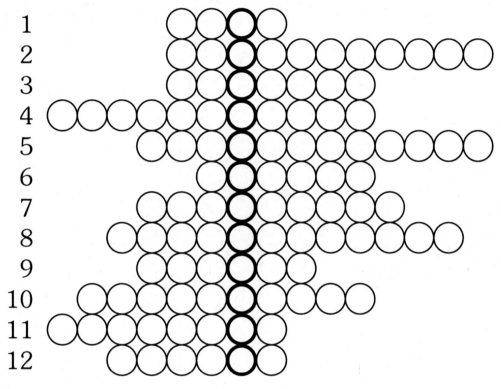

1. "The Wolverine State"

2. "The Buckeye State"

3. "The Flickertail State"

4. "Hawkeye State"

5. "The Cornhusker State"

6. "The Sunflower State"

7. "The Sunshine State"

8. "The Bread and Butter State"

9. "The Show Me State"

10. "The Hoosier State"

Puzzler Word:_____

The Southwest

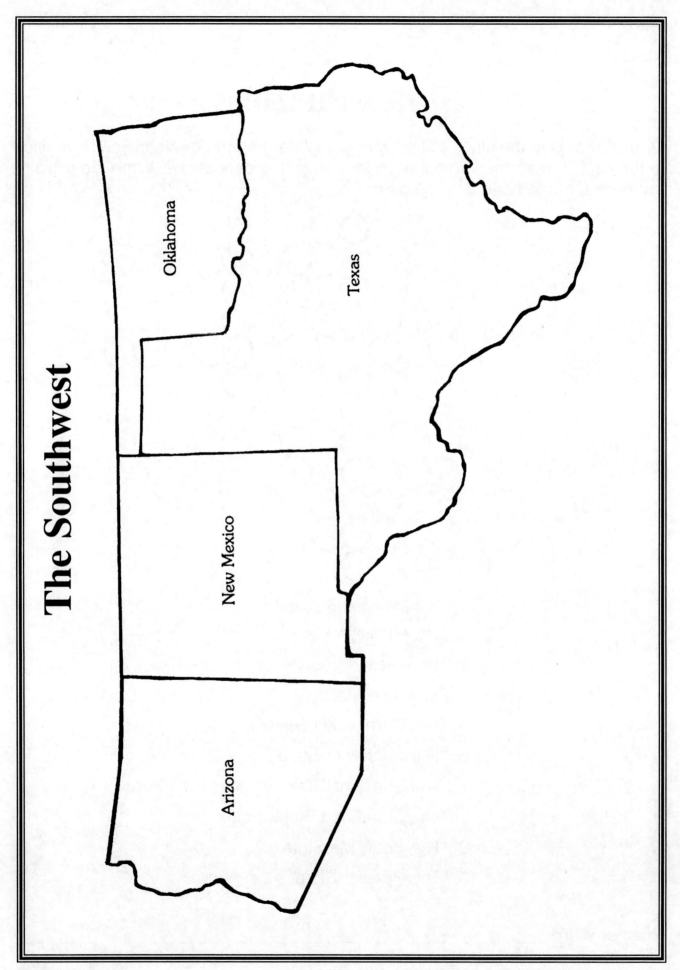

Oklahoma

Texas

New Mexico

Arizona

Arizona

"The Grand Canyon State"

Basic Facts

Capital: *Phoenix*
Statehood: *February 14, 1912*
Admittance: *48th state*
Motto: *God Enriches*
Song: *"Arizona"*
Bird: *Cactus Wren*
Flower: *Saguaro cactus blossom*
Tree: *Paloverde*
Abbreviation: *AZ*

Area: *114,000 square miles (295,260 sq. km)*
Elevation: *(above sea level)*
 Highest: 12,633ft.(3,851 m)-Humphreys Peak
 Lowest: 70 ft. (21 m) – Yuma County
Average Temperatures:
 July: 80°F. (27°C)
 January: 41°F. (5°C)
Average Yearly Precipitation: *13 in. (33 cm)*

Population

How Many: *3,677,985 (1990 Census)*
Where They Live: *84% urban, 16% rural*
Largest Cities: *Phoenix, Tucson, Mesa*

State Government

Governor: *4-year term*
Senators *(30): 2-year term*
Representatives *(60): 2-year term*
Counties: *15*

Federal Government

Senators *(2): 6-year term*
Representatives *(5): 2-year term*
Electoral Votes: *8*

Arizona State Flag

Economy

Agriculture: *beef cattle, cotton and cottonseed, hay, lettuce, pecans, milk*
Manufacturing: *electric machinery and equipment, transportation equipment, metals, food products, printed materials*
Mining: *copper, gold*

Interesting Facts

• The planet Pluto was discovered from the Lowell Observatory in Flagstaff by Clyde W. Tombough in 1930.

• The first organized rodeo was held in Prescott on July 4, 1888. lt was called a "Cowboy Tournament."

Interesting Arizonan

• Sandra Day O'Conner was the first woman to be elected to the Supreme Court of the United States. This historic event took place in 1981.

Arizona

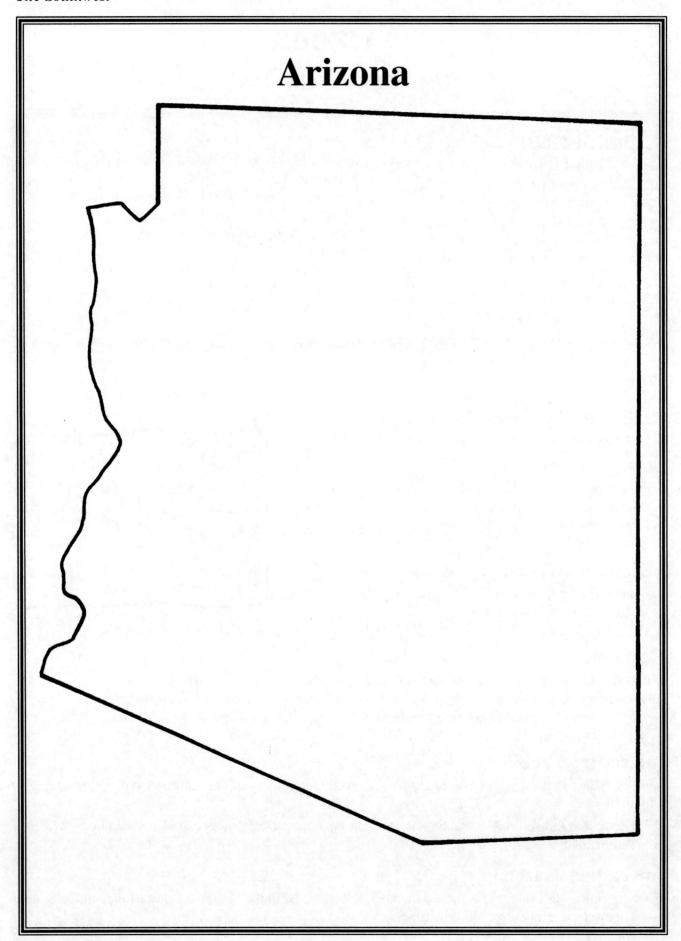

The Grand Canyon: A Natural Wonder

The Grand Canyon was created by natural forces. It was formed over millions of years by the incredible strength of the Colorado River. The canyon stretches for 277 miles (44.3 km). This is larger than the state of Rhode Island. The tallest building, the Sears Tower, stands 1,454 feet (443 m) high. It would take four Sears Towers stacked on top of each other to reach from the bottom to the top of the Grand Canyon.

The Grand Canyon is made up of many layers of granite, sandstone, limestone, and shale. The Colorado River cuts away at this material creating these layers and forms the Grand Canyon walls. Over the years these layers hardened into rock. Today you can see these rock layers exposed in the walls of the Grand Canyon.

Activity: A Closer Look at the Grand Canyon

Locate pictures of the Grand Canyon in science magazines, travel brochures, or library reference books. The Grand Canyon provides us with one of the best examples of layers of sandstone in the world. Sandstone is a type of sedimentary rock. It is very soft. Count the layers of sandstone rock in the pictures of the Grand Canyon. The older sandstone is at the bottom of the canyon, while the newest sandstone is at the top. Choose one of the Grand Canyon pictures you found. On a piece of drawing paper, illustrate a part of it, showing the layers that have formed in the canyon walls.

Colorful Sand Paintings

Sand is actually small pieces of rock. Sandstone starts off as beach or river sand. After millions of years, minerals grow between the tiny grains and "cement" them together to form solid rock. Since minerals come in lots of colors, the layers of sandstone (like in the Grand Canyon) come in lots of colors, too.

Activity: Make Your Own Sand Paintings

Essentials

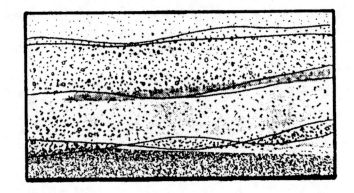

- pencils
- white construction paper
- sand
- paper cups
- liquid food coloring
- water
- plastic spoons
- paper towels
- liquid white glue
- small paintbrushes
- newspaper to cover work surface

Note: You can pre-dye sand a few days before this activity by filling paper cups half full with sand. Add water to the cup until sand is completely covered. Add drops of one food coloring per cup. (The more drops you use, the more vibrant the color will become.) Stir the sand, water, and food coloring with a spoon. Let the ingredients set for 20 minutes. Pour off as much liquid as possible without pouring out the sand. Spread drained sand on paper towels and let it dry completely. For variety, you can try different color combinations.

Directions

1. Use a pencil to draw lines across construction paper.

2. Squirt a small amount of glue in one area. Shake off excess glue.

3. Sprinkle one color of dyed sand in the area where glue was added.

4. Repeat steps 2 and 3 with other sands to create colorful layers. Set aside to dry. Display your sand paintings around one or more large pictures of the Grand Canyon.

New Mexico
"The Land of Enchantment"

Basic Facts

Capital: *Santa Fe*
Statehood: *January 6, 1912*
Admittance: *47th state*
Motto: *It Grows as It Goes*
Song: *"O, Fair New Mexico"*
Bird: *Roadrunner*
Flower: *Yucca Flower*
Tree: *Pinon*
Abbreviation: *NM*

Area: *121,593 square miles (314,295 sq. km)*
Elevation: *(above sea level)*
 Highest: *13,161 ft. (4,011 m) – Wheeler Peak*
 Lowest: *2,817 ft. (859 m) – Eddy County*
Average Temperatures:
 July: *74°F. (23°C)*
 January: *34°F. (1°C)*
Average Yearly Precipitation: *13 in. (33 cm)*

Population

How Many: *1,521,779 (1990 Census)*
Where They Live: *72% urban, 28% rural*
Largest Cities: *Albuquerque, Sante Fe, Las Cruces*

New Mexico State Flag

State Government

Governor: *4-year term*
Senators *(42): 4-year term*
Representatives *(70): 2-year term*
Counties: *33*

Federal Government

Senators *(2): 6-year term*
Representatives *(3): 2-year term*
Electoral Votes: *5*

Economy

Agriculture: *beef cattle, hay, milk, cotton*
Manufacturing: *food products, electric machinery and equipment, printed material, lumber and wood products*
Mining: *natural gas, petroleum, coal, copper, potash, uranium*

Interesting Facts

• The first atomic bomb was built at Los Alamos in 1945.
• The Smokey Bear Historical State Park is located in Capitan. A little bear was found clinging to a tree during a forest fire and Smokey the Bear became a symbol to help prevent forest fires.

Interesting New Mexican

• Laura Gilpin is a well-known New Mexican photographer who captured the lives of the Navajo and Pueblo Indians who live in this state.

New Mexico

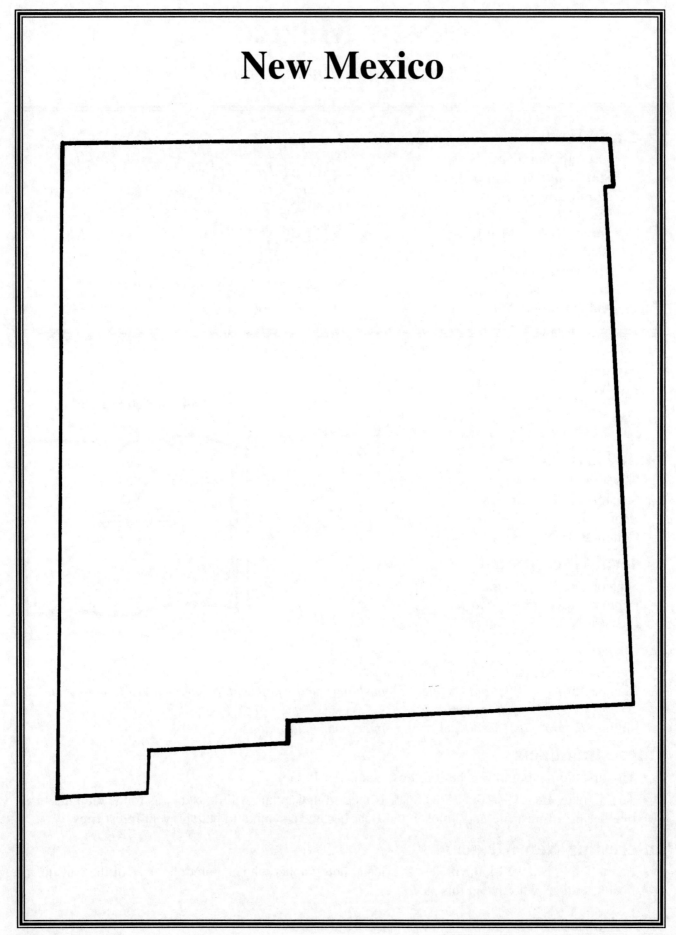

Hot-Air Enchantment

The International Balloon Fiesta is a captivating, annual affair held in Albuquerque, New Mexico. The event is held in October. The fiesta attracts hundreds of participants and thousands of spectators, dazzling them with its early morning mass ascensions, daily races, and spectacular evening festivities.

How do the magnificent balloons that fill the sky at the Fiesta move about? Hot-air balloons rise because the air inside the bag is warmer and lighter than the air outside. Heat for the hot-air balloon comes from a burner that uses a gas called propane. This is a safe and inexpensive gas. The burner provides the flame which in turn heats the bag. Many balloons today are filled with helium, which is lighter than air. The bag is the brightly-colored balloon part of the hot-air balloon. The bag of the hot air balloon is made of nylon or polyester. The size of the bag depends upon how much weight the hot air balloon is carrying. The basket is another part of a hot-air balloon. It hangs from strong tapes that are sewn into the bag. The basket is made of wicker or aluminum. Ballooning is a popular sport for some but is a job to others. Balloons can be used for carrying scientific instruments high into the atmosphere. These instruments collect information about the weather and air pollution.

Activity 1: Make Your Own Hot-Air Balloon

Essentials

- pattern on page 194
- scissors
- glue
- hair dryer
- tissue paper

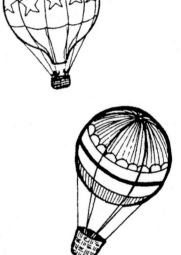

Directions

Trace the pattern onto tissue paper. Enlarge the pattern first if you wish to make a larger balloon. Lift the rectangular shapes up by folding them along the dashed lines. To form the box shape of the balloon, fold the tabs in and glue them to the appropriate sides. Allow glue to dry. Holding the open end of the balloon down, inflate it with the heat from a hair dryer. Watch your balloon rise!

Activity 2: Rising To the Occasion

Essentials

- balloons
- felt-tip marker

Directions

Choose a personal or academic goal you would like to achieve this year. Inflate a balloon and write your name and the goal you have selected on a balloon. Attach the balloon to a wall or bulletin board displaying other students' balloons. When you have reached your goal, pop the balloon, indicating that you have been successful!

Hot-Air Enchantment *(cont.)*

Follow the directions on page 193 to make your own hot-air balloon.

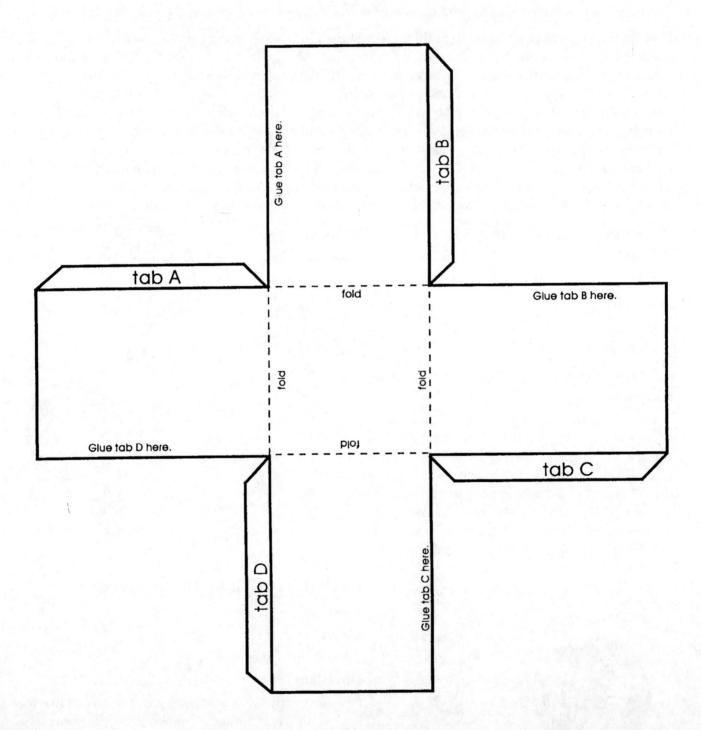

Oklahoma
"The Sooner State"

Basic Facts

Capital: *Oklahoma City*
Statehood: *November 16, 1907*
Admittance: *46th state*
Motto: *Labor Conquers All Things*
Song: "Oklahoma"
Bird: *Scissor-tailed flycatcher*
Flower: *Mistletoe*
Tree: *Redbud*
Abbreviation: *OK*

Area: *69,956 square miles (181,186 sq. km)*
Elevation: *(above sea level)*
  Highest: 49,973 ft. (1,516 m) – Black Mesa
  Lowest: 287 ft. (87 m) – McCurtain County
Average Temperatures:
  July: 82°F. (28°C)
  January: 37°F. (3°C)
Average Yearly Precipitation: *33 in. (84 cm)*

Population

How Many: *3,157,604 (1990 Census)*
Where They Live: *67% urban, 33% rural*
Largest Cities: *Oklahoma City, Tulsa, Lawton*

Oklahoma State Flag

State Government

Governor: *4-year term*
Senators *(48): 4-year term*
Representatives *(101): 2-year term*
Counties: *77*

Federal Government

Senators *(2): 6-year term*
Representatives *(6): 2-year term*
Electoral Votes: *8*

Economy

Agriculture: *beef cattle, wheat, hay, milk, cotton*
Manufacturing: *transportation equipment, electric equipment, rubber products*
Mining: *natural gas, petroleum, coal*

Interesting Facts

• There are more than 60 Native American tribes living in Oklahoma.

• The Oklahoma State Capitol is the only state house with working oil wells on the grounds.

Interesting Oklahoman

• Will Rogers was a cowboy and humorist. He gave lectures, did rope tricks, and worked in both the political and business world. He wrote a newspaper column and starred in many movies. He is most famous for saying, "I never met a man I didn't like."

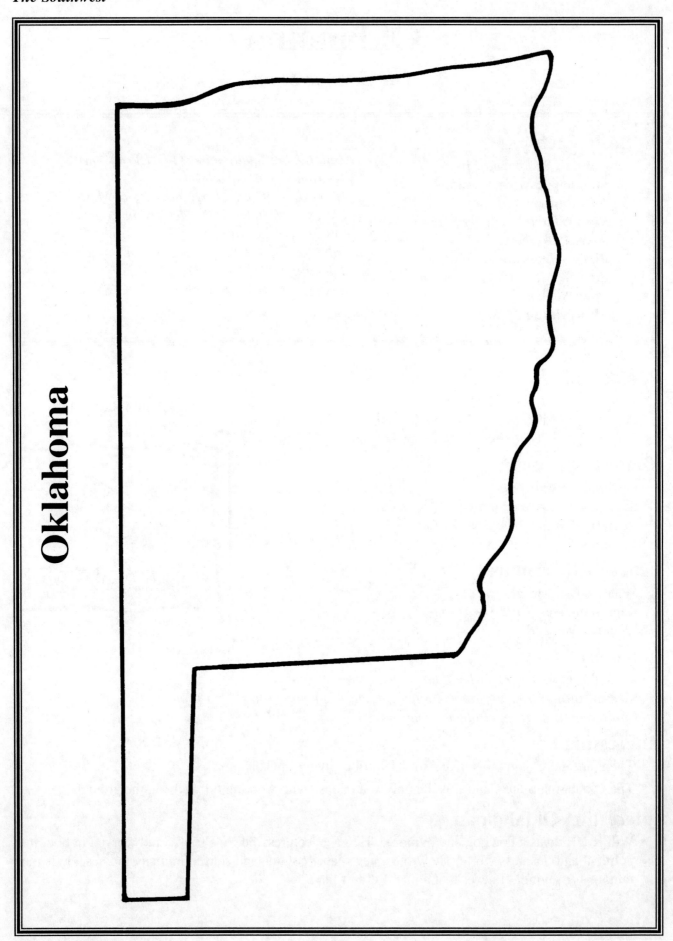

Oklahoma

Sooners and Boomers

"As long as grass shall grow and rivers run ..." These were the words of the United States Government, guaranteeing the Indians of the lands of the Oklahoma Territory forever. However, at noon on April 22, 1889, this promise was broken. Two million acres of unassigned lands were opened to all white settlers. This was called the Oklahoma "Land Run." At noon, 50,000 people stampeded the borders. Oklahoma city was founded in a day, becoming a tent city of 10,000 occupants. That same day, the town of Guthrie was born as well with over fifty thousand occupants.

Companies hired professional promoters to organize and lead homesteaders into the unassigned lands of Oklahoma. The promoters were called boomers. Unassigned lands are areas of rich cattle-grazing land, that were not assigned to any particular tribe. Once the homesteaders had occupied the land, the boomers would set up the companies and open up businesses in the territory. A few famous boomer leaders were C.C. Carpenter, David L. Payne, and William L. Couch.

Many people tried to sneak onto the unassigned lands sooner than the official starting time. These "early birds" were called sooners. Some sooners were officials, such as land-office men, soldiers, or marshals who took advantage of the "inside track." Others were simply homesteaders. If the federal troops caught a sooner, the troops marched the sooners back to the border. Many got away with their ploy. Just before law-abiding landrunners appeared, sooners would stake their claims and then run their horses to exhaustion. The sooner would show a tired horse to those pioneers who legally entered the territory as proof that the sooner had just arrived.

Activity: Sooner and Boomer Role-Play

In the late 1800's, boomers convinced the government to open Oklahoma lands to white settlers and the Oklahoma "Land Run" had begun. Imagine thousands of settlers waiting at the state borders!

Locate additional information about sooners, boomers, and the effect of the "Land Run" on Native American tribes. Work in groups of three for this activity. Have each member take one of the following roles: sooner, boomer, or Native American who lost land. After researching your part, have your group dramatize what it might have been like at the time of the "Sooners and Boomers."

Texas
"The Lone Star State"

Basic Facts

Capital: *Austin*
Statehood: *December 29, 1845*
Admittance: *28th state*
Motto: *Friendship*
Song: *"Texas, Our Texas"*
Bird: *Mockingbird*
Flower: *Bluebonnet*
Tree: *Pecan*
Abbreviation: *TX*

Area: *266,807 square miles (691,030 sq. km)*
Elevation: *(above sea level)*
 Highest: 8,751 ft. (2,667 m) – Guadalupe Peak
 Lowest: Sea level along coastline
Average Temperatures:
 July: 83°F. (28°C)
 January: 46°F. (8°C)
Average Yearly Precipitation: *27 in. (67 cm)*

Population

How Many: *17,059,805 (1990 Census)*
Where They Live: *80% urban, 20% rural*
Largest Cities: *Houston, Dallas, San Antonio*

State Government

Governor: *4-year term*
Senators *(31): 4-year term*
Representatives *(150): 2-year term*
Counties: *254*

Federal Government

Senators *(2): 6-year term*
Representatives *(27): 2-year term*
Electoral Votes: *29*

Economy

Agriculture: *beef cattle, cotton*
Fishing: *shrimp*
Manufacturing: *chemicals, food products, electric equipment, petroleum products, machinery, transportation*
Mining: *natural gas, petroleum*

Texas State Flag

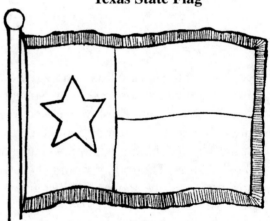

Interesting Facts

- The first round-the-world airplane flight started at Carswell Air Force Base in Fort Worth. It began on February 26th and ended March 2nd, 1949. It took 94 hours and one minute for the Lucky Lady II to complete the flight.
- "Remember the Alamo" became a battle cry during the Spanish-American War. The restored fort is now a National Park in San Antonio.

Interesting Texan

- Sam Houston fought for the independence of Texas from Mexico and for the admittance of Texas as a state. Houston is named after him.

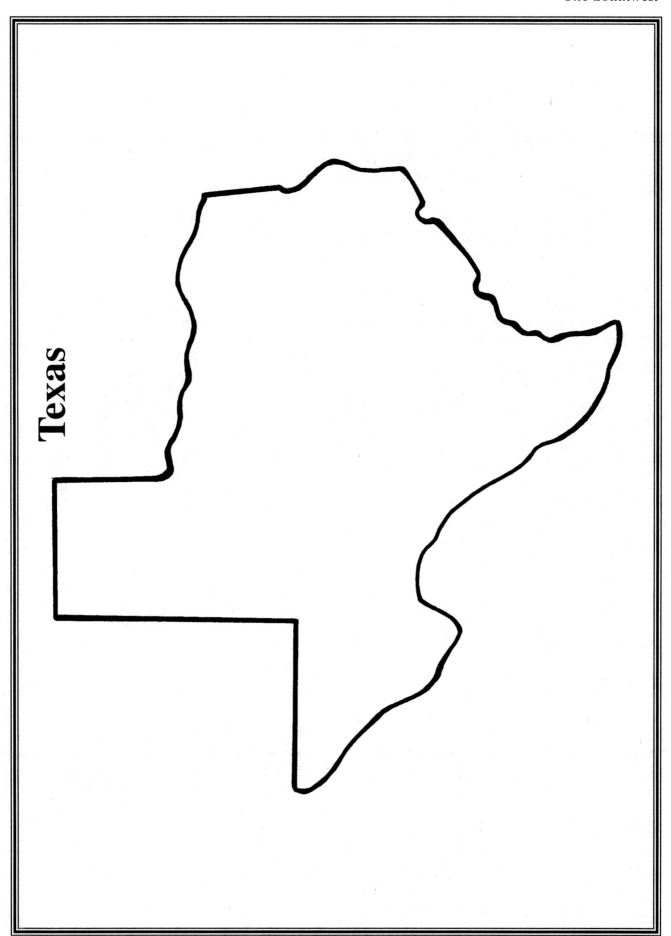

Texas

The Competent Cowboy

At one time, the words "Texas" and "cowboy" were synonymous.

The height of the cowboy period was from the 1860's to the mid 1880's.

The job of the cowboys, or frontier cowboys as they were often called, was to conduct a cattle drive by getting the cattle to the railroads. First there was the roundup or gathering of the cattle from the open plains. When the herd was together, the cowboys branded the cattle with the ranch's symbol in order to keep track of them.

When the cattle were ready for the drive (a task that required six to twelve cowboys and involved a herd of 1,000 to 3,000 cattle) the cattle were moved toward their destination. A cattle drive would take approximately two to three months.

Cowboys prepared for their journey by packing essential equipment, including a 10-gallon hat to keep them cool, leather trousers over jeans to protect their legs, and tapered-heel boots to prevent the cowboy's foot from catching in a stirrup. A bandanna was worn to stop the dirt and dust from getting into the cowboy's nose and mouth.

The cowboy's rope, or lariat, became an important tool during a cattle drive. The lariat was used to pull cattle from the mud, to tie up horses, and to drag wood to a campfire.

The cattle drive was strenuous, dangerous work and was often lonely for the cowboy. Cowboys had to keep the cattle together and headed in the right direction. A cowboy's worst danger was a stampede. A stampede occurred when one frightened cow began to run and the rest of the cattle followed. To stop a stampede, cowboys had to ride in front of the cattle and try to turn them around.

Once they reached the railroad, the cattle drive was over. The cattle were then sold and loaded onto the train. The cowboy was now looking forward to a shave, a haircut, a bath, and a good meal. Cowboy hats and boots are still part of the everyday dress of many Texans, and you can still spot cowboys, and now cowgirls, herding cattle across the plains of Texas. However, today, Texans are just as likely to be workers in an oil field or scientists in a lab as they are cowboys or cowgirls.

Activity: Fact or Fiction?

After reading the information above and other accounts of the cowboy's life in the 1800's, read some fictional tales about cowboys, such as the stories about Slue Foot Sue and Pecos Bill.

Compare the lives of the fictional characters with those of real cowboys by completing the Venn diagram on page 201.

Venn Diagram

Directions: Compare the lives of real cowboys with fictional stories of cowboys. In the appropriate sections of the diagram, write your ideas about how they are alike and how they are different.

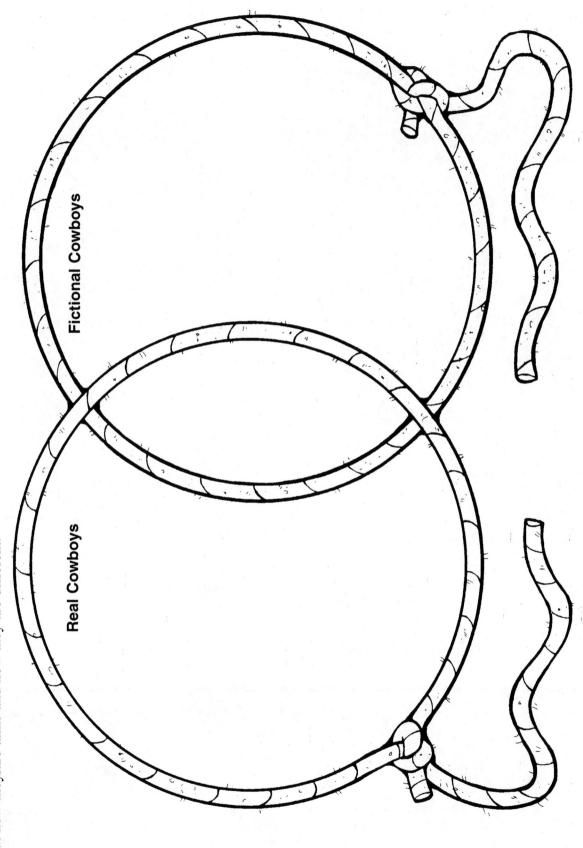

Fictional Cowboys

Real Cowboys

Southwestern Clip Art

Arizona

Grand Canyom

silver mining

kachina doll

Cemetery at Tombstone

International
Ballon Fiesta

New Mexico

First atomic bomb
exploded (July 16, 1945
near Alamogordo

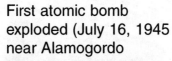

Gila Cliff Dwellings
National Monument

Carlsbad Caverns

Southwestern Clip Art *(cont.)*

Oklahoma

6½ million acre
land rush

National Cowboy
Hall of Fame

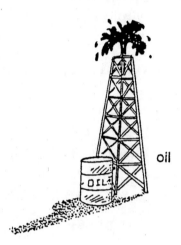

oil

Texas

oil

Alamo

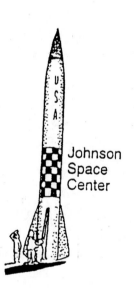

Johnson
Space
Center

Padre
Seashore

Name _____   Date _____

Which State Am I?

Directions: Identify the state described. Write its name on the line.

1. I was among the first 30 states admitted to the Union. If you like beef, you should like me, because I am home to a huge number of beef cattle. I am also famous for the great amount of petroleum and natural gas that is mined within my borders. My neighbors are one foreign country, four states, and a large body of water.

   Which state am I? _____

2. I was one of the last states to join the Union. Some of my valuable natural resources are petroleum, natural gas, and uranium. I have many cattle, but I also produce crops like hay and cotton. The first atomic bomb was set off on my land in 1945 and the heat turned my sands into glass. The state to the east of me is not part of the southwestern region.

   Which state am I? _____

3. I became a state in a winter month, on February 14, 1912, Valentine's Day, to be exact. I was one of the last 5 states to join the Union. One of my most valuable resources is gold. Some of my most important agricultural products are beef cattle, cotton, lettuce, pecans, and milk. I also have the third largest Native American population in the United States.

   Which state am I? _____

4. I was among the last states to join the Union. More than 60 Native American tribes live in my state. I like to think that I point the way to the lands of the west. Like my neighbors, I produce a lot of beef cattle, wheat, and other agricultural products, as well as petroleum, natural gas, and coal. I hold a World Championship Watermelon Seed Spitting Contest.

   Which state am I? _____

Name _____   Date _____

Identifying Southwestern States

Directions: Outlines of the states in the southwestern region of the United States are mixed up with those of other regions. Identify the southwestern states by coloring them yellow.

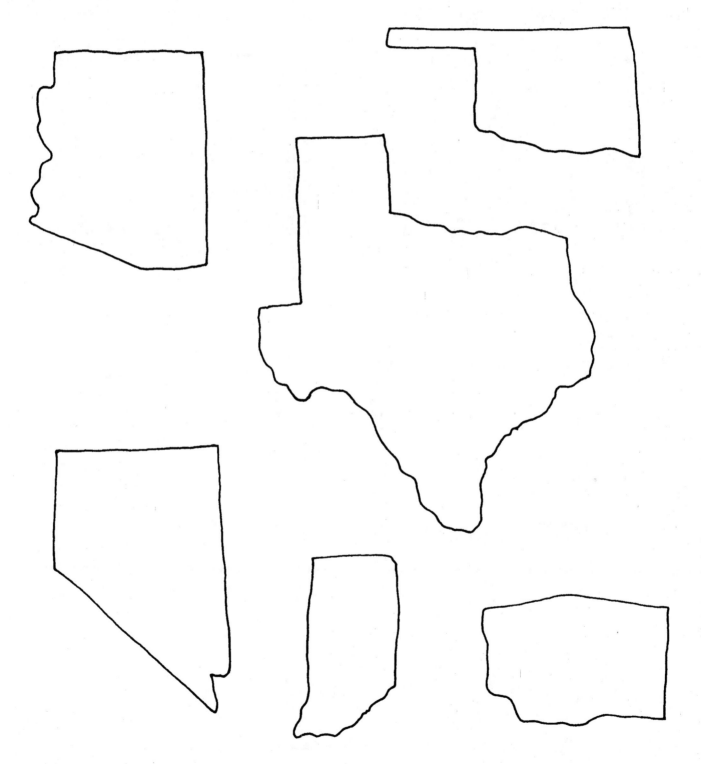

Name _____   Date _____

Flag Match

Directions: Write the number of the flag next to the state to which it belongs. Color the flags correctly.

1.

3.

2.

4.
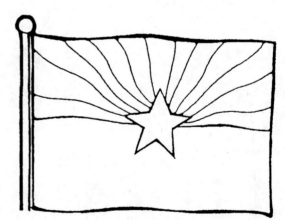

New Mexico_____   Oklahoma _____

Texas_____   Arizona _____

Name _____   Date _____

City Match

Directions: Match the cities with their states by writing the numbers of the cities on the appropriate lines.

1. Albuquerque	9. Phoenix
2. Dallas	10. Bartlesville
3. Santa Fe	11. Scottsdale
4. Houston	12. Austin
5. Lawton	13. Tulsa
6. Los Alamos	14. San Antonio
7. Tucson	15. Las Cruce
8. Oklahoma City	16. Tempe

Arizona

Oklahoma

_____   _____

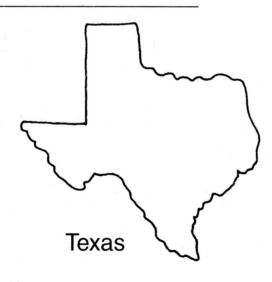

Texas

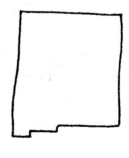

New Mexico

_____   _____

Name _____   Date _____

How Far Is It?

Directions: Choose ten pairs of cities from the map below. Write their names in the blanks. Then use the map of the southwest and the scale on this page to find the distances between the cities you listed.

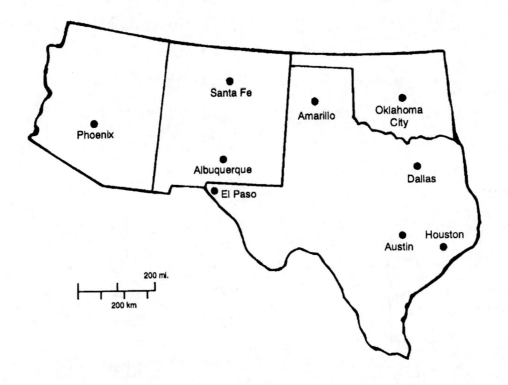

1. _____ to _____ = _____ mi./km

2. _____ to _____ = _____ mi./km

3. _____ to _____ = _____ mi./km

4. _____ to _____ = _____ mi./km

5. _____ to _____ = _____ mi./km

6. _____ to _____ = _____ mi./km

7. _____ to _____ = _____ mi./km

8. _____ to _____ = _____ mi./km

9. _____ to _____ = _____ mi./km

10. _____ to _____ = _____ mi./km

Name _____   Date _____

Admission Days

Directions: Complete the following exercises to learn more about when each of the southwestern states received statehood.

A. Research to find out when the southwestern states below were granted statehood. Record their admission dates next to the states' names.

Name	**Month**	**Day**	**Year**
1. Arizona			
2. New Mexico			
3. Oklahoma			
4. Texas			

B. The admission dates of the southwestern states can be plotted on a time line. Plot them on the time line below, making sure to label each one.

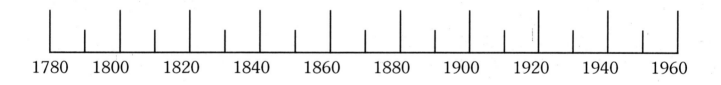

1780   1800   1820   1840   1860   1880   1900   1920   1940   1960

1. Which southwestern state was the first to receive statehood?

   _____

2. How many days after New Mexico became a state did Arizona receive its statehood?

   _____

3. How many years after Texas became a state did Oklahoma receive its statehood?

   _____

4. How many southwestern states received statehood in this century?

   _____

Name _____   Date _____

States Puzzler

Directions: Use the clues at the bottom of the page to complete the puzzle.

Across

3. New Mexico's largest city
5. "Land of Enchantment"
7. one of Arizona's most spectacular scenic wonders
8. "The Lone Star State"
9. capital of Texas
10. Arizona's state bird

Down

1. precipitation (New Mexico does not get much of this each year.)
2. "The Sooner State"
4. largest Texas city
6. one of Arizona's chief products

The West

Washington

Montana

Oregon

Idaho

Wyoming

Nevada

Utah

Colorado

California

Hawaii

Kahoolawe

Maui →

Lanai

Molokai →

Oahu →

Hawaiian
Islands

Kauai →

Nihau

Alaska

Alaska
"The Frontier State"

Basic Facts

Capital: *Juneau*
Statehood: *January 3, 1959*
Admittance: *49th state*
Motto: *North to the Future*
Song: *"Alaska's Flag"*
Bird: *Willow Ptarmigan*
Flower: *Forget-me-not*
Tree: *Sitka spruce*
Abbreviation: *AK*

Area: *591,004 square miles (150,700 sq. km)*
Elevation: *(above sea level)*
 Highest: 20,320 ft. (6,194 m) -Mount McKinley
 Lowest: Sea level along coastline
Average Temperatures:
 July: 55°F. (13°C)
 January: 5°F. (-13°C)
Average Yearly Precipitation: *55 in. (140 cm)*

Population

How Many: *551,947 (1990 Census)*
Where They Live: *64% urban, 36% rural*
Largest Cities: *Anchorage, Fairbanks, Juneau*

State Government

Governor: *4-year term*
Senators *(20): 4-year term*
Representatives*(40): 2-year term*
Boroughs: 15

Federal Government

Senators *(2): 6-year term*
Representatives *(1): 2-year term*
Electoral Votes: *3*

Alaska State Flag

Economy

Agriculture: *milk, timber* Fishing: *salmon, herring, halibut*
Manufacturing: *food products, lumber and wood products, metal products, printed materials*
Mining: *petroleum, natural gas, sand and gravel, stone, gold*

Interesting Facts

• Alaska has the longest coastline of any state. It is 6,640 miles (10,686 kilometers) long.

• More bald eagles nest along the Chilkat River than anywhere else in the world.

Interesting Alaskan

• Joseph Juneau discovered gold in Alaska in 1880. Finding the gold led to the development of Alaska. The city, Juneau, was built near his discovery and is named after him.

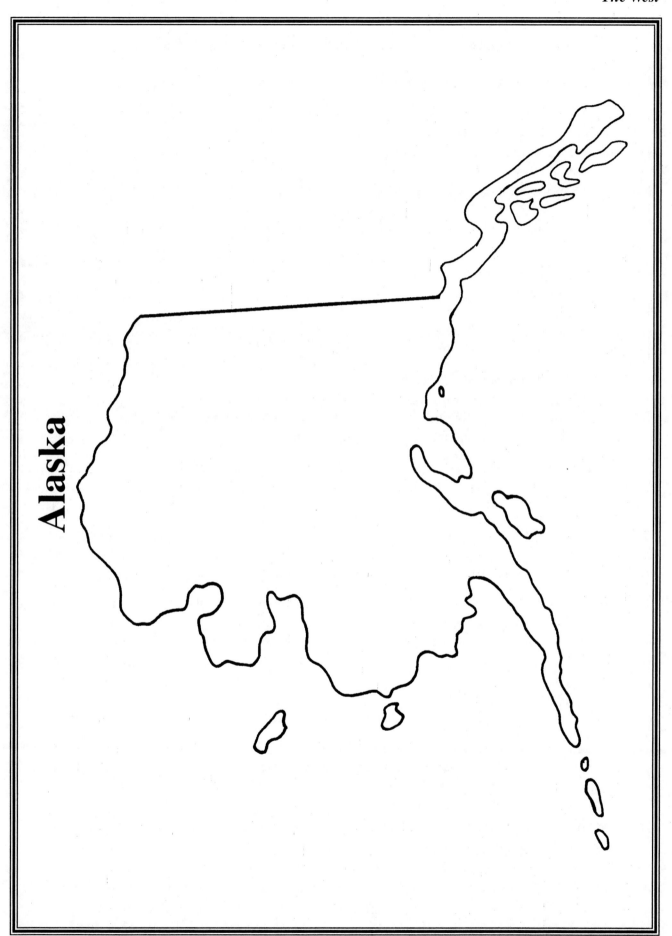

Alaska

The Eskimos of Alaska

Eskimos are people who live in or near the Arctic. The name Eskimo comes from an American Indian word meaning "eaters of raw meat." Eskimos in Alaska call themselves "Inupiat" or "Yupik"; these words mean "people."

For many years, Eskimos lived near the sea, which provided them with numerous food sources: seals, walruses, polar bears, whales, and fish. They also hunted a land animal called the caribou, using its skins for clothing, homes, and boats.

Eskimos lived in cultural groups, not in tribes. There were different cultural groups for different regions. Some families would have as many as 20 people in each family. Each cultural group shared special traditions.

There were rules of conduct rather than laws. The Eskimos' most important motto was that everyone must help in the struggle to survive and that each person must live peacefully with others in his/her group. Sometimes, when fights were unavoidable, the men would sing insults at one another, and whoever got upset would lose.

The language of the Alaskan Eskimo groups was similar. They constructed their language by stringing words together. A one syllable word could form up to a five syllable word. Eskimos had no system of writing.

The Eskimos' way of life started changing around the 1800's as Europeans arrived and Eskimos began to do the fishing and trapping for them. In return, the Europeans offered rifles, furs, and other useful goods. Many resources the Eskimos needed were destroyed due to the increase in trapping and whaling.

This ended the traditional way of life for many Eskimos. Now most Eskimos live in small towns or settlements. They wear modern clothing, live in present-day houses, and eat store-bought food. Many Eskimos now work for wages, and the ones that can't find jobs need the assistance of the government to live.

Activity: A New Cultural Group

Work together with a few other students to create your own cultural group. Make up a name for the group. Make it as unique as possible.

- Try writing your own alphabet and some common words for your language. Or you may wish to prepare a rebus dictionary, in which the pictures you draw represent words or parts of words that can be combined to make sentences or complete ideas.

- Have your own group motto. Try to choose one that reflects an important value or goal that your group will work to achieve.

- Prepare some recreational activities. (The Eskimos loved to tell stories and dance to the beat of drums. Perhaps your group could create some original stories, dances, and songs, too.)

When you have put together your ideas and projects, share your new cultural group with the class.

California

"The Golden State"

Basic Facts

Capital: *Sacramento*
Statehood: *September 9, 1850*
Admittance: *31st state*
Motto: *Eureka (I Have Found It)*
Song: *"I Love You, California"*
Bird: *California valley quail*
Flower: *Golden poppy*
Tree: *California redwood*
Abbreviation: *CA*

Area: *158,706 square miles (411,049 sq. km)*
Elevation: *(above sea level)*
 Highest: 14,494 ft. (4,418 m) -Mount Whitney
 Lowest: 282 ft. (86 m) – Death Valley
Average Temperatures:
 July: 75°F. (24°C)
 January: 44°F. (7°C)
Average Yearly Precipitation: *22 in. (56 cm)*

Population

How Many: *29,839,250 (1990 Census)*
Where They Live: *91% urban, 9% rural*
Largest Cities: *Los Angeles, San Diego, San Jose*

California State Flag

State Government

Governor: *4-year term*
Senators *(40): 4-year term*
Representatives*: (80): 2-year term*
Counties: *58*

Federal Government

Senators *(2): 6-year term*
Representatives *(52): 2-year term*
Electoral Votes: *54*

Economy

Agriculture: *milk, beef cattle, greenhouse and nursery products, cotton, grapes*
Fishing: *tuna, salmon, crab*
Manufacturing: *electric machinery and equipment, transportation equipment, metal products,*
  printed material, chemicals
Mining: *petroleum, natural gas, sand and gravel*

Interesting Facts

• The world's oldest tree, the General Sherman, located in the Sequoia National Park, is about 2,500 years old.

• The first cable-car street system was introduced in San Francisco in 1873.

Interesting Californian

• Sally Ride made history in 1983 as the first American woman to travel in space. She was born in Los Angeles.

California

All That Glitters

California's nickname is "The Golden State." In addition to the golden hills that grace this third-largest state, California is famous for the "Gold Rush" of 1849. "Gold rush" is the term used to describe the swift movement, or rush, of people to a place where gold has been discovered.

On January 24, 1848, gold was discovered in California at Sutter's mill by James Marshall. By 1849, the "Gold Rush" was on! Prospectors (those in search of gold) came to seek their fortunes, towns sprang up almost overnight, transportation networks developed, and new territories were born. With the 1848 discovery of gold, California set the stage for other gold rushes in the West.

Activity 1: Mine For Gold

Start your own Gold Rush! Conceal small pieces of gold-yellow construction paper around the classroom (about half as many "nuggets" as there are students in the class). Tell the rest of the class that the pieces of construction paper represent gold, and that they have only a short time to locate the treasure. Then give the class three to five minutes to search the room. When time is up, ask each "miner" to count his or her "nuggets." Talk about the experience.

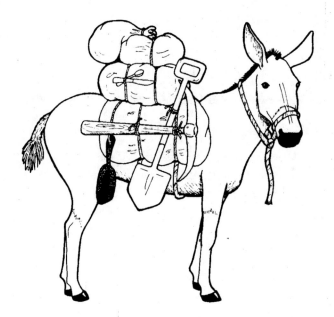

"Gold fever," the excited, restless feeling experienced by a gold miner, was a common condition in the gold rush days. Did you experience "gold fever"?

Activity 2: A Shoe-Box Mining Town

Locate information about the mining towns that existed during the Gold Rush—what they looked like, who lived there, etc. Construct a shoe-box diorama of a mining town. You might include the following items: miner's camps, staked-out claims, and various mining techniques.

Colorado
"The Centennial State"

Basic Facts

Capital: *Denver*
Statehood: *August 1, 1876*
Admittance: *38th state*
Motto: *Nothing Without Providence*
Song: *"Where the Columbines Grow"*
Bird: *Lark bunting*
Flower: *Rocky Mountain columbine*
Tree: *Blue spruce*
Abbreviation: *CO*

Area: *104,091 square miles (269,592 sq. km)*
Elevation: *tabove sea level)*
 Highest; 14,433 ft. (4,399 m) – Mount Elbert
 Lowest: 3,350 ft. (1021 m) – Prowers County
Average Temperatures:
 July: 74°F: (23°C)
 January. 28°F. (-2°C)
Average Yearly Precipitation: *15 in. (38 cm)*

Population

How Many: *3,307,912 (1990 Census)*
Where They Live: *81% urban, 19% rural*
Largest Cities: *Denver, Colorado Springs, Aurora*

State Government

Governor: *4-year term*
Senators *(35); 4-year term*
Representatives *(65): 2-year term*
Counties: *63*

Federal Government

Senators *(2): 6-year term*
Representatives *(6): 2-year term*
Electoral Votes: *8*

Colorado State Flag

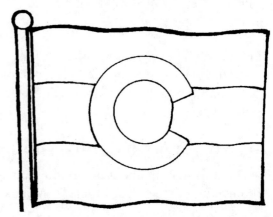

Economy

Agriculture: *beef cattle, wheat, corn, milk, hay, sheep*
Manufacturing: *food products, rubber and plastic products, printed material, metal products*
Mining: *coal, petroleum, stone*

Interesting Facts

• Colorado is often called the "highest state," because it has over 1,000 mountains that are more than 10,000 feet (3000 m) above sea level.

• The largest silver nugget was discovered in Aspen in 1894. It weighed 1,840 pounds (828 kg).

Interesting Coloradan

• Jack Dempsey was a famous heavyweight boxer. He started fighting professionally when he was 19 years old. He was born in Manassa.

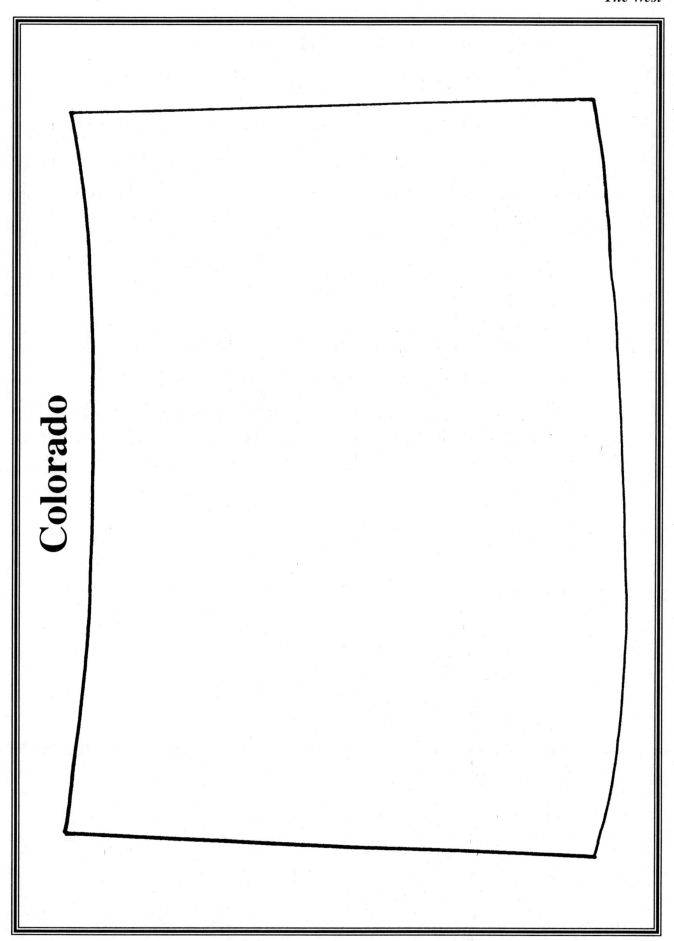

Colorado

The Magnificent Mountains

A mountain is a landform that stands much higher than its surroundings. It has steep slopes and sharp or rounded peaks. Mountains occur in the ocean as well as on land. Whether on land or under water, mountains are created over long periods of time by great forces in the earth.

Much of the state of Colorado is located in the spectacular Rocky Mountains, making it the nation's overall highest-elevation state. The Rockies are the largest mountain system in North America. It has more than a thousand peaks that are over ten thousand feet (300 m) high. The Rocky Mountains' range is often called the "Roof of North America." The sides of the mountains are filled with fossils of animals that once lived in the sea, and rocks that were formed in the hot interior of the earth. Rich lodes of silver were found in these mountains, not to mention a few nuggets of gold. Visitors to the Rockies enjoy its beautiful lakes, ski resorts, and wild game.

Activity: Rocky Mountain Relief Map

The Rockies form the largest mountain system in North America. They stretch across the United States and Canada for more that 3,000 miles (4,800 km). In some areas, the mountains extend about 350 miles (563 km) wide. The provinces and states through which the Rocky Mountains stretch include Alaska, Washington, Montana, Idaho, Wyoming, Utah, Colorado, New Mexico, Alberta, British Columbia, and the Northwest and Yukon Territories.

To see just how large an area the Rocky Mountain Range occupies in the United States, follow the directions below to make a relief map. You may wish to work in a group for this activity.

- Locate a relief map in an encyclopedia, atlas, or other reference book.
- Cut out an 18" x 24" (46 cm x 61 cm) piece of cardboard (cover with white paper) or white poster board.
- Make an outline of the United States on the cardboard or poster board.
- Using modeling clay (or the play clay recipe on page 165), form the mountain range across the states through which it extends. If possible, include the Appalachian Mountains on your map. Try to show the difference in the elevations and size of the two mountain ranges.
- Share your relief map with the class. Tell some interesting facts about this magnificent mountain range.

Hawaii

"The Aloha State"

Basic Facts

Capital: *Honolulu*
Statehood: *August 21, 1959*
Admittance: *50th State*
Motto: *The Life of the Land is Perpetuated in Righteousness*
Song: *"Hawaii Ponoi" ("Hawaii's Own")*
Bird: *Nene (Hawaiian Goose)*
Flower: *Hibiscus*
Tree: *KuLui*
Abbreviation: *HI*

Area: *6,471 square miles (16, 759 sq. km)*
Elevation: *(above sea level)*
 Highest: 13, 796 ft. (4,205 m) – Mauna Kea
 Lowest: Sea level along coastline
Average Temperatures:
 July: 75°F. (24°C)
 January: 68°F. (20°C)
Average Yearly Precipitation: *110 in. (279 cm)*

Population

How Many: *1,115,274 (1990 Census)*
Where They Live: *87% urban, 13% rural*
Largest Cities: *Honolulu, Hilo, Kailua*

State Government

Governor: *4-year term*
Senators *(25): 4-year term*
Representatives *(51): 2-year term*
Counties: *5*

Federal Government

Senators *(2): 6-year term*
Representatives *(2): 2-year term*
Electoral Votes: *4 r*

Hawaii State Flag

Economy

Agriculture: *sugar cane, pineapples, beef cattle*
Fishing Industry: tuna, snapper
Manufacturing: *food products, clothing, chemicals, textiles, metals, printed materials, transportation equipment*
Mining: *stone, sand and gravel*

Interesting Facts

• Haleakala is one of the world's largest inactive volcanoes. It is on the island of Maui and measures about 25 miles (40 km) around its rim.

• The Hawaiian alphabet has only 12 letters—a, e, h, i, k, l, m, n, o, p, u, and w.

Interesting Hawaiian

• King Kamehameha I united the Hawaiian islands in 1795. He was born on the island of Hawaii.

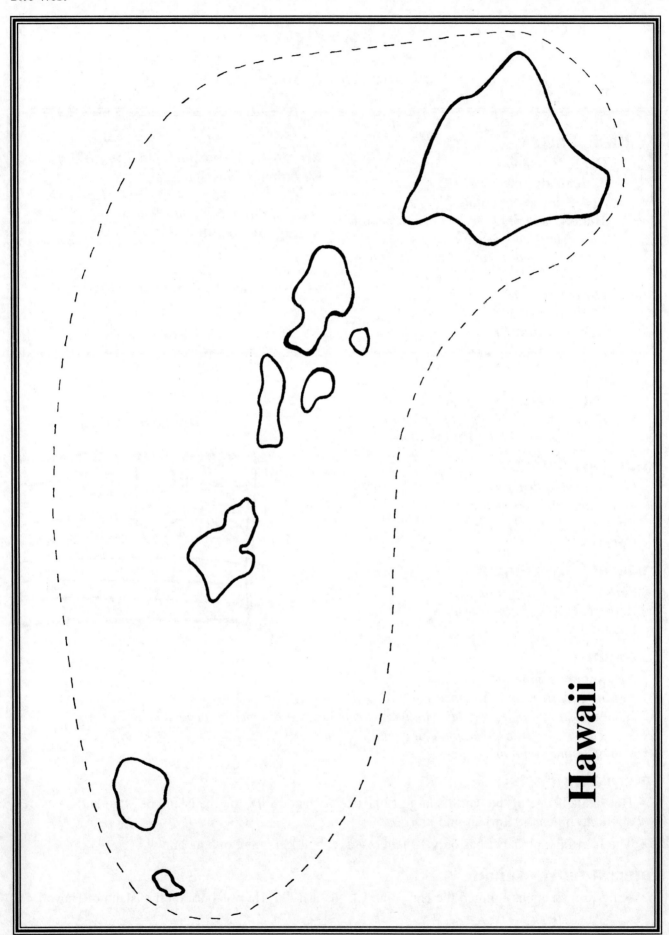

Hawaii

Go Hawaiian

Hawaii was formed many centuries ago by volcanic activity.

Hawaii has a tropical climate cooled by trade winds. Normal daily temperatures in Honolulu average 72 degrees Fahrenheit (22 degrees Celsius) in January and 80 degrees Fahrenheit (26 degrees Celsius) in July.

Hawaii's earliest inhabitants were Polynesians who came to the islands in double-hulled canoes between 1,000 and 1,400 years ago, either from Southeast Asia or from the Margues in the South Pacific.

The Hawaiian Alphabet

Although Hawaii has been part of the United States since August 21, 1959, it still retains its own culture, customs, language, and alphabet. The Hawaiian alphabet is as unique as the people who first inhabited the islands. The alphabet contains only 12 letters: five vowels (a, e, i, o, u) and seven consonants (h, k, l, m, n, p, w).

In the early 1800's, missionaries sent to the islands worked with the Hawaiians to put together a language in written form. Based on the existing language, only 12 letters were needed to complete the Hawaiian alphabet.

Today, most of the people of Hawaii speak English. However, it is not uncommon to hear such familiar words as "hula" and "aloha" spoken on the islands.

Activity: A Hawaiian Picture Dictionary

Below you will find some frequently used words in the Hawaiian language. Use some of them, and/or invent words of your own, using the Hawaiian alphabet to make your own picture dictionary of Hawaiian words.

haole—HOWlay, foreigner	**Oe**—OH ee, you
kal—KAH ee, the sea	**moana**—moh AH nah, ocean
kane—KAH neh, man	**kokua**—koh KOO uh, help (cooperation)
mahimahi—MAH hee MAH hee, tasty fish	**nui**—NOO ee, large (great)
manu—MAH noo, bird	**keiki**—KAY kee, child
mauna—MOW nah, mountain	**lei**—/ay, garland (wreath)
nani—NAH nee, beautiful	**mahalo**—mah HAH loh, thanks

To prepare your picture dictionary, staple several pieces of blank white 8½" x 11" (20 cm x 28 cm) paper together to form the picture pages. On each page write a word and add an illustration relating to the word. (You may wish to explain something about the origin or meaning of the word, too.) Cut out and color the cover on page 224. Attach the cover to the pages of the dictionary. Share your Hawaiian picture dictionary with the class.

My Hawaiian Picture Dictionary

224

Idaho
"The Gem State"

Basic Facts

Capital: *Boise*
Statehood: *July 3, 1890*
Admittance: *43rd state*
Motto: *It Is Forever*
Song: *"Here We Have Idaho"*
Bird: *Mountain bluebird*
Flower: *Syringa (mock orange)*
Tree: *Western pine*
Abbreviation: *ID*

Area: *83,564 square miles (216,432 sq. km)*
Elevation: *(above sea level)*
  Highest: 12,662 ft. (3,859 m) – Borah Peak
  Lowest: 710 ft. (216 m) – Snake River
Average Temperatures:
  July: 67°F. (19°C)
  January: 23°F. (-5°C)
Average Yearly Precipitation: *16 in. (41 cm)*

Population

How Many: *1, 011, 986 (1990 Census)*
Where They Live: *54% urban, 46% rural*
Largest Cities: *Boise, Pocatello, Idaho Falls*

State Government

Governor: *4-year term*
Senators *(42): 4-year term*
Representatives *(84): 2-year term*
Counties: *44*

Federal Government

Senators *(2): 6-year term*
Representatives *(2): 2-year term*
Electoral Votes: *4*

Idaho State Flag

Economy

Agriculture: *beef cattle, potatoes, wheat, milk, hay, barley*
Manufacturing: *lumber and wood products, food products, chemicals, rubber and plastic products, printed materials*
Mining: *silver, lead, zinc*

Interesting Facts

- Idaho is the potato capital of the United States. It produces over 10 billion pounds of potatoes each year.
- Electricity from atomic energy was first generated in a laboratory near Idaho Falls in 1951.

Interesting Idahoan

- Chief Joseph, the leader of the Nez Perce Indians, is known as a great leader and humanitarian who worked for peace.

Idaho

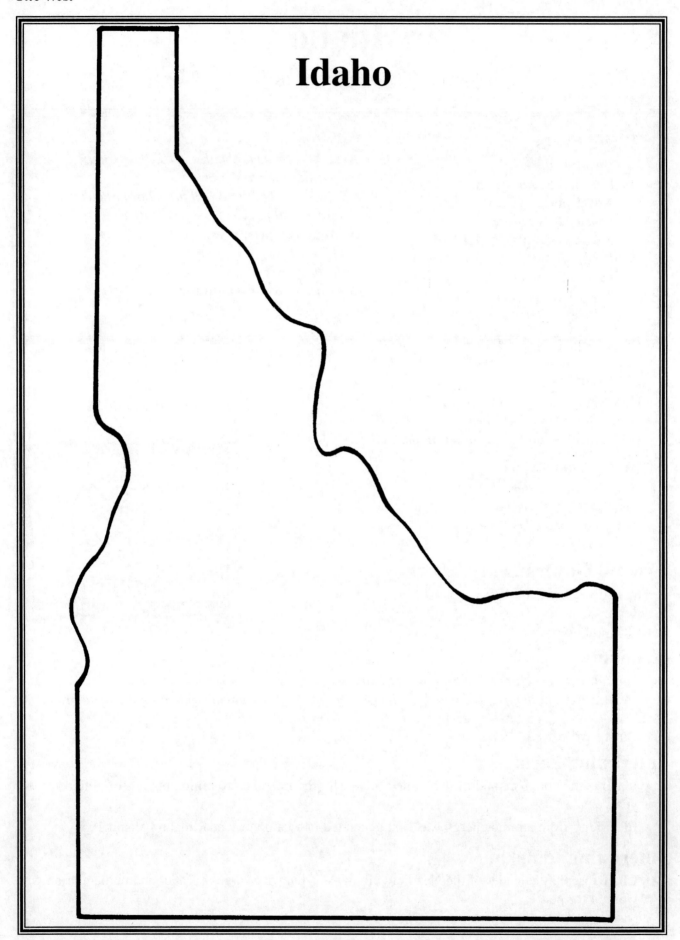

The Scoop On Spuds!

Idaho produces more of the world's most popular vegetable than any other state in the country. It leads the country in potato-growing. When you eat French fries at a fast food restaurant or even baked or mashed potatoes at home, there is a very good chance that they are from Idaho.

A potato is high in nutritional value and is made up of 80% water and 205to solid matter. It has no more calories than an apple. Starch makes up 85% of the solid material and the rest is made up of protein and many other minerals and vitamins. Most Idaho potatoes are grown in the Snake River region.

How to Grow a Potato

The edible parts of the potato plant are found underground and are called tubers. There are three to six tubers per plant. After the tubers mature, the plant dies. Most potato growers plant small, whole tubers and segments called seed pieces that are cut from the tuber. A gas-powered planter makes a trough, gently drops in the potato, and drops fertilizer on each side of the potato. Most of the time a farmer will cultivate the crops. Cultivation helps air purify the soil, kill weeds, and provide a soil covering.

Interesting Facts and Myths

Fact: Americans spend almost four billion dollars a year on potato chips.

Myth: If a woman is expecting a baby, she should not eat potatoes because the baby will be born with a big head.

Fact: Potatoes can be used to make petroleum.

Myth: If you have a wart, rub it with a cut potato, then bury the potato. As the potato rots in the ground, your wart will disappear.

Fact: People who eat potatoes as the main part of their diet have fewer cavities in their teeth.

Activity: Starch Storing

Every human body needs starch. One of the ways we get starch is through the foods we eat. You can tell where the starch is stored in a potato by trying the following experiment.

Essentials

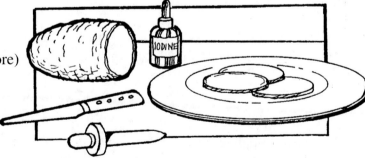

- a slice of potato
- tincture of iodine (available at a drug store)
- paper plate
- kitchen knife
- eye dropper

Directions

Place the potato slice on a paper plate. Scrape a little of the surface of the potato slice. On the knife you will see a whitish liquid; this is starch. Use an eye dropper to add some iodine to the surface of the potato slice. (Caution: Iodine is poison. Handle with care. Do not eat any of the foods with iodine on them; throw them away.) What happens to the area where the iodine was added?

Explanation: Tincture of iodine is used as an indicator to test for starch. A food product will turn a blue-black color in the presence of iodine. There is starch in the potato where the iodine turns color.

Montana

"The Treasure State"

Basic Facts

Capital: *Helena*
Statehood: *November 8, 1889*
Admittance: *41st state*
Motto: *Gold and Silver*
Song: *"Montana"*
Bird: *Western meadowlark*
Flower: *Bitterroot*
Tree: *Ponderosa pine*
Abbreviation: *MT*

Area: *147,046 square miles (380,848 sq. km)*
Elevation: *(above sea level)*
 Highest: 12,799 ft. (3,901 m) – Granite Peak
 Lowest: 1,800 ft. (549 m) – Lincoln County
Average Temperatures:
 July: 68°F. (20°C)
 January: 18°F. (-8°C)
Average Yearly Precipitation: *15 in. (38 cm)*

Population

How Many: *803,655 (1990 Census)*
Where They Live: *53% urban, 47% rural*
Largest Cities: *Billings, Great Falls, Butte*

State Government

Governor: *4-year term*
Senators *(50): 4-year term*
Representatives *(100): 2-year term*
Counties: *56*

Federal Government

Senators *(2): 6-year term*
Representatives *(1): 2-year term*
Electoral Votes: *3*

Montana State Flag

Economy

Agriculture: *beef cattle, wheat, hay, barley, milk, sugar beets*
Manufacturing: *lumber and wood products, food products, petroleum and coal products, glass products*
Mining: *clay, stone, petroleum, copper, natural gas, silver*

Interesting Facts

• More gem sapphires are found in Montana than anywhere else in the United States.

• Grasshopper Glacier, near Cooke City, is named for the grasshoppers that became trapped in the ice hundreds and thousands of years ago and can still be seen today.

Interesting Montanan

• Jeannette Rankin was the first woman in the United States Congress. She was elected in 1916.

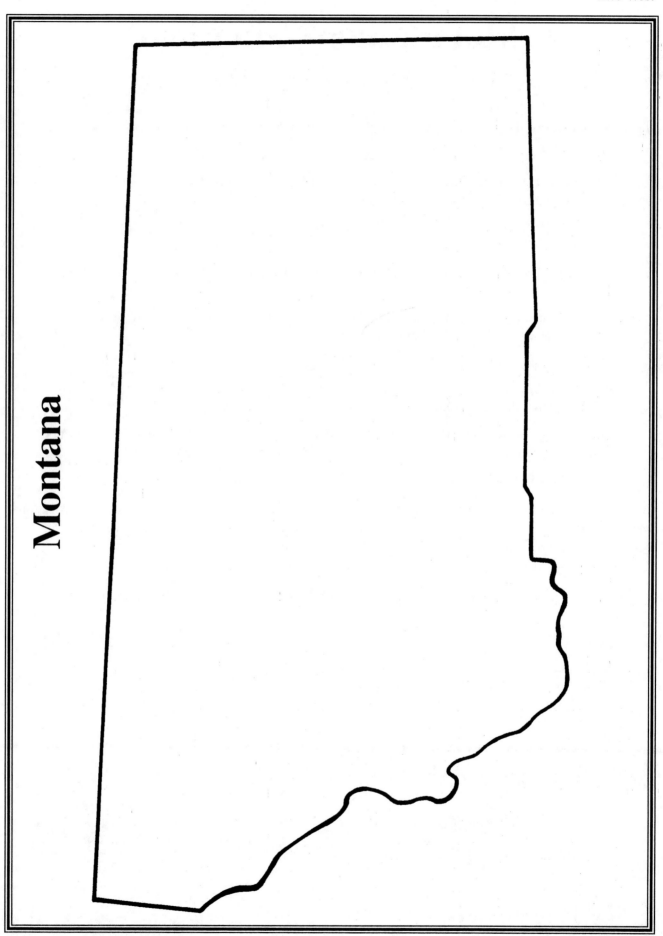

Montana

Mountainous Montana

Montana's name is derived from the Latin word meaning "mountainous."

It was in 1803, when president Thomas Jefferson dispatched the Lewis and Clark Expedition to explore the upper reaches of the Missouri River, that the written history of Montana began.

Activity: "Claim to Fame" Reports

Each of the items listed below has facts about famous people or events from Montana's history. Choose one item and do some research to find out more.

1. Grasshopper Glacier is named for the swarms of grasshoppers that became trapped in its ice years ago and can still be seen.

2. Custer's Last Stand took place in this state in 1876 when Custer and over 200 of his troops were killed in the Battle of Little Bighorn.

3. Jeannette Rankin became the first woman to serve in the United States Congress. She was elected to the United States House of Representatives in 1916.

4. Just about every town in Montana has a rodeo.-

5. The fur trade dominated Montana's economy until 1858, when gold was discovered near the present community of Drummond.

6. The railroads brought a rush of homesteaders between 1900 and 1910, increasing the number of farms and ranches.

7. Today, many tourists seek out the former gold rush camps, ghost towns, and dude ranches.

Write some of the information you discovered on large index cards. (You may wish to add illustrations.) Make a "Claim To Fame Booklet" by stapling the fact cards together. To make a cover, cut out the box below and glue it to a blank index card. Attach it to the front of the booklet.

Claim to Fame Booklet

Nevada

"The Silver State"

Basic Facts

Capital: *Carson City*
Statehood: *October 31, 1864*
Admittance: *36th state*
Motto: *All for Our Country*
Song: *"Home Means Nevada"*
Bird: *Mountain bluebird*
Flower: *Sagebrush*
Tree: *Single-leaf pinon*
Abbreviation: *NV*

Area: *110,561 square miles (286,352 sq. km)*
Elevation: *(above sea level)*
  Highest: 13,143 ft. (4,006 m) – Boundary Peak
  Lowest: 470 ft. (143 m) – Clark County
Average Temperatures:
  July: 73°F. (23°C)
  January: 30°F. (-1°C)
Average Yearly Precipitation: *9 inches (23 cm)*

Population

How Many: *1,206,152 (1990 Census)*
Where They Live: *85% urban, 15% rural*
Largest Cities: *Las Vegas, Reno, Paradise*

State Government

Governor: *4-year term*
Senators *(32)*: *4-year term*
Assembly Members *(42)*: *2-year term*
Counties: *17*

Federal Government

Senators *(2)*: *6-year term*
Representatives *(7)*: *2-year term*
Electoral Votes: *9*

Nevada State Flag

Economy

Agriculture: *hay, beef cattle, milk, potatoes, sheep*
Manufacturing: *machinery, printed materials, food products*
Mining: *gold, silver, barite, sand and gravel*

Interesting Facts

- The United States Federal Government owns more than three-fourths of the land in the state of Nevada.
- Of all the states, Nevada gets the least amount of rainfall during the year.

Interesting Nevadan

- James Warren Nye was the only territorial governor of Nevada. He had the honor of leading Nevada into statehood in 1864.

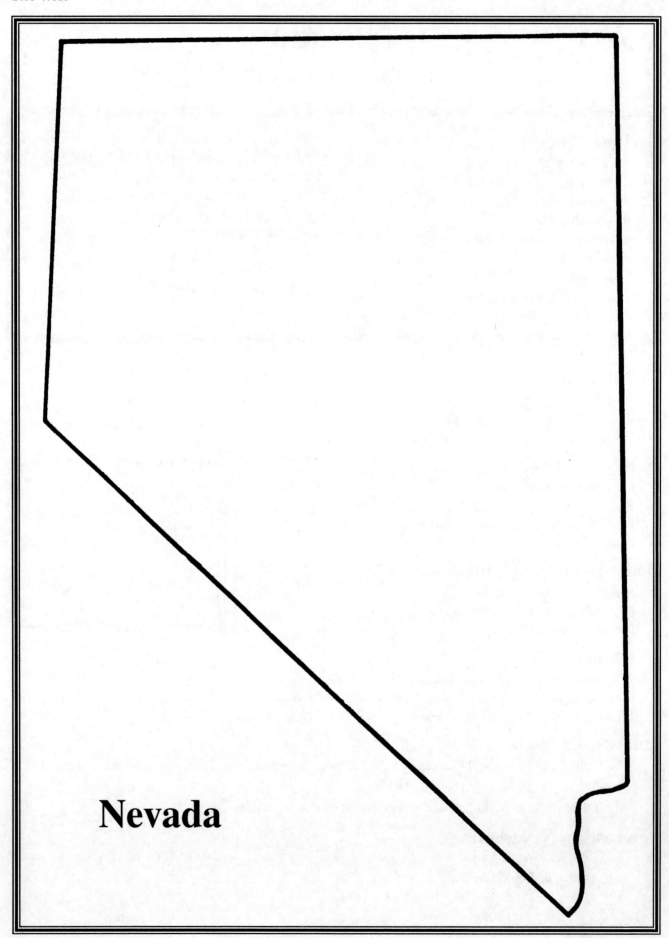

Nevada

The Ghost Towns of Nevada

In 1859, a large concentration of silver and gold was discovered in what is now Virginia City. The discovery attracted thousands of fortune seekers and helped make the region a thriving mining center.

By the late 1870's, the lode's rich ores were exhausted and Nevada slipped into a 20-year depression. People began to leave Nevada by the thousands, and several thriving communities became ghost towns.

Activity: Simulated Ghost Town

Make a ghost town in your classroom. Use a tape recorder to record appropriate sounds. For example, you might record ghostly voices spelling words, an eerie-sounding bell ringing, echoing laughter, the scraping of a chalkboard with fingernails, etc. Decorate the classroom to look as if it had been deserted for a long time. Add cobwebs, and other "ghost-town touches" to make the room look as though it was left abruptly. Have other classes visit your "ghost town." Play the tape as you guide visitors through. Be a tour guide, explaining to the visitors how and why the town became a ghost town.

Suggestions for other sound effects:

- Galloping horse: Tap open palms against legs in a galloping rhythm.
- Banging shutters or saloon door: Open and close a wooden folding chair.
- Train: Fill a metal box with small items and shake in the rhythm of a train. Have students use their voices to add the whistle sounds.

Oregon
"The Beaver State"

Basic Facts

Capital: *Salem*
Statehood: *February 14, 1859*
Admittance: *33rd state*
Motto: *She Flies with Her Own Wings*
Song: *"Oregon, My Oregon"*
Bird: *Western meadowlark*
Flower: *Oregon grape*
Tree: *Douglas fir*
Abbreviation: *OR*

Area: *97,073 square miles (251,419 sq. km)*
Elevation: *(above sea level)*
 Highest: 11,239 ft. (3,426 m) – Mount Hood
 Lowest: Sea level along coastline
Average Temperatures:
 July: 66°F. (19°C)
 January: 32°F. (0°C)
Average Yearly Precipitation: *28 in. (71 cm)*

Population

How Many: *2,853,733 (1990 Census)*
Where They Live: *68% urban, 32% rural*
Largest Cities: *Portland, Eugene, Salem*

State Government

Governor: *4-year term*
Senators *(30): 4-year term*
Representatives *(60): 2-year term*
Counties: *36*

Federal Government

Senators *(2): 6-year term*
Representatives *(5): 2-year term*
Electoral Votes: *7*

Oregon State Flag

Economy

Agriculture: *timber, beef cattle, greenhouse and nursery products, milk, hay, wheat*
Fishing: *salmon, tuna, shrimp*
Manufacturing: *wood products, food products, paper products, machinery, scientific instruments, electric equipment*
Mining: *sand and gravel, nickel, stone*

Interesting Facts

• Crater Lake is the deepest lake (1,932 ft./580 m) in the United States.

• The world's smallest official park is found in Portland. The park covers an area of 452 square inches (3.4 sq. cm).

Interesting Oregonian

• Although John McLoughlin was born in Quebec, he became known as the "Father of Oregon." He played an important role in settling the Oregon territory and was the director of the famous trading business, The Hudson's Bay Company.

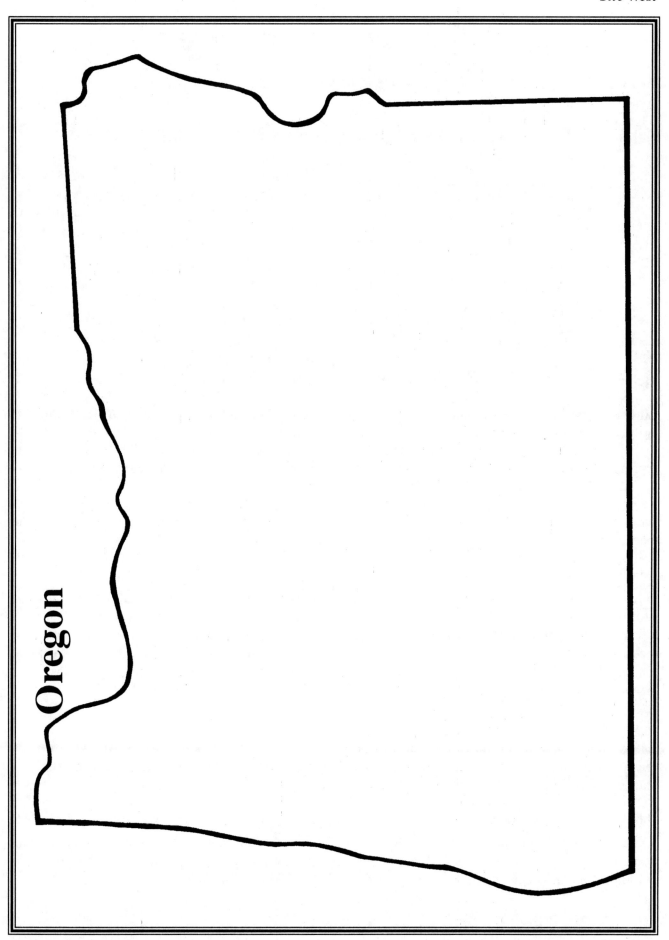

Oregon

"Pioneer's Paradise"

In 1843, many people headed west in search of the "Pioneer's Paradise." The Oregon Trail was still a treacherous stretch of land that hadn't been traveled by many people. So why go west? Oregon fever! The pioneers of the mid 1800's left their homes in hopes of better opportunity, better land, and a better life altogether. Oregon offered free land and jobs for skilled workers and farm hands.

These pioneers rode in wagons, on horses, pulled handcarts, and a few even pushed wheelbarrows. The trail stretched northwestward from Missouri for 2,000 miles (3,200 km). The pioneers were on this trail for as long as six months. Many of the inexperienced pioneers did not know of the hazards that lay ahead. Some turned around and went home, but many of the pioneers faced the dangers with courage.

The Beginning

Before leaving on the trip, the necessities needed to be purchased.

At least $600 was needed to purchase these supplies which included food, cooking utensils, clothing, tools, bedding, weapons, and luxury items if there was any space left over.

Spring was the time to begin the trip; this gave the pioneers just enough time to cross the mountains before the snows closed the mountain passes.

Missouri was the starting point for the Oregon Trail. This is where civilization ended and the unknown began.

The Hardships

Some pioneers fell, wagons and all, into deep mountain passes and were unable to get out. A prairie storm often struck without warning. Eighty mile-an-hour (128 km per hour) winds would tear canvas off the wagons. The wheels of transportation would get stuck in the mud and the rivers and creeks became impassable. Prairie blizzards were even worse than storms. Disease was the greatest killer of all on the Oregon Trail. Unsafe water was exceptionally dangerous. Clean water was scarce and was needed for survival.

The Journey

Many pioneers traveled from dawn to dusk, in a wagon train of fifty or more wagons. At night the pioneers would position their wagons in a circle, for safety. They would tell stories, sing, and even dance to forget the troubles of the day.

The End of the Journey

Once the pioneers reached Oregon, they had to file a claim. A claim is a request to own a tract of land. Each family could get 640 acres (256 ha) of land; and to keep it the family would have to build a cabin within six months. This was hard work and the whole family had to pitch in to finish the cabin.

"Pioneer's Paradise" *(cont.)*

Activity 1: An Oregon Trip

Work in pairs for this activity. With your partner, make a list of the things you would pack in a wagon if you were to journey along the Oregon Trail. Include things that you have to take in order to survive and things that you would like to take if you have room.

Share and compare your list with other groups. As a class, decide on the "top ten" supplies that would have probably been most essential on the Oregon Trail.

Activity 2: Pioneer transportation

Essentials

- construction paper (brown and white)
- tagboard or lightweight cardboard
- pencil
- scissors
- paper punch
- glue or tape
- yarn scraps
- brass paper fastener

Directions

- Take a brown piece of paper. Cut four slits two inches (5 cm) from each of the four corners. Fold the sides up and glue (or tape) them together.
- Measure and cut a white piece of paper for the top of the wagon. Fold the paper, and glue (or tape) the sides to the inside bed of the wagon.
- Cut out four wagon wheels from whichever type of cardboard you chose.
- For movable wheels, use brass paper fasteners to attach the wheels to the wagon. Put the fasteners through the center of the wheel, and attach them to the bed of the wagon.
- To make a seat for your wagon, cut out a rectangle and fold it into a seat shape.

You can decorate your wagon with sayings like "Oregon or Bust." You can also make a wagon train by connecting the wagon together.

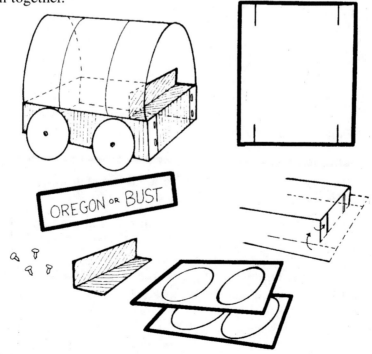

Utah

"The Beehive State"

Basic Facts

Capital: *Salt Lake City*
Statehood: *February 14, 1859*
Admittance: *45th state*
Motto: *Industry*
Song: *"Utah, We Love Thee"*
Bird: *Sea gull*
Flower: *Sego lily*
Tree: *Blue spruce*
Abbreviation: *UT*

Area: *84,899 square miles (219,809 sq. km)*
Elevation: *(above sea level)*
 Highest: 13,528 ft. (4,123 m) – Kings Peak
 Lowest: 2,000 ft. (610 m) – Beaverdam
Average Temperatures:
 July: 73°F. (23O C)
 January: 25°F. (-4°C)
Average Yearly Precipitation: *12 in. (30 cm)*

Population

How Many: *1,727,784 (1990 Census)*
Where They Live: *84% urban, 16% rural*
Largest Cities: *Salt Lake City, Provo, West Valley City*

Utah State Flag

State Government

Governor: *4-year term*
Senators *(29): 4-year term*
Representatives *(75): 2-year term*
Counties: *29*

Federal Government

Senators *(2): 6-year term*
Representatives *(3): 2-year term*
Electoral Votes: *5*

Economy

Agriculture: *beef cattle, milk, hay, sheep, turkeys*
Manufacturing: *machinery, transportation equipment, food products, electric equipment*
Mining: *petroleum, coal, copper, uranium, gold*

Interesting Facts

- The Rainbow Bridge located in the Glen Canyon National Recreation Area is the largest known natural stone bridge in the world.

- The Great Salt Lake, located near Salt Lake City, is four times more salty than any ocean.

Interesting Utahan

- Brigham Young led a group of Mormons west across the young United States in search of religious freedom. He and his followers arrived and settled where Salt Lake City now stands on July 24, 1847.

Utah

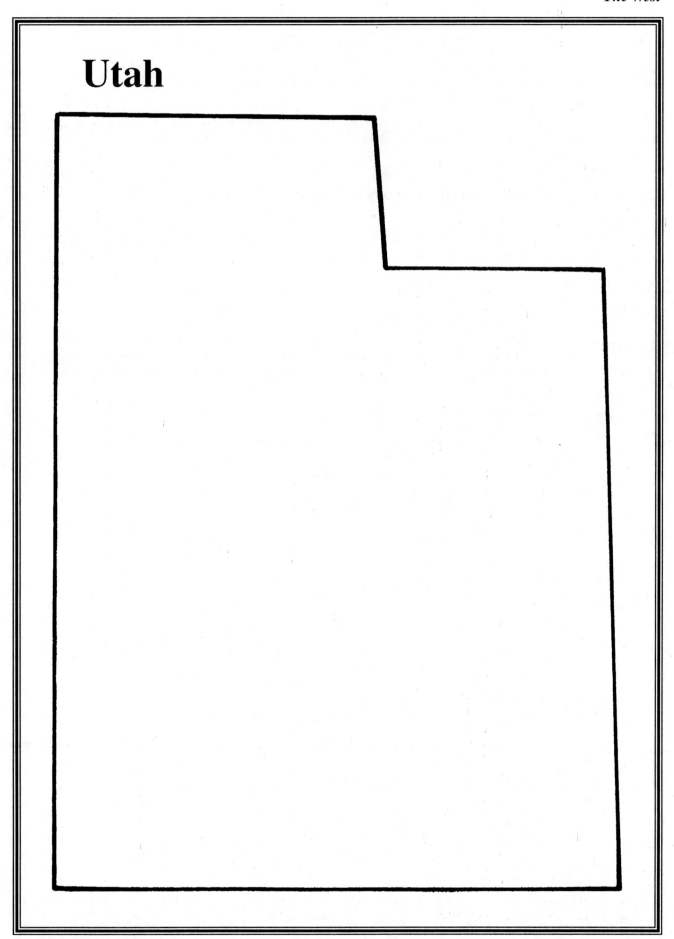

The Great Salt Lake

The Great Salt Lake is fed by freshwater streams, and is saltier than the oceans because its waters do not drain away. It becomes salty because evaporation removes water in the form of water vapor and leaves behind a residue of salt. The Great Salt Lake is the largest saline lake in North America. Read the following fascinating facts about the Great Salt Lake. Then try the activity below.

- There are five billion tons of minerals worth about $90 billion dollars in Utah's Salt Lake.
- The Great Salt Lake is seven times as salty as the ocean.
- Salt makes water buoyant. A swimmer can float like a cork in the Salt Lake.
- The Great Lake has flooded many times in the 1980's. The water level raised 2.6 meters (8.5 ft.) in just two years.

Activity: Reappearing Salt Lick

The following activity may be done individually, as a whole class, or in groups.

Essentials

- salt
- sugar
- Epsom salts (available at drug stores)
- laundry detergent flakes
- 4 recycled glass jars
- spoons
- magnifying glass
- thread or thin string
- very hot water
- pencils
- paper clips
- food coloring (optional)

Directions

1. Boil some water and pour the very hot water into a jar about half full.
2. Slowly stir in about a cup (250 mL) of salt, until no more will dissolve.
3. Tie a string onto the middle of a pencil, and tie a paper clip onto the other end.
4. Moisten the string and rub some salt onto the string.
5. Drop the string into the hot water, paper clip end first.
6. Lay the pencil across the jar.
7. Put the glass jar in a cool place, where it will not be bumped. Watch the jar over the next two days and do not touch! Follow this same process with Epsom salts, sugar, and laundry detergent flakes. **Note:** You might want to try adding food coloring to one of the solutions.

Does the salt reappear? Keep a record or draw a picture of what you see in each of the solutions. Which one grew the largest?

Explanation: Salt dissolves in hot water, and so it seems to disappear. When the water turns cold again it cannot hold salt like hot water can, so the salt reappears on the string.

Washington
"The Evergreen State"

Basic Facts

Capital: *Olympia*
Statehood: *November 11, 1889*
Admittance: *42nd state*
Motto: *Aliki (Bye and Bye)*
Song: *"Washington, My Home"*
Bird: *Willow goldfinch*
Flower: *Coast rhododendron*
Tree: *Western hemlock*
Abbreviation: *WA*

Area: *68,139 square miles (176,479 sq. km)*
Elevation: *(above sea level)*
  Highest: 14,410 ft (4,392 m) Mount Rainier
  Lowest: Sea level along coastline
Average Temperatures:
  July: 66°F. (10°C)
  January: 30°F. (-1°C)
Average Yearly Precipitation: *38 in. (97 cm)*

Population

How Many: *4,887,941 (1990 Census)*
Where They Live: *74% urban, 26% rural*
Largest Cities: *Seattle, Spokane, Tacoma*

State Government

Govemor: *4-year term*
Senators *(49): 4-year term*
Representatives *(98): 2-year term*
Counties: *39*

Federal Government

Senators *(2): 6-year term*
Representatives *(9): 2-year term*
Electoral Votes: *11*

Washington State Flag

Economy

Agriculture: *chickens, beef cattle, eggs, soybeans, peanuts, cotton, wheat*
Fishing: *shrimp, oysters, salmon, tuna*
Manufacturing: *paper products, chemicals, rubber and plastic products, textiles, metals, transportation equipment*
Mining: *coal, sand and gravel, gold, gemstones*

Interesting Facts

• The state of Washington is the only state named after a president of the United States.

• The greatest snowfall in North America occurred in Washington between July 1971 and June 1972. A total of 1,122 inches (2805 cm) of snow fell in just over one year.

Interesting Washingtonian

• Sonora Louise Smart Dodd, of Spokane, was the originator of a special holiday, Father's Day. It was first officially celebrated on June 19, 1910.

Washington

The Olympic Mix

The Olympic National Park, established in 1938, is one of the most beautiful national parks the United States has to offer. This park is a mixture of environments which includes tall mountains, eternally snowcapped and overrun with amazing glaciers, a 50-mile (80 km) stretch of some of the most unrestrained beaches in the country, and a rain forest as green and shadowy as an Amazon jungle.

Rain Forest

Moisture from the clouds blows inland from a warm Pacific current and forces the clouds to rise by the barrier of the Olympics. As they move upward, they cool and the moisture creates rain and snow. The rain forest of this region results from exceptional soil and massive amounts of rainfall. A hike along the coastline of Olympic National Park takes you into a completely different realm.

Coastline

The coastline is leisurely and almost magical. The trees along the shore are bent almost flat due to the high winds. Along the beach, you can stop to visit the tidepools full of fascinating marine life. You may even see a migration of whales swimming from California to Alaska.

Glaciers

Yet another completely different environment is left to explore. Mount Olympus is nearly 8,000 feet (2,400 m) tall. It has seven glaciers on its flanks with ice 900 feet (270 m) thick. Here autos can no longer travel. Backpackers and mountain climbers are all you will see. The Olympic National Park is a wild experience, with three very diverse environments.

Activity: Create Your Own Environment Poster

Essentials

- poster board
- small sheets of paper
- glue
- writing utensils (pencils, pens, markers, crayons)

Directions

On one piece of paper draw a picture of Washington State and mark where Olympic National park is located. On separate sheets of paper trace a scene of each of the three environments. Include animals, plants, mountains, beaches, trees, weather, and other essential items. On another sheet of paper create a sign warning people to take care of the environment. Glue each of the sheets of paper onto a poster board. Display your poster and share it with the class.

Wyoming
"The Equality State"

Basic Facts

Capital: *Cheyenne*
Statehood: *July 10, 1890*
Admittance: *44th state*
Motto: *Equal Rights*
Song: *"Wyoming"*
Bird: *Western meadowlark*
Flower: *Indian paintbrush*
Tree: *Cottonwood*
Abbreviation: *WY*

Area: *97,809 square miles (253,326 sq km)*
Elevation: *(above sea level)*
 Highest: 13,804 ft. (4,207 m) – Gannett Peak
 Lowest: 3,001 ft. (945 m) – Crook County
Average Temperatures:
 July: 67°F. (19°C)
 January: 19°F. (-7°C)
Average Yearly Precipitation: *13 in. (33 cm)*

Population

How Many: *455,975 (1990 Census)*
Where They Live: *63% urban, 37% rural*
Largest Cities: *Casper, Cheyenne, Laramie*

Wyoming State Flag

State Government

Governor: *4-year term*
Senators *(30): 4-year term*
Representatives *(64): 2-year term*
Counties: *23*

Federal Government

Senators *(2): 6-year term*
Representative *(1): 2-year term*
Counties: *23*
Electoral Votes: *3*

Economy

Agriculture: *beef cattle, sheep, sugar beets, hay, wheat, milk, barley*
Manufacturing: *chemicals, petroleum products, food products*
Mining: *clay, coal, natural gas, petroleum, stone, uranium*

Interesting Facts

• Independence Rock, a large granite boulder located near Casper, has names carved in it by settlers who were moving during the early 1800's.

• In 1869, Wyoming women were given the right to vote in elections.

Interesting Wyomingian

• Nellie Tayloe Ross was the first woman governor of any state. In 1933, she became the first female director of the United States Mint.

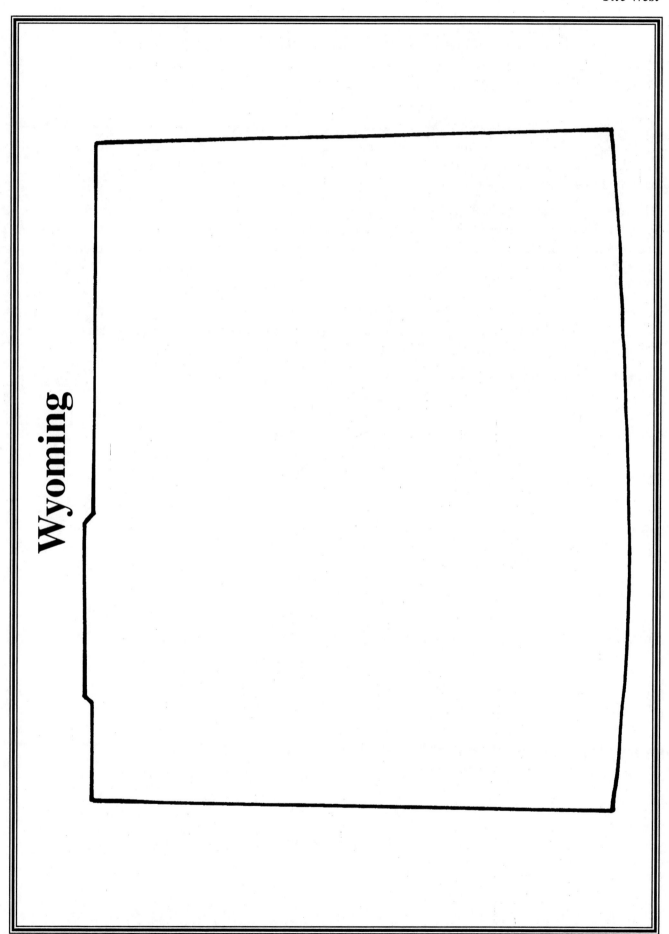

Wyoming

Rambunctious Rodeo Riders

A door on a fence flies open. A few seconds later, a bucking, kicking bronco speeds out. The horse kicks its rear feet into the air, then spins around in circles. Will the rider be knocked to the ground or will he or she survive this rugged ride?

Welcome to the rodeo, where men and women, boys and girls alike test their riding and roping ability. A rodeo features bronco riding, bull riding, calf roping, and steer wrestling. These events have been recreated to capture the spirit of the Old West.

The rodeo events are separated into two main groups. The first of the events are the rough stock events. Rough stock events feature riders on bucking horses or bulls for a specified number of seconds. Riders are awarded points according to how long they ride (higher points for longer amounts of time). The second group of events are timed events, judged according to how quickly the contestants complete a required task (such as calf roping, barrel racing, or steer wrestling).

Rodeos were developed in the 1800's when after a hard day's work, the cowboys gathered together to have some fun. Wyoming's most popular annual event is the Frontier Days Celebration. This celebration lasts for ten days in July and features a widely known rodeo.

Find out as much as you can about rodeos, especially on the topic of roping. Then try the rope spinning activitity on page 247.

Rambunctious Rodeo Riders *(cont.)*

Roping is a very important part of the rodeo. Learning how to rope cattle takes a great deal of practice and skill. Try your hand at roping with the following activity.

Activity: Rope Spinning

Essentials

- braided rope (often called sash cord), 10 or 12 feet (about 4 m) long and about ¼ to ⅜ inch (.7 cm) in diameter (available at hardware store)
- scissors
- large, flat washer

Directions

At one end of the rope, tie a slip knot known as the "honda." (See illustration.) Make sure you snip off the end of the knot. Feed the other end of the rope through the honda knot; then pull the honda knot tight. Put a washer over the other end of the rope; then tie the end sticking out from the washer in a simple knot.

Note: This is an activity to be done outside. Wear clothing that will not get caught in the rope. Never put the rope around someone's head or body. Do not get discouraged; rope spinning takes a lot of practice.

How To Spin the Rope

Hold the rope at the honda knot; the loop should hang down. The length of the rope from the honda knot to the washer is called the "spoke." When the loop is the correct size, the spoke should hang down from the honda halfway to the bottom of the loop. After this is done, pull the honda knot tight.

To make the "flat loop" spin, stand with your feet slightly apart and your body leaning a little bit forward. Hold the rope with the honda knot in your left hand. Place the knotted end of the spoke with the washer loosely between the second and the third fingers of your right hand so that the knot faces the palm of your hand. Now bring the loop over to your right hand and let it lie loosely across your fingers. You are now ready to throw out the rope to spin. Throw out your right hand in a right-hand direction, away from your body.

At the same time release the loop from both hands, while still loosely holding the spoke. Your right hand should continue to travel in the right-hand direction while the loop spins parallel to the ground and the spoke slips and turns between your fingers. If the rope is too big, make it smaller. Take it slow, get the rhythm, and keep practicing.

Western Clip Art

Alaska

Mount McKinley

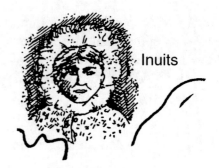

Inuits

fishing

oil

California

Hollywood

Disneyland

Golden Gate Bridge

San Juan Capistrano

Western Clip Art *(cont.)*

Colorado

U.S.A. Air Force
Academy

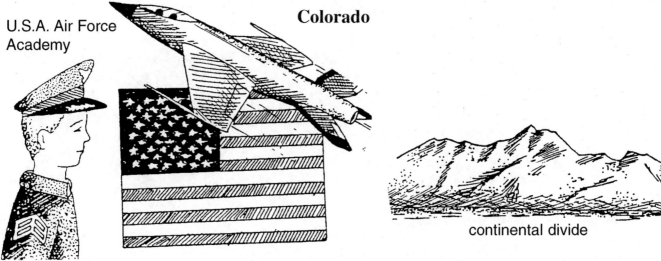

continental divide

Pike's Peak

Hawaii

U.S.S. Arizona
Memorial
Pearl Harbor

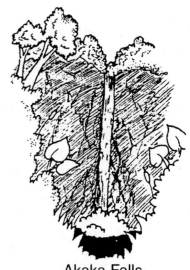

Diamond Head

fishing

Akaka Falls

Western Clip Art *(cont.)*

Idaho

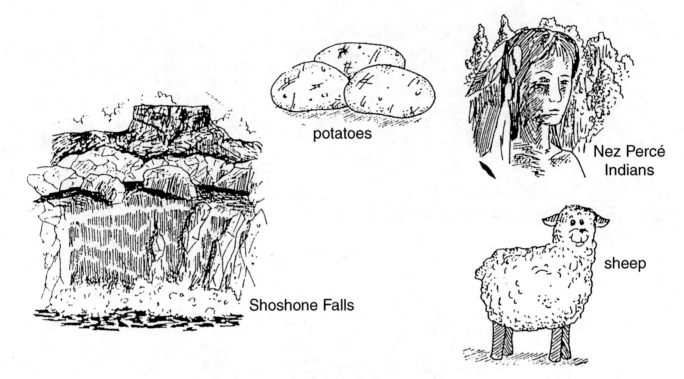

potatoes

Nez Percé Indians

sheep

Shoshone Falls

Montana

beef cattle

Glacier National Park

Custer Hill

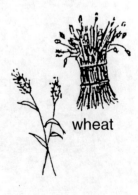

wheat

250

© *Teacher Created Materials, Inc.*

Western Clip Art *(cont.)*

Nevada

Las Vegas

Lake Tahoe

Virginia City

Oregon

Crater Lake

Mount Hood

salmon fish ladder

Sea Lion Caves

Oregon Trail

Western Clip Art *(cont.)*

Utah

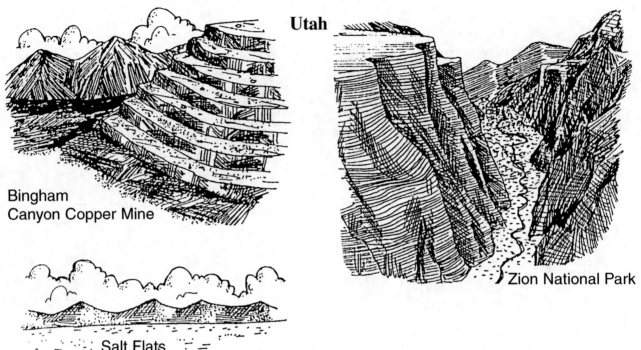

Bingham
Canyon Copper Mine

Salt Flats

Zion National Park

Washington

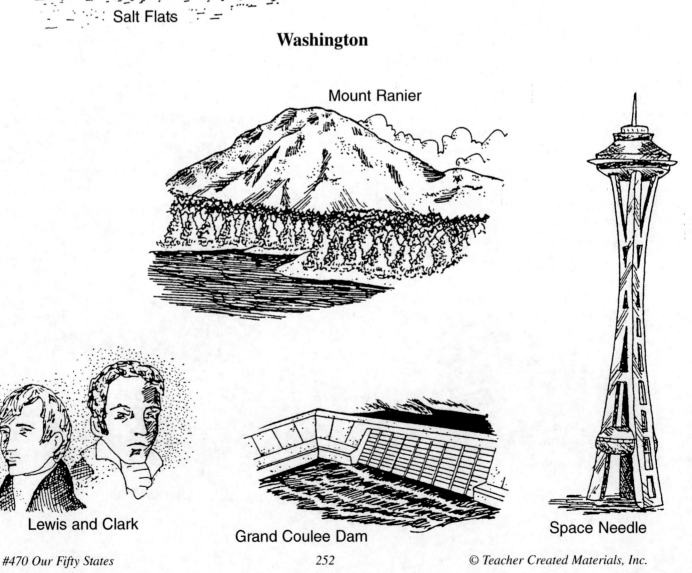

Mount Ranier

Lewis and Clark

Grand Coulee Dam

Space Needle

Western Clip Art *(cont.)*

Wyoming

rodeos

Wind River Indian
Reservation

Devil's Tower

Yellowstone National
Park

Name _____ Date _____

Which State Am I?

Directions: Identify the state described. Write its name on the line.

1. I was one of the last two states to join the Union. Some of my most valuable natural resources are petroleum, natural gas, timber, and seafood. My climate prevents me from producing many agricultural products. A foreign country is on my eastern boundary. I am closer to Russia than any other state.

   Which state am I? _____

2. I was the 31st state to join the Union. Although I have many valuable resources, I think my most important is my climate. My climate helps me produce many crops, such as cotton, grapes, oranges, and tomatoes. Some people often associate me with gold. The world's oldest tree is located in one of my parks.

   Which state am I? _____

3. More than 30 states joined the United States before me. One of my most valuable natural resources is coal. Some of the important agricultural products that I produce are beef cattle, milk, wheat, and sheep. A major river and I share the same name. I am also the highest state of the United States.

   Which state am I? _____

4. I was one of the last states to join the Union. I am well-known for agricultural products such as pineapples and sugar cane. My volcanoes are famous, too. If you want to visit me, you have to cover a lot of water. I am the only state not located in North America.

   Which state am I? _____

5. I was one of the last 40 states in our country. Many people think my most famous product is potatoes. I also produce wheat, hay, and barley. You can find precious and semi-precious stones all over. I am bordered by no less-than six states and one foreign country!

   Which state am I? _____

6. More than 40 states joined the U.S. before me. If you love jewelry, then I'm your state. I have incredible deposits of copper and silver. I am sometimes called the treasure state.

   Which state am I? _____

Name _____ Date _____

Which State Am I?

7. More than 30 states joined the Union before me. I am the only state whose laws allow most kinds of gambling, and this attracts many tourists. Less rain falls here than in any other state. As a result, all my farming requires irrigation.

   Which state am I? _____

8. I was one of the first 40 states in the United States. Some of my valuable natural resources are timber, nickel, and seafood. Among the crops grown within my borders are hay and wheat. I have the deepest lake in the United States, Crater Lake.

   Which state am I? _____

9. More than 40 states joined the Union before I did. I am well-known for my forest products, but I also produce wheat, beef cattle, and coal. The greatest snowfall amount in North America occurred in my state. I am the only state named after a President.

   Which state am I? _____.

10. I was one of the last 10 states to join the Union. Among my most important agricultural products are sheep, beef cattle, and sugar beets. A large granite boulder located in my state has settler's names carved on it. American women first voted here.

    Which state am I? _____

11. I, too, was one of the last states to join the Union. I am well-known for my beef cattle, but I also produce petroleum and coal. The Great Salt Lake, located within my borders, is four times more salty than the ocean.

    Which state am I? _____

Name _____ Date _____

Identifying Western States

Directions: Outlines of some of the states of the western region are mixed with those of other states. Identify the western states by coloring them orange.

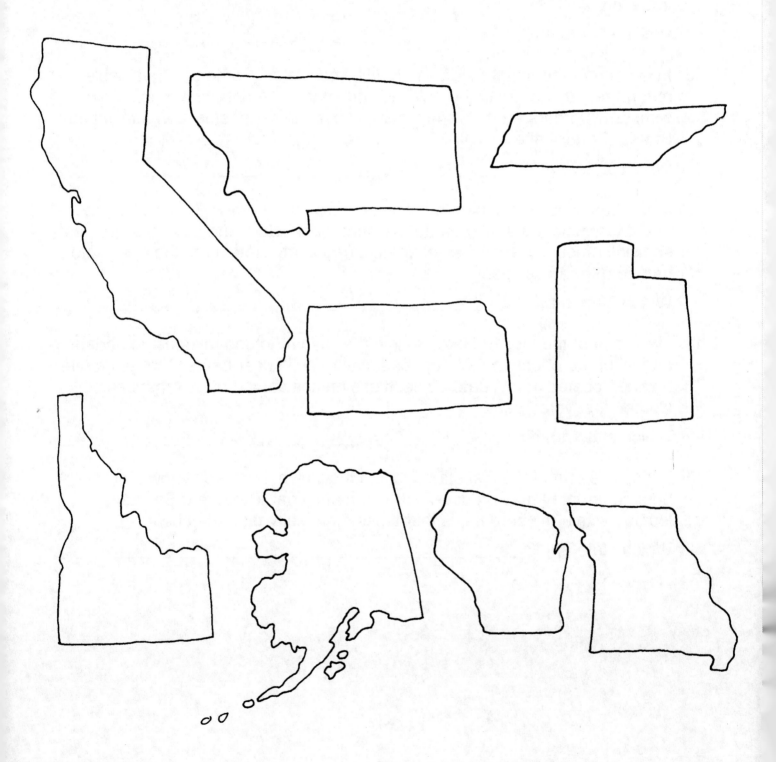

Name _____   Date _____

Flag Match

Directions: Write the number of the flag next to the state to which it belongs. Color the flags correctly.

1.

4.

2.

5.

3.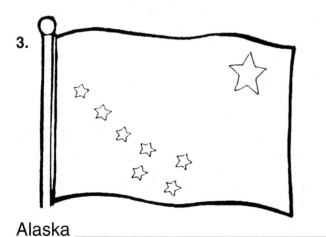

6.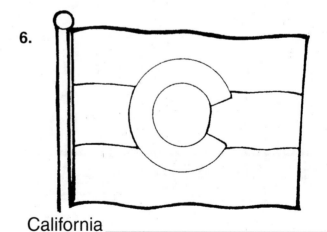

Alaska _____

Colorado _____

Idaho _____

California _____

Hawaii _____

Montana _____

Name _____ Date _____

Flag Match *(cont.)*

Directions: Write the number of the flag next to the state to which it belongs.
Color the flags correctly.

7.

10.

8.
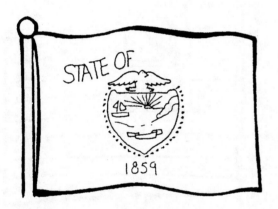

11.

9.

Nevada _____ Oregon _____

Utah_____ Washington _____

Wyoming _____

Name _____   Date _____

City Match

Directions: Match the cities with their states by writing the numbers of the cities on the appropriate lines.

1. Casper   5. Cheyenne   9. Anchorage
2. Hilo   6. Hana   10. Juneau
3. Fairbanks   7. San Francisco   11. Honolulu
4. San Diego   8. Laramie   12. Los Angeles

Alaska

_____

California

_____

Hawaii

_____

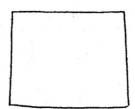

Wyoming

_____

Name _____   Date _____

City Match

Directions: Match the cities with their states by writing the numbers of the cities on the appropriate lines.

13. Boise   17. Idaho Falls   21. Reno

14. Billings   18. Pocatello   22. Butte

15. Moab   19. Las Vegas   23. Great Falls

16. Paradise   20. Provo   24. Salt Lake City

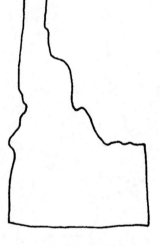

Idaho

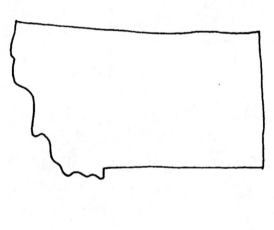

Montana

_____

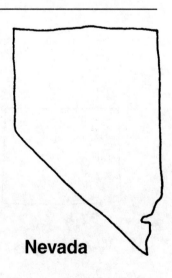

Nevada

_____

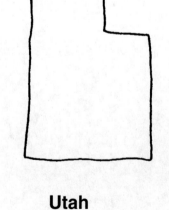

Utah

_____

Name _____   Date _____

How Far Is It?

Directions: Choose ten pairs of cities from the map below. Write their names in the blanks. Then use the map of the west and the scale on this page to find the distances between the cities you listed.

1. _____ to _____ = _____ mi./km
2. _____ to _____ = _____ mi./km
3. _____ to _____ = _____ mi./km
4. _____ to _____ = _____ mi./km
5. _____ to _____ = _____ mi./km
6. _____ to _____ = _____ mi./km
7. _____ to _____ = _____ mi./km
8. _____ to _____ = _____ mi./km
9. _____ to _____ = _____ mi./km
10. _____ to _____ = _____ mi./km

Name _____   Date _____

Comparing Highest Elevations

Directions: Record the highest elevation (in feet) of each state on the numbered lines. Round off these numbers to the nearest 100. Write the rounded numbers on the lettered lines. Complete the bar graph using the rounded numbers

Alaska	1. _____	a. _____
California	2. _____	b. _____
Colorado	3. _____	c. _____
Hawaii	4. _____	d. _____
Idaho	5. _____	e. _____
Montana	6. _____	f. _____
Nevada	7. _____	g. _____
Oregon	8. _____	h. _____
Utah	9. _____	i. _____
Washington	10. _____	j. _____
Wyoming	11. _____	l. _____

Highest Elevations in Western States

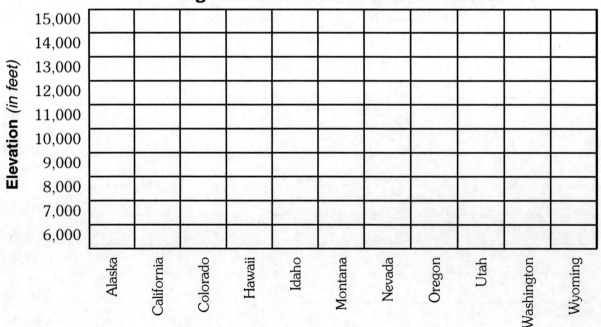

Name _____   Date _____

Admission Days

Directions: Complete the following exercises to learn more about when each of the western states received statehood.

  A. When were the western states granted statehood? Record their admission dates next to the states' names.

Name	Month	Day	Year
1. Alaska	_____	_____	_____
2. California	_____	_____	_____
3. Colorado	_____	_____	_____
4. Hawaii	_____	_____	_____
5. Idaho	_____	_____	_____
6. Montana	_____	_____	_____
7 Nevada	_____	_____	_____
8. Oregon	_____	_____	_____
9. Utah	_____	_____	_____
10. Washington	_____	_____	_____
11. Wyoming	_____	_____	_____

B. The admission dates of the Western states can be plotted on the time line. Plot them on the time line below, making sure to label each one.

1780   1800   1820   1840   1860   1880   1900   1920   1940   1960

Name _____   Date _____

States Puzzler

Directions: Fill in the blanks with the correct words. Ring the words in the puzzle.

```
L  A  N  Q  U  W  E  A  S  T  B  R  H  W  C
O  R  E  G  O  N  N  D  E  H  I  N  P  B  A
S  T  U  M  Q  S  B  O  A  H  A  W  A  I  I
A  L  A  S  K  A  T  T  L  E  R  S  N  U  P
N  N  N  E  H  L  O  U  K  F  T  R  W  E  M
G  P  C  T  O  E  S  S  M  J  O  L  A  C  Y
E  O  H  H  N  M  B  O  F  R  G  S  S  L  L
L  R  O  D  O  E  J  A  I  F  R  K  H  E  O
E  T  R  K  L  R  M  L  I  L  P  P  I  A  I
S  L  A  G  U  S  A  C  R  A  M  E  N  T  O
T  A  G  A  L  C  G  G  B  J  E  O  G  C  W
S  N  E  D  U  J  U  N  E  A  U  R  T  S  H
W  D  H  K  L  F  B  K  J  I  F  M  O  P  N
U  H  S  E  A  T  T  L  E  C  N  K  N  O  D
```

1. _____ is the northernmost state in the western region. Its

   capital is _____ and its largest city is_____.

2. The state of_____ is a chain of islands in the Pacific Ocean.

   Its capital and largest city is_____ .

3. _____ is the capital of_____, the

   "Golden State." _____ is the largest city in this state.

4. Because of its many forests, _____is called "The

   Evergreen State." Its capital, _____, is located near the

   southern end of Puget Sound._____, the largest city, is

   north of the capital.

5. _____ , the "Beaver State," has its capital in _____ .

   _____ is its largest city.

Name _____ Date _____

Western Puzzler

Directions: Find your way from the start to the finish by tracing a path through the rectangles that contain names of features found in the western region.

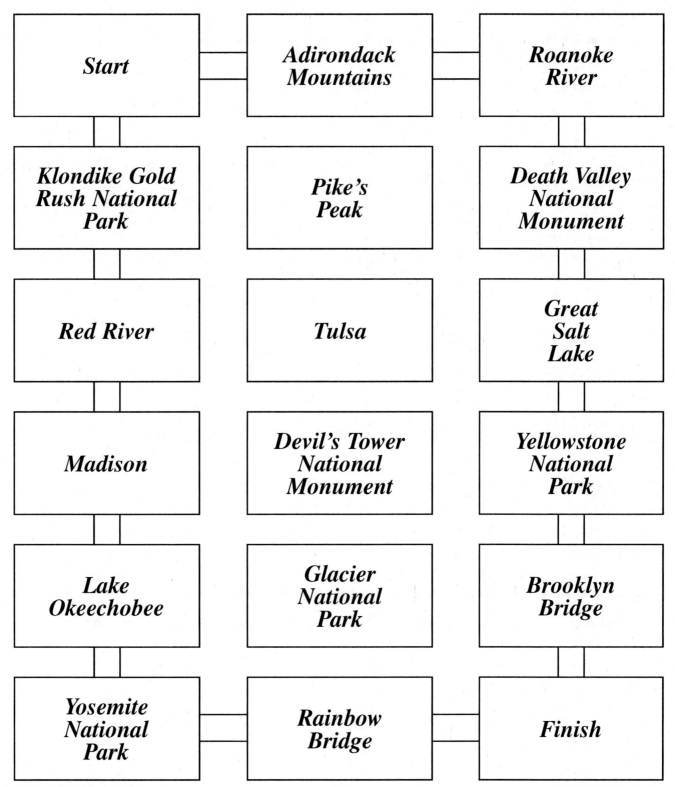

Start	*Adirondack Mountains*	*Roanoke River*
Klondike Gold Rush National Park	*Pike's Peak*	*Death Valley National Monument*
Red River	*Tulsa*	*Great Salt Lake*
Madison	*Devil's Tower National Monument*	*Yellowstone National Park*
Lake Okeechobee	*Glacier National Park*	*Brooklyn Bridge*
Yosemite National Park	*Rainbow Bridge*	*Finish*

States Trivia Game

Game Summary

The States Trivia Game is a board game played by two to six individuals or teams. It is designed to test your students' knowledge of basic facts about the states of the United States. The object of the game is to be the first individual or team to complete the circuit around the United States. This is done by combining luck (rolls of the die) with skill (the ability to correctly answer questions about the states).

Equipment

Game Board—The game board (pages 268-271) consists of a trail of 50 states printed on a map of the United States. Each state represents a move of one space on the game board.

Question Cards—The question cards are divided into four sets (state, largest city, state abbreviation, and capital). Each set contains 18 cards. To make the game cards, reproduce six copies of page 272 onto heavy paper and cut out the cards. Sort the cards into four piles so that all of the cards in a set have the same question printed on them. The questions are applicable to all of the states. The answers to the questions as they apply to each state are listed on the game answer key (pages 273-274). Provide a die and game markers for each group of players.

Rules

Beginning Play. If it is desirable to practice only one form of identification, such as the names of the states, no cards are needed and the participants can be expected to attempt to provide the desired information without prompting. If two or more forms of identification are expected, choose the sets of question cards that are applicable. Shuffle these cards thoroughly and set them aside in a stack.

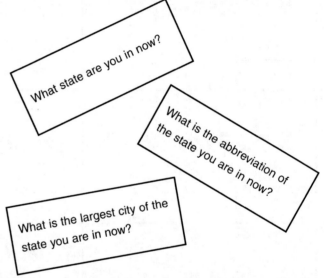

Each player or team places the individual or team marker on one of the six different start/finish spaces on the game board. The spaces are numbered 1 through 6.

Play Sequence: To begin each turn, the teacher (or student "caller") draws a question card and reads it to the player/team whose turn it is. The question applies to whichever state is occupied by the player/team's marker.

If the player/team answers incorrectly or is unable to answer, the marker may not be moved. If after three turns the player/team has not given a correct answer for the state in which his/her marker is located, the die is rolled on the following turn and the marker is moved.

Once a player/team answers correctly, the die is rolled and the marker is moved the appropriate number of spaces along the trail. (The number of spaces in each circuit is the same in both directions; therefore, it does not matter which direction a player/team moves their marker to complete the trail.)

Markers may "jump" other markers, and more than one marker may occupy a space.

End of Game: The game is over as soon as a player or team returns to the original starting place for that player or team.

States Trivia Game Board

Directions: Cut each map section along the lines, as indicated. Do not cut off tabs. Put map together before gluing to prevent wrong tabs from being glued. Glue the pieces of the States Trivia Game Board on pages 268-271 together, matching up letters. Mount on a 24" x 36" (61 cm x 91 cm) piece of tag board, color, and laminate.

Follow the game board model below to help assemble the game board map. Note: Cut out the outlines of Alaska and Hawaii (below), and attach them to the game board as shown.

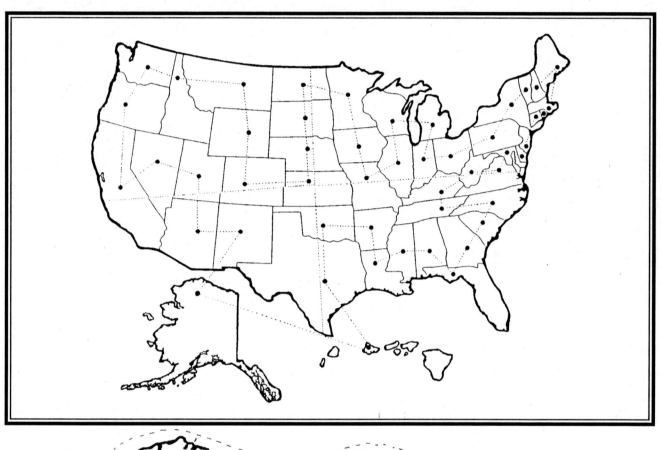

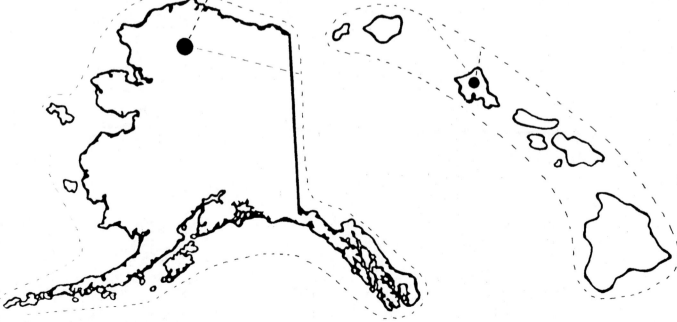

States Trivia Game Board *(cont.)*

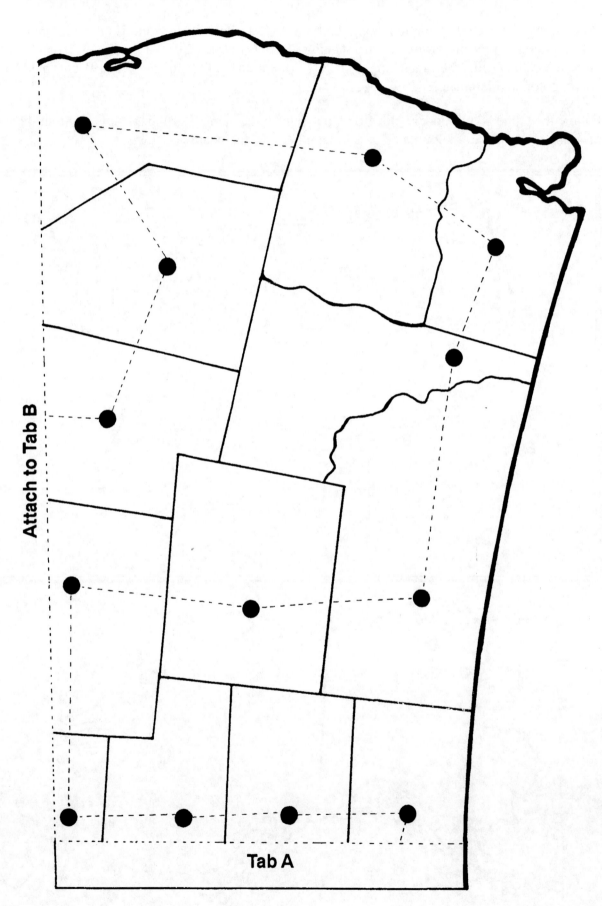

Attach to Tab B

Tab A

States Trivia Game Board *(cont.)*

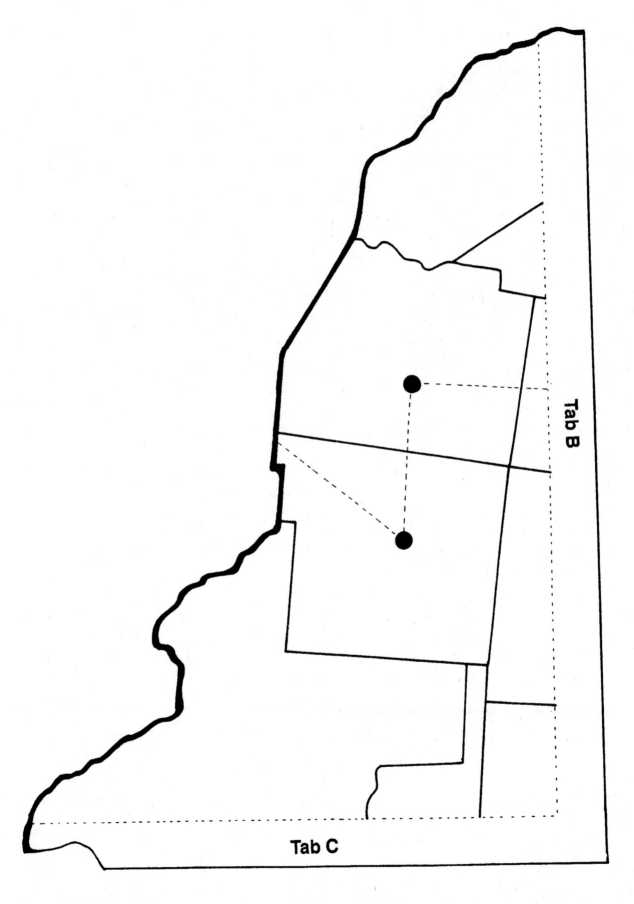

Tab B

Tab C

States Trivia Game Board *(cont.)*

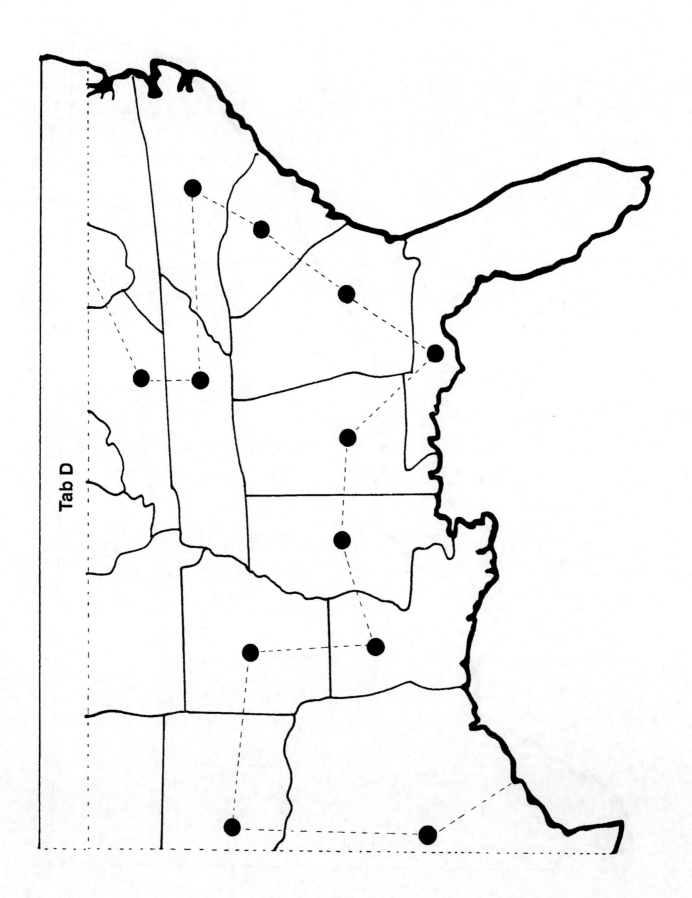

States Trivia Game Board

(cont.)

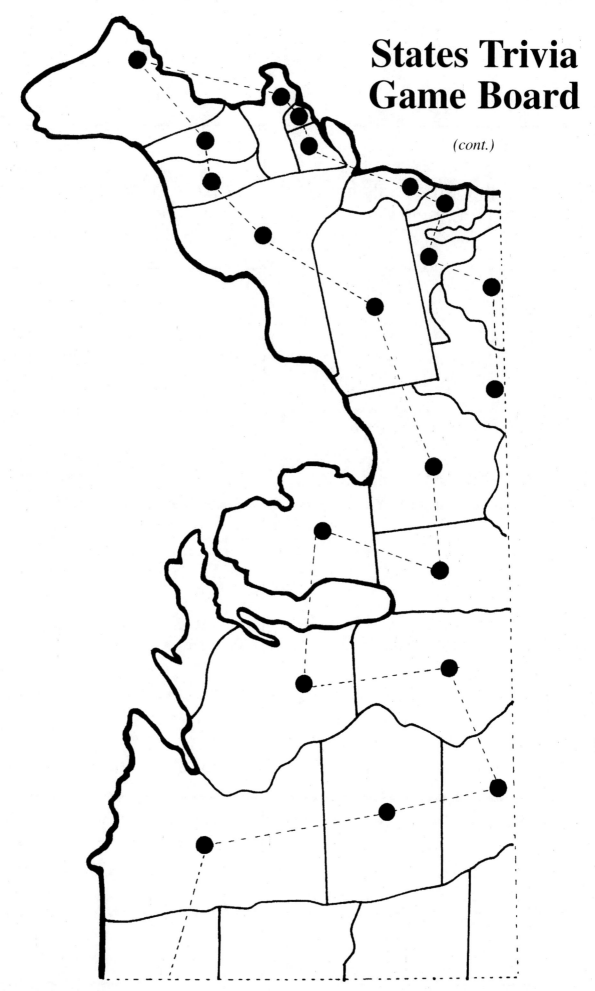

States Trivia Game Cards

See page 266 for directions.

What is the largest city in the state you are in now?	What is the largest city in the state you are in now?
What is the largest city in the state you are in now?	What is the abbreviation of the state you are in now?
What is the largest city in the state you are in now?	What is the abbreviation of the state you are in now?
What is the capital of the state you are in now?	What is the capital of the state you are in now?
What is the capital of the state you are in now?	What state are you in now?
What state are you in now?	What state are you in now?

Game Answer Key

Use the following information with the States Trivia Game on pages 266-272.

State	Abbreviations	Capital	Largest City
Alabama	AL	Montgomery	Birmington
Alaska	AK	Juneau	Anchorage
Arizona	AZ	Phoenix	Phoenix
Arkansas	AR	Little Rock	Little Rock
California	CA	Sacramento	Los Angeles
Colorado	CO	Denver	Denver
Connecticut	CT	Hartford	Bridgeport
Delaware	DE	Dover	Wilmington
Florida	FL	Tallahassee	Jacksonville
Georgia	GA	Atlanta	Atlanta
Hawaii	HI	Honolulu	Honolulu
Idaho	ID	Boise	Boise
Illinois	IL	Springfield	Chicago
Indiana	IN	Indianapolis	Indianapolis
Iowa	IA	Des Moines	Des Moines
Kansas	KS	Topeka	Wichita
Kentucky	KY	Frankfort	Louisville
Louisiana	LO	Baton Rouge	New Orleans
Maine	ME	Augusta	Portland
Maryland	MD	Annapolis	Baltimore
Massachusetts	MA	Boston	Boston
Michigan	MI	Lansing	Detroit
Minnesota	MN	St. Paul	Minneapolis
Mississippi	MS	Jackson	Jackson
Missouri	MO	Jefferson City	St. Louis

Game Answer Key *(cont.)*

Use the following information with the States Trivia Game on pages 266-272.

State	Abbreviations	Capital	Largest City
Montana	MT	Helena	Billings
Nebraska	NE	Lincoln	Omaha r
Nevada	NV	Carson City	Las Vegas
New Hampshire	NH	Concord	Manchester
New Jersey	NJ	Trenton	Newark
New Mexico	NM	Santa Fe	Albuquerque
New York	NY	Albany	New York City
North Carolina	NC	Raleigh	Charlotte
North Dakota	ND	Bismarck	Fargo
Ohio	OH	Columbus	Cleveland
Oklahoma	OK	Oklahoma City	Oklahoma City
Oregon	OR	Salem	Portland
Pennsylvania	PA	Harrisburg	Philadelphia
Rhode Island	RI	Providence	Providence
South Carolina	SC	Columbia	Columbia
South Dakota	SD	Pierre	Sioux Falls
Tennessee	TN	Nashville	Memphis
Texas	TX	Austin	Houston
Utah	UT	Salt Lake City	Salt Lake City
Vermont	VT	Montpelier	Burlington
Virginia	VA	Richmond	Norfolk
Washington	WA	Olympia	Seattle
West Virginia	WV	Charleston	Charleston
Wisconsin	WI	Madison	Milwaukee
Wyoming	WY	Cheyenne	Casper

Idea Bank

United States Map Ideas

1. Use the blank map (page 280) to introduce state information or evaluate students' knowledge of the states. Let students use a copy of the blank map to practice writing each state's pertinent information.

2. Have students fill in state names and add the names of the countries to the north and south of the United States and the bodies of water to the east and west.

3. Have students color each state in alphabetical order.

4. Have students work in teams using an encyclopedia, to divide the map into Time Zones. For convenience, a time zone map is provided below. Ask students time questions like, "If it is 7:00 p.m. in California, what time is it in Massachusetts?" Have students make up their own questions.

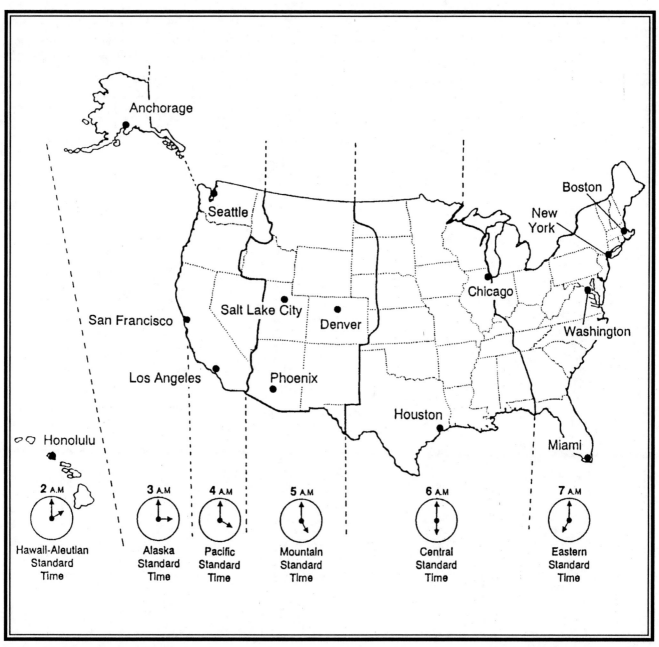

Idea Bank *(cont.)*

United States Map Game

Preparation: Copy and laminate the blank United States map (page 280) on white construction paper. This will serve as the game board. Make two copies of the labeled United States map (page 281), one on yellow and one on orange construction paper.

Cut the colored maps apart into states. To make one set of playing pieces, count out 25 yellow states and 25 orange states to create the entire United States. (Store the pieces in self-sealing plastic bags.) Have students create state fact question cards by gluing the remaining state pieces on one side of an index card and writing a fact about the state on the other side.

Directions: The game is played by two students (or teams). One student uses the 25 yellow state playing pieces, the other, the 25 orange state playing pieces. The fact cards are shuffled and students take turns answering the questions. If the question is answered correctly, the student places one of his/ her state playing pieces onto the blank map game board. (Note: It does not have to be the same state as in the state fact question.) If the answer is incorrect, it becomes the other student's turn. The winner is the first to get all of his/her own 25 state playing pieces onto the game board. Or, to make it a real team effort, end the game when both players get all 50 state playing pieces on the board.

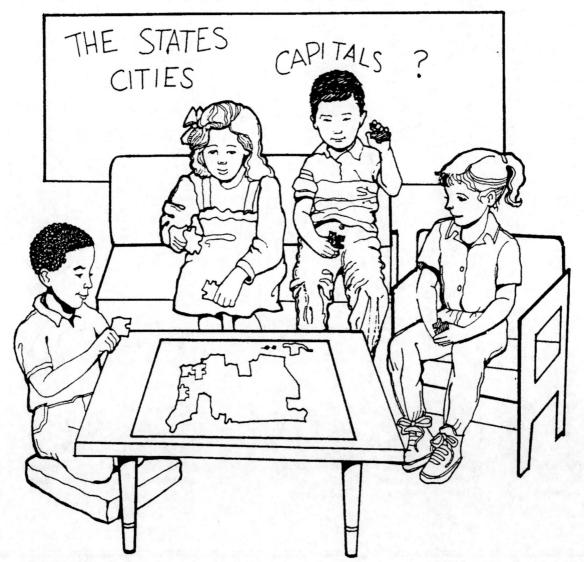

Idea Bank *(cont.)*

Learning United States Regions

The United States may be divided into the following regions:

- **The Southeast:** Alabama, Arkansas, Florida, Georgia, Kentucky, Louisiana, Mississippi, North Carolina, South Carolina, Tennessee, Virginia, West Virginia

- **The Northeast:** Connecticut, Delaware, Maine, Maryland, Massachusetts, New Hampshire, New Jersey, New York, Pennsylvania, Rhode Island, Vermont

- **The Midwest:** Illinois, Indiana, Iowa, Kansas, Michigan, Minnesota, Missouri, Nebraska, North Dakota, Ohio, South Dakota, Wisconsin

- **The Southwest:** Arizona, New Mexico, Oklahoma, Texas

- **The West:** Alaska, California, Colorado, Hawaii, Idaho, Montana, Nevada, Oregon, Utah, Washington, Wyoming

Use this regional division, or one represented in another source, to help students learn and remember information about the United States. Try one of the following ideas:

Fifty States Book

Create a book of the fifty states with regional chapters. Begin by tracing the outline of each state from the patterns in this book. Hand out a set of blank state outlines to each student. Provide colorful construction paper for a book cover. Discuss the concept of regions and the use of a table of contents. Have students make a table of contents with regional chapters.

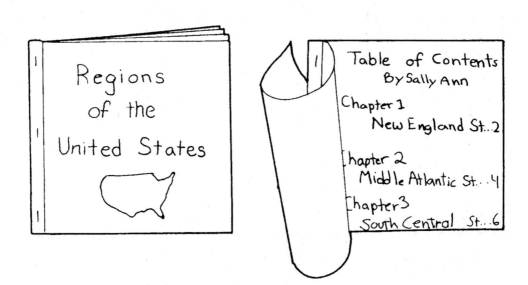

Have students put the states in correct regional order according to the table of contents. Have them number their pages and write the appropriate page numbers in the table of contents. This blank book can now be used for a variety of activities such as creative writing, math practice, or basic state facts and/or review. (Option: Divide the class into several groups for the five regions. Have each group prepare its section. Assemble the sections into a class book.)

Idea Bank *(cont.)*

Learning United States Regions *(cont.)*

Make Regional Rings

Reduce the size of the state pattern pieces until you can fit about four states on one piece of paper. Reproduce these smaller versions of the states and provide each student with a set. Discuss regions of the United States. Assign a color to each region and have students color the states accordingly. Have students cut out and punch a hole near one end of each state.

Provide five twist ties or small metal rings, and have students make "regional rings" to help them review. (**Option:** You may wish to make one large set of seven "regional rings" to act as a model. Use the size of each state as it appears in this book.)

Language Arts Activities

Guess Who I Am?

Pretend to be one of the fifty states. Have students line up in spelling bee fashion. Ask students to guess what state you are by the state clues that you give. (Note: For review, have students come up with their own Guess Who I Am? clues to be given during the game!)

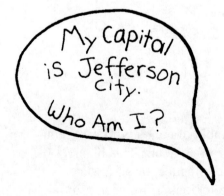

Idea Bank *(cont.)*

Language Arts Activities *(cont.)*

Where Are You From?

Create a "United States Hall of
Fame" by having students draw
pictures of themselves and
placing their pictures under their
birth state name and map in the
hallway. (For extra fun, provide
extra paper near each state so
passers-by can add where they
are from as well!)

Math Activities

Measure and Make

Practice measuring by obtaining cookbooks from the various states and making special dishes which
represent each state or region. Have a special State Tasting Party. Invite another class and share oral
reports written by individual students or student teams.

Compare and Share

Create graphs to show information about individual states, or create comparison graphs of more than
one state. Have students share the information they have gathered.

 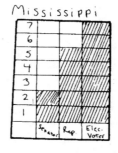 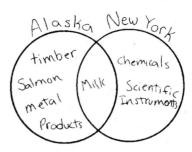

Guest Speakers

Involve the community as your students learn about the fifty states. Schedule guest speakers throughout
the unit as a way of introducing students to a state or as part of a culminating activity. Try some of the
following suggestions:

- Invite parents from different states to come and share about their lives while living in that state.
  (Don't forget to write thank-you letters! You can use the state patterns provided. Have students
  color the "art" side and write their "thank you" message on the other!)

- Invite a meteorologist from a local television news station to come and discuss how he/she analyzes
  the United States weather forecast. After the guest speaker is finished, have students watch a
  videotape of the special guest in action!

- Travel agents love to come and share information on vacationing in our fifty states! After the
  presentation, have students create travel posters or brochures for the fifty states to try to get people
  to want to travel to that state for a special holiday vacation!

The United States

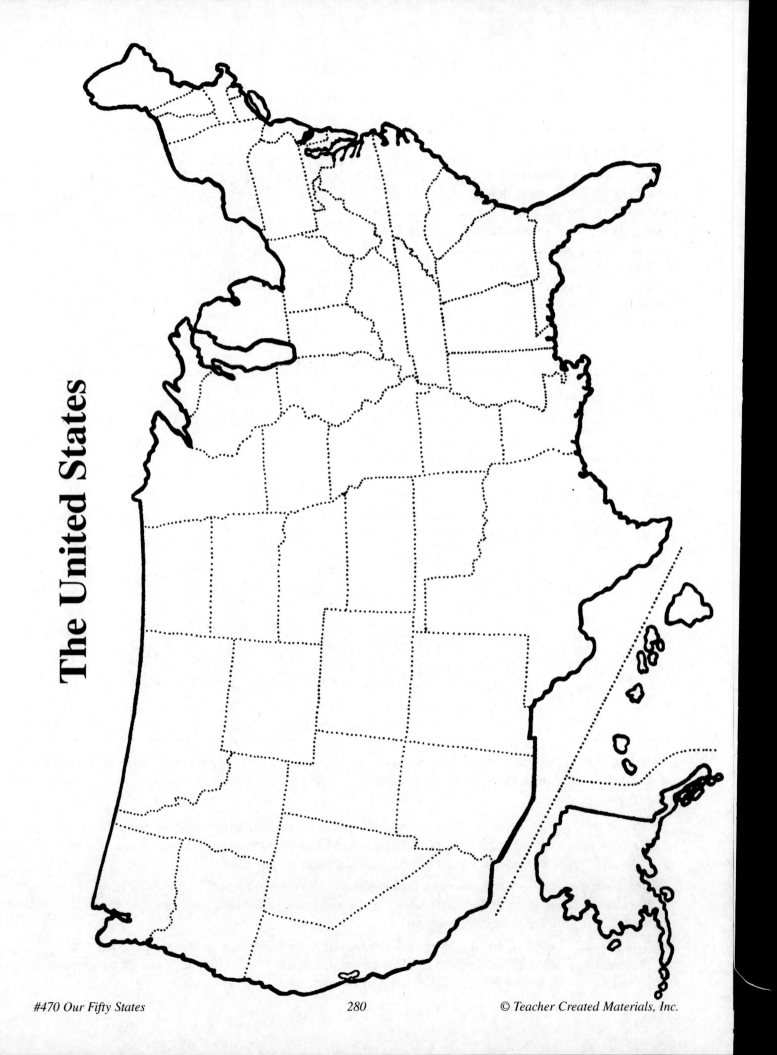

The United States *(cont.)*

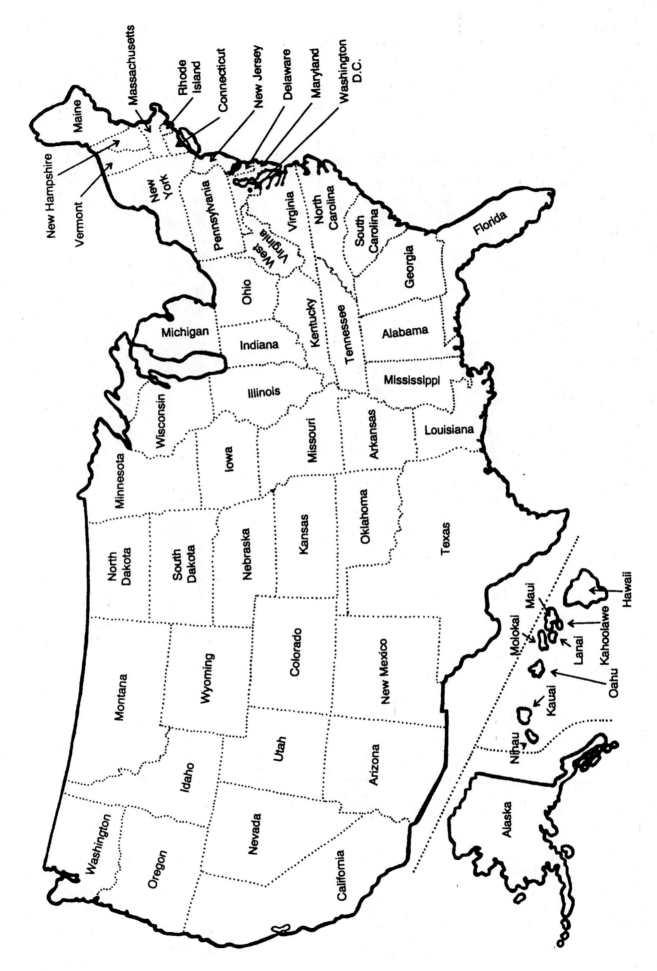

Regions of the United States

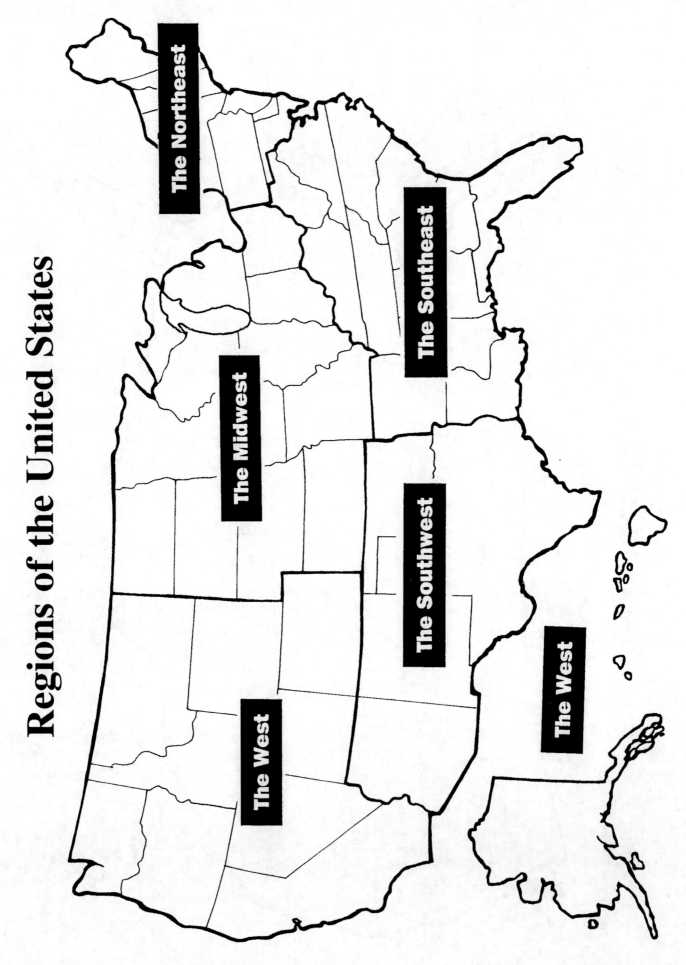

The Northeast

The Southeast

The Midwest

The Southwest

The West

The West

Answer Key

Page 34—The Flight

Clue words will vary.

Flight: 2,3,5,7,9

Flyer: 1,4,6,8,10

Pages 54-55—Which State Am I?

1. Alabama
2. Florida
3. Kentucky
4. Louisiana
5. Arkansas
6. Georgia
7. South Carolina
8. North Carolina
9. West Virginia
10. Virginia
11. Tennessee
12. Mississippi

Page 56—Identifying Southeast States

Kentucky

Mississippi

Alabama

Georgia

Louisiana

Pages 57-58 Flag Match

Virginia: 3

Mississippi: 4

Arkansas: 6

Louisiana: 1

Kentucky: 2

West Virginia: 5

Tennessee:10

North Carolina: 9

Alabama: 11

South Carolina: 12

Florida: 8

Georgia: 7

Pages 59-60—City Match

Georgia: 3,5,9

Mississippi: 2,8,12

Louisiana: 6,7,11

Arkansas: 1,4,10

South Carolina: 15,16,21

Florida: 19, 20, 22

Alabama: 13, 14, 17

Virginia: 18, 23, 24

Page 61—How Far Is It?

Answers will vary.

Page 62—Comparing Areas of the Southeast

1. 51,705   a. 52,000
2. 53,187   b. 53,000
3. 58,664   c. 59,000
4. 58,910   d. 59,000
5. 40,409   e. 40,000
6. 47,752   f. 48,000
7. 47,689   g. 48,000
8. 52,669   h. 53,000
9. 31,113   i. 31,000
10. 42,114   j. 42,000
11. 40,767   k. 41,000
12. 24,231   l. 24,000

Page 63—Admission Days

A.

1. December 14, 1819
2. June 15, 1836
3. March 3, 1845
4. January 2, 1788
5. June 1, 1792
6. April 30, 1812
7. December 10, 1817
8. November 21, 1789
9. May 23, 1788
10. June 1, 1796
11. June 25, 1788
12. June 20, 1863

Page 64—States Puzzler

1. Florida
2. Mississippi
3. North Carolina
4. Alabama
5. South Carolina
6. Georgia
7. Tennessee
8. Kentucky
9. West Virginia
10. Virginia
11. Arkansas
12. Louisiana

Page 70—First Written Constitution

1. no; Mr. X is 22 years old. To be a representative, a citizen must be 25 years old; Article 1, Section 2.2.
2. no; Miss Y h-as been a citizen of the United States for six years. To be a senator, a person must have been a citizen for nine years; Article 1, Section 2.3.
3. no; Even though Mrs. W is a citizen, she has been living in the United States for only four years. To be eligible to run for President, a citizen must have been living in the country for 14 years; Article 2, Section 1.5.
4. yes; Representation in Congress is determined by population. If the population of a state decreases, the number of representatives from that state may be reduced; Article 1, Section 23.

Answer Key *(cont.)*

Pages 112-113—Which State Am I?

1. Connecticut
2. Maryland
3. Delaware
4. New Hampshire
5. Maine
6. Massachusetts
7. Pennsylvania
8. Rhode Island
9. Vermont
10. New York
11. New Jersey

Page 114—Identifying

Northeastern States

Maine

Pennsylvania

Vermont

Maryland

New York

Pages 115-116— Flag Match

Pennsylvania: 1

New York: 4

Massachusetts: 6

New Jersey: 3

Delaware: 2

Maine: 5

New Hampshire: 7

Rhode Island: 8

Vermont: 9

Maryland: 10

Connecticut: 11

Pages 117-118—City Match

Massachusetts: 1, 10, 11

New York: 2, 4, 5

Maine: 3, 6, 7

Maryland: 8, 9, 12

Pennsylvania: 14, 19, 20

Connecticut: 16, 17, 23

Rhode Island: 13, 15, 21

Delaware: 18, 22, 24

Page 119—How Far Is It?

Answers will vary.

Page 120 Comparing

Population

1. 3,295,669   a. 3,300,000
2. 668,696   b. 700,000
3. 1,233,223   c. 1,200,000
4. 4,798,622   d. 4,800,000
5. 6,029,051   e. 6,000,000
6. 1,113,915   f. 1,100,000
7. 7,748,634   g. 7,700,000
8. 18,044,505   h. 18,000,000
9. 11,924,710   i. 11,900,000
10. 1,005,984   j. 1,000,000
11. 564,964   k. 600,000

Page 121—Admission Days

1. January 9, 1788
2. December 7, 1787 3. March 15, 1820
4. April 28, 1788
5. February 6, 1788
6. June 21, 1788
7. December 18, 1787
8. July 26, 1788
9. December 12, 1787
10. May 29, 1790
11. March 4, 1791

Page 122—States Puzzler

1. Maine
2. Rhode Island
3. Vermont
4. Connecticut
5. New Hampshire
6. Newark
7. Annapolis
8. Pennsylvania
9. Boston
10. Montpelier
11. Delaware
12. Albany

Puzzler Word: northeastern

Page 165—Is That a Fact?

1. l mi. (l km)
2. 14 years
3. about 12 feet (4 m) high
4. 5,225 feet (1,745 m) above sea level

Pages 176-177—Which State

1. South Dakota
2. Michigan
3. Indiana
4. Ohio
5. Minnesota
6. Illinois
7. Iowa
8. Missouri
9. Kansas
10. North Dakota
11. Nebraska
12. Wisconsin

Pages 178—Identifying Midwestern States

Wisconsin

Iowa

Ohio

Kansas

Michigan

Missouri

Nebraska

North Dakota

South Dakota

Minnesota

Pages 179-180—Flag Match

Illinois: 5

Indiana: 6

Iowa: 4

Kansas: 3

Michigan: 1

Minnesota: 2

Missouri: 12

North Dakota: 9

South Dakota: 7

Nebraska: 10

Ohio: 11

Wisconsin: 8

Answer Key (cont.)

Pages 181-182—City Match

Illinois: 2,13,14
Indiana: 7,8, 10
Iowa: 1,3, 4
Kansas: 11, 16,18,
Michigan: 5,9,17
Minnesota: 6, 12,15
Missouri: 28, 34, 36
Nebraska: 26, 29, 32
North Dakota: 20, 24, 25
Ohio: 21, 22, 23
South Dakota: 19, 33, 35
Wisconsin: 27, 30, 31

Page 183—How Far Is It?

Answers will vary.

Page 181—Admission Days

1. December 3, 1818
2. December 11, 1816
3. December 28, 1846
4. January 29, 1861
5. January 26, 1837
6. May 11, 1858
7. August 10, 1821
8. March 1, 1867
9. November 21, 1789
10. March 1, 1803
11. November 2, 1889
12. May 29, 1848

Page 185—States Puzzlers

A.

1. Michigan
2. Ohio
3. North Dakota
4. Iowa
5. Nebraska
6. Kansas
7. South Dakota
8. Minnesota
9. Missouri
10. Indiana

Puzzler Word: midwestern

Page 20—Which State Am I?

1. Texas
2. New Mexico
3. Arizona
4. Oklahoma

Page 205—Identifying Southwestern States

Arizona
Texas
Oklahoma
New Mexico

Page 206—Flag Match

New Mexico: 3
Texas: 2
Oklahoma: 1
Arizona: 4

Page 207—City Match

Arizona: 7, 9, 11, 16,
Texas: 2, 4, 12, 14
Oklahoma: 5, 8, 10, 13
New Mexico: 1, 3, 6, 15

Page 208—How Far Is It?

Answers will vary.

Page 209—Admission Days

A.

1. February 14, 1912
2. January 6, 1912
3. November 16, 1907
4. December 29, 1845

C.

1. Texas
2. 39 days
3. 62 years
4. 3 states

Page 210—States Puzzler

Across

3. Albuquerque
5. New Mexico
7. Grand Canyon
8. Texas
9. Austin
10. Cactus Wren

Down

1. Rain
2. Oklahoma
4. Houston
6. Gold

Pages 254-255—Which State Am I?

1. Alaska
2. California
3. Colorado
4. Hawaii
5. Idaho
6. Montana
7. Nevada
8. Oregon
9. Washington
10. Wyoming
11. Utah

Page 256—Identifying Western States

California
Montana
Utah
Idaho
Alaska

Answer Key *(cont.)*

Pages 257-258—Flag Match

Alaska: 3

California: 1

Colorado: 6

Hawaii: 5

Idaho: 4

Montana: 2

Nevada: 11

Oregon: 8

Utah: 10

Washington: 7

Wyoming: 9

Pages 259-260—City Match

Alaska: 3, 9, 10

Hawaii: 2, 6, 11

California: 4, 7, 12

Wyoming; 1, 5, 8

Idaho: 13, 17, 18

Nevada: 16, 19, 21

Montana: 14, 22, 23

Utah: 15, 20, 24

Page 261—How Far Is It?

Answers will vary.

Page 262—Comparing Highest Elevation

1. 20,320   a. 20,300
2. 14,495   b. 14,500
3. 14,433   c. 14,400
4. 13,796   d. 13,800
5. 12,662   e. 12,700
6. 12,799   f. 12,800
7. 13,143   g. 13,000
8. 11,239   h. 11,200
9. 13,528   i. 13,500
10. 14,410   j. 14,400
11. 13,804   k. 13,800

Page 263—Admission Days

1. January 3, 1959
2. September 9, 1850
3. August 1, 1876
4. August 21, 1959
5. July 3, 1890
6. November 8,1889
7. October 31, 1864
8. February 14, 1859
9. January 4, 1896
10. November 11, 1889
11. July 10, 1890

Page 264—States Puzzler

1. Alaska, Juneau, Anchorage
2. Hawaii, Honolulu
3. Sacramento, California, Los Angeles
4. Washington, Olympia, Seattle
5. Oregon, Salem, Portland

Page 265—Western Puzzler

Klondike Gold Rush National Park

Pike's Peak

Death Valley National Monument

Great Salt Lake

Yellowstone National Park

Devil's Tower National Monument

Glacier National Park

Rainbow Bridge

Related Bibliography

The Southeast

Branley, Franklin. *Hurricane Watch* (Harper Collins, 1985).

Celsi, Teresa. *Rosa Parks and the Montgomery Bus Boycott* (Millbrook Press, 1991).

Milton, Joyce. *Marching to Freedom: The Story of Martin Luther King, Jr.* (Dell, 1987).

Moore, Eva. *Story of George Washington Carver* (Scholastic, 1971).

The Northeast

Ackerman, Karen. *Leaves in October* (Macmillan Child Group, 1991).

Allison, Linda. *Sunshine Makes the Seasons* (Little Brown, 1975).

Caney, Steven. *Steven Caney's Invention Book* (Workman Publishing, 1985).

Carter, Katherine. *Ships & Seaports* (Children's Press, 1983).

Fisher, Leonard. *Ellis Island Gateway to the American Dream* (Holiday, 1986).

Fisher, Leonard. *Symbol Art: Thirteen Squares, Circles and Triangles from Around the World* (Macmillan, 1986).

Jones, Charlotte Foltz. *Mistakes That Worked* (Doubleday, 1991).

Miller, Natalie. *The Story of the Liberty Bell* (Children's Press, 1965).

TCM 234 *Thematic Unit—Immigration* (Teacher Created Materials, 1993).

The Midwest

Adler, David. *A Picture Book of Abraham Lincoln* (Holiday House, 1989).

Aliki. *The Story of Johnny Appleseed* (Prentice Hall, 1963).

Brown, Marion M. Sacagawea: *Indian Interpreter to Lewis and Clark* (Childrens Press, 1988).

D'Aulaire, Ingri & Edgar. *Abraham Lincoln* (Doubleday, 1987).

Freedman, Russell. *Lincoln: A Photobiography* (Ticknor, 1987).

Kellogg, Stephen, retold by. *Johnny Appleseed* (Morrow Junior Books, 1988).

San Souci, Robert. *Adventures of America Legendary Heroes: Larger Than Life* (Doubleday, 1991).

Seymour, Flora W. *Sacagawea: American Pathfinder.* (Macmillan Child Group, 1991).

Skurzynski, Gloria. *Honest Andrew* (Harcourt, Brace, Jovanovich, 1980).

Stoutenburg, Adrien. *American Tall Tales* (Puffin Books, 1976).

TCM Thematic Unit: Apples (Teacher Created Materials, 1990).

The Southwest

Byers, Betsy. *The Blossoms and the Green Phantom* (Delacorte, 1987).

Calhoun, Mary. *Hot-Air Henry* (Morrow, 1979).

Freedman, Russell. *Cowboys of the Wild West* (Ticknor, 1983).

Gorsline, Marie & Douglas. *Cowboys* (Random House, 1980).

Martini, Teri. *Cowboys* (Childrens, 1981).

Mell, Jan. Grand *Canyon.* (Macmillan Child Group, 1988).

Peterson, David. *Grand Canyon National Park* (Childrens, 1993).

Saunders, Rupert. *Balloon Voyage* (Rourke, 1988).

The West

Alexander, Bryan & Cherry. *An Eskimo Family* (Lerner, 1985).

Bellvile, Cheryl Walsh. *Rodeo* (Carolrhoda, 1985).

Coombs, Charles. *Let's Rodeo* (Henry Holt, 1986).

The Eskimo: *The Inuit & Yupik People* (Childrens, 1985)

Fisher, Leonard. *Oregon Trail* (Holiday House, 1990).

Gorsline, Marie & Douglas. *The Pioneers* (Random, 1982).

Johnson, Sylvia A. *Potatoes* (Lerner, 1984).

Mackintosh, Berry. *The National Park Service* (Chelsea, 1987).

Mithutsch, Ali. *From Sea to Salt* (Carolrhoda, 1985).

Peters, Lisa Westberg. *The Sun, the Wind, & the Rain* (Henry Holt, 1988).

Radlauer, Ruth. *Olympic National Park* (Childrens, 1978).

Smith, Greg J. H. *Eskimos: The Inuit of the Arctic* (Rourke, 1987).

Steiner, Barbara. *Whale Brothers* (Walker, 1988).

Stone, Lynn M. *Mountains* (Childrens, 1983).

Watts, Barrie. *Potato* (Silver, 1988).

Resources

The following ideas can be used as resources to gain information in your studies of the fifty states.

General Information

Look through your local television guide for documentaries and specials featuring the fifty states. Public television stations are often a good source for these shows.

Contact the various state capitals. Address letters to state legislators, state offices of agriculture, or tourism. Addresses can be obtained from sources at the local library or in telephone books.

Write letters to federal legislators. Address letters to individual legislators.

Letters sent to senators should be addressed in the following way:

The Honorable_____
(Senator's Name)

United States Senate
Washington, D.C. 20510

Address letters to representatives as follows:

The Honorable_____
(Representative's Name)

United States House of Representatives
Washington, D.C. 20515

Many museums have displays and exhibits about their states. The Smithsonian Institution in Washington, D. C. is one such museum.

The address is:

The Smithsonian Institution
1000 Jefferson Dr. S.W.
Washington, D. C. 20506

For more information about areas of local interest, contact city halls or the Chamber of Commerce.

Travel agencies are an excellent source of tourist information. They are often willing to give teachers pamphlets and posters for student use.

Research Information

Almanacs, atlases, and encyclopedias offer a wealth of information about the states. Keep them in the classroom for easy reference.

In addition, state road maps are a good resource for research. Besides providing geographical information, they often list places of interest and information about special state events.

In large cities the telephone book is filled with reference materials that students can use, including numbers and names of government agencies.

Teacher Created Materials Publications

The following products may be useful in learning more about the United States.

TCM 094—*Patriotic Graph Art*
TCM 112—*Hooray for the USA!*
TCM 113—*Patriotic Holidays*
TCM 142—*Patriotic Patterns and Clip Art*
TCM 160—*United States Geography*
TCM 162—*Writing a State Report*
TCM 163—*Writing a Country Report*
TCM 185—*Big & Easy Art for Patriotic Holidays*
TCM 276—*NativeAmericans* (Primary)
TCM 285—*NativeAmericans* (Intermediate)
TCM 282—*Westward Ho* (Intermediate)
TCM 295—*Transcontinental Railroad*
TCM 367—*Patriotic Wordsearches, Codes, & Crossword Puzzles*
TCM 480—*American History Simulations*
TCM 738—*Award Ribbon Shape Note Pad*
TCM 755—*Earth Shape Note Pad*